305.896 G983b
GUTERMAN   FV
 BLACK PSYCHE; THE MODAL
PERSONALITY PATTERNS OF BLACK
AMERICANS   7.95

BLACK PSYCHE

THE GLENDESSARY PRESS — Berkeley

Consulting Editor:
Donald A. Hansen *University of California, Berkeley*

Black Psyche

The Modal Personality Patterns
of Black Americans

Edited by

Stanley S. Guterman

RUTGERS UNIVERSITY

The Glendessary Press, Inc.
2512 Grove, Berkeley, California

Library of Congress Card Catalog No.: 72-186268
ISBN: 0-87709-218-4 paperbound   0-87709-718-6 clothbound

For Marilyn

Contents

PREFATORY NOTE *xi*

INTRODUCTION *xiii*

PART ONE: THE SOCIAL AND HISTORICAL BACKDROP

1 THE SITUATION OF BLACKS IN AMERICAN SOCIETY *5*
National Advisory Committee on Civil Disorders

2 CRUCIBLE OF IDENTITY:
THE NEGRO LOWER-CLASS FAMILY *31*
Lee Rainwater

PART TWO: THE CHARACTERISTICS
OF THE MODAL PERSONALITY

3 RACE AWARENESS AMONG
AMERICAN AND HONG KONG CHILDREN *67*
J. Kenneth Morland

4 RACE, ETHNICITY, AND SELF-ESTEEM *87*
Morris Rosenberg

5 RACE, ETHNICITY, AND
THE ACHIEVEMENT SYNDROME *101*
Bernard C. Rosen

6 ALIENATION, RACE, AND EDUCATION *129*
Russell Middleton

7 WHAT GHETTO MALES ARE LIKE: ANOTHER LOOK *139*
Ulf Hannerz

8   RACIAL DIFFERENCES ON THE MINNESOTA
     MULTIPHASIC PERSONALITY INVENTORY   *163*
     E. Earl Baughman and W. Grant Dahlstrom

PART THREE: PERSONALITY INFLUENCES ON BEHAVIOR

9   THE PSYCHOLOGICAL CONTEXT OF MILITANCY   *191*
     Gary T. Marx

10   THE SIGNIFICANCE OF "SOUL"   *215*
     Ulf Hannerz

11   THE STUDY OF URBAN VIOLENCE:
     SOME IMPLICATIONS OF LABORATORY
     STUDIES OF FRUSTRATION AND AGGRESSION   *231*
     Leonard Berkowitz

12   CIVIL RIGHTS ACTIVITY AND
     REDUCTION IN CRIME AMONG NEGROES   *245*
     Fredric Solomon, Walter L. Walker,
     Garrett J. O'Connor, and Jacob R. Fishman

13   THE LOCUS OF CONTROL AND ACADEMIC
     PERFORMANCE AMONG RACIAL GROUPS   *271*
     James S. Coleman, Ernest Q. Campbell, Carol J. Hobson,
     James McPartland, Alexander M. Mood, Frederic D. Weinfeld,
     and Robert York

14   INTERNAL-EXTERNAL CONTROL IN THE
     MOTIVATIONAL DYNAMICS OF NEGRO YOUTH   *289*
     Patricia Gurin, Gerald Gurin,
     Rosina C. Lao, and Muriel Beattie

SELECTED BIBLIOGRAPHY   *307*

REFERENCES   *315*

Prefatory Note

I am indebted to several agencies and individuals for aid of various sorts in preparing this anthology.

Much of the work on the book was done with financial assistance from the Rutgers University Research Council. This assistance took the form of a Faculty Fellowship during the summer of 1970 and of a research grant during the following academic year.

Two truly excellent secretaries, Eleanor Hornor and Emily Kosobucki, typed the bulk of the manuscript and of the voluminous correspondence required to assemble an anthology.

I have benefited from extended conversations about black modal personality with two of my colleagues at Rutgers University, Wilbur H. Watson and Helen Safa, and with Rae Carlson of the National Institute of Mental Health.

My brother-in-law, Robert J. Lefkowitz, provided stylistic advice, which proved helpful.

Thoughtful counsel was given by my editor at The Glendessary Press, C. H. Gustafson. Even when I didn't wholly agree with him, his comments forced me to come to grips with important issues of style and substance. The book is significantly better for his efforts.

Finally, I am grateful to my wife, Marilyn, for her suggestions about style and for helping out with the typing.

Some of the selections were considerably edited to fit this book. The phrase "excerpted from" in a permission note means I have abridged a publication and have perhaps brought together and rearranged passages from different parts of the original. Except for works put out by the United States Government Printing Office, all such editing was done with the consent of the author and the publisher.

An italicized number with a citation refers to a selection in the book. For example, "Middleton 6" refers to selection six.

Introduction

It has been observed that "every man is in certain respects (a) like all other men, (b) like some other men, (c) like no other man" (Kluckhohn and Murray 1956, p. 53). This anthology will explore the ways a black American is like other black Americans. The most appropriate tool for this exploration is the concept of modal personality.* This concept refers to those characteristics and patterns of personality that are shared by large numbers of individuals in any group and that may be typical of the group. More specifically it denotes the average score of members of a group on one or more personality variables (Inkeles and Levinson 1969, pp. 423–28; Child 1968, p. 96).† In general, do members have relatively high self-esteem? Or low self-esteem? Compared to the members of other groups, are members likely to direct their aggressions "inward," perhaps as depression or self-blame? Or "outward," perhaps as anger against others or verbal abuse of others? Does the typical member feel that it pays to put forth effort in most situations? Or does he feel that events in his life are usually beyond his control? It is to questions such as these that the study of modal personality seeks answers.

To argue that members of a group may have certain personality characteristics in common is not to deny the uniqueness of each individual. For one thing, there is variability around the average.

* Without attempting to give a rigorous definition of personality, we can in general say that it refers to a combination of the relatively enduring psychological characteristics of an individual that influence his behavior. Some aspects of personality are motivations (e.g., need Achievement), attitudes (e.g., alienation, attitude toward one's racial group), aspects of the self (e.g., self-esteem), aptitudes (e.g., intelligence), and defenses (e.g., methods of handling aggression).

† Ideally, each modal personality characteristic of a group is ascertained by giving a representative sample from the group a measure of personality and then finding the average score of that sample on the measure. The term "average," of course, encompasses several statistical measures—for example, the mode, the median, and the mean. For our purpose here, there is no need to be more precise and talk about specific measures of the average.

For example, even though the typical black feels alienated (Middleton 6), some blacks will be extremely disaffected while others will be reasonably content. Even more important for individuality is that any given aspect of personality is always part of a constellation of personality tendencies, and this constellation is never identical for any two persons.

Though each individual is unique, individuals in a group exposed to the same social conditions may, in response, develop similarities in personality. As a consequence, members of the group may, on the average, differ in certain respects from the members of another group not exposed to these conditions. Blacks, of course, have individual personalities. Yet since they have been subject to discrimination and minority group status, it is not surprising that many would have low need Achievement (i.e., feeble strivings to master tasks).*

How does an investigator go about uncovering such similarities in personality among the members of a group? In practice, he does so by comparing that group with another group—a "control group." In the study of blacks the control group has implicitly or explicitly been American whites. The justification for this is that such research aims to ascertain the effects on personality of a complex of conditions commonly associated with being black (discrimination, poverty, etc.). This requires comparing American blacks with a group that does not live under those conditions. Blacks living in societies in which they are more fully accepted (e.g., Mexico or Puerto Rico) could conceivably serve as a control group. But as a practical matter the not-discriminated-against group that has been most readily available for research is American whites.

If we assume that the modal personality patterns of blacks are due to social influences, our interest should be in blacks not as a race in the biological sense (if, indeed, there is such a thing) but as a race in the sociological sense. Social race refers to a group regarded as distinct by its own members and by other members of the society and whose distinctiveness is based on skin color and

*For a more detailed definition of "need Achievement," see the prefatory note to Rosen's article 5.

other physical features. A group that is looked upon as a race in one society may not be in another society. Blacks in the United States, for example, would not be recognized as a distinctive racial group in Mexico (Van den Berghe 1967, pp. 42–58). Therefore, race, as we use the term here, signifies not the sharing of hereditary characteristics per se but the consciousness of being a distinctive group.

This sociological view of race underscores the differences between stereotypes and modal personality. Historically stereotypes about the behavior and personalities of minority group members have occupied a prominent place in racist thought. Blacks have been pictured as "uppity," insolent, dirty, oversexed, inferior, and dangerous. Central to racist thought has been the view that these stereotyped qualities are biologically innate. As part of racist ideology, stereotypes have served the function of justifying discrimination and prejudice and thereby of keeping the blacks "in their place" (Simpson and Yinger 1965, pp. 119–21; Van den Berghe 1967, pp. 25–34).

The concept of modal personality is fundamentally different from racist stereotyping. Underlying studies of modal personality is the assumption that the personality tendencies shared by blacks are not rooted in genetics but are a response to patterned social conditions. In addition, the specific characteristics of the modal personality rest on scientific evidence. Although particular studies may contain defects of one sort or another, social scientists endeavor to base their generalizations about the personality characteristics of blacks on sound procedures of data collection, measurement, and analysis. Unlike the folklore of stereotypes, moreover, the scholarship on the modal personality of blacks is not designed to justify prejudice and discrimination. On the contrary, to the extent that this line of research enables us to assess the impact of discrimination and minority group status on the inner recesses of the individual, it makes us conscious of the psychological damage that racism has caused.

This consideration accents one rationale for studying the modal personality of blacks. For such study pinpoints the ways in which conditions associated with minority group status have affected the psyche. Discrimination, for example, entails that blacks be thwarted in a variety of ways, such as not being treated with the respect that an individual ordinarily expects in his relations with others. This thwarting, in part, explains the anger and aggression blacks may vent (Berkowitz *11*). Another meaning of discrimination is that blacks have very little prestige in the society. And because the society thinks very little of blacks, they—at least up until recently—have thought very little of themselves as a racial group (Morland *3*).

A further reason for studying the modal personality of blacks is to inform public policy. We know, for example, that blacks who feel powerless in influencing the larger social environment sympathize with rioting and civil disorder more than blacks who do not feel powerless (Ransford 1968). This sense of powerlessness is a reflection of reality, a reflection of the lack of responsiveness on the part of government and of the society generally to the needs and interests of black Americans. Thus, if the society wants to reduce the incidence of civil disorders, it can do so by increasing the responsiveness of government and of other institutions to the wishes and interests of blacks.

Another example of the way the study of modal personality illuminates public policy comes from the area of education. It appears that one reason that black children have not done as well in school as whites is that they believe that their environment does not reward effort (Coleman and others *13*). This belief, too, is based on reality. Historically discrimination has meant that blacks working as hard as whites would not get the same rewards. Thus one way to raise the academic performance of blacks is to create more equality of reward.

To understand just how discrimination affects the psyche of the black man, we need to study the intervening processes by which this impact makes itself felt. Most research on the modal personality patterns of black Americans, however, fails to go beyond a mere delineation of the respects in which blacks and whites differ in personality. The studies tell us, for example, that blacks tend to feel more alienated than whites (Middleton *6*) or that they feel less control over events in their personal lives (Gurin and others *14*).

What is largely missing is attention to the intervening processes by which these differences have come about.

One illustration of this deficiency concerns socioeconomic status (SES). Because of the direct and indirect effects of discrimination, blacks have lower SES than whites. SES correlates with many personality variables on which racial differences have been found. Thus it is reasonable to presuppose that SES mediates some of the effects of minority group membership on personality. This presupposition receives support in Rosen's study (5). His data suggest that one reason that blacks tend to score lower than whites on need Achievement is that blacks have lower socioeconomic status, and individuals with low SES tend to score relatively low on need Achievement. But our knowledge on this point is the exception, not the rule. Unfortunately, the design of all but a few studies makes it impossible to detect to what degree racial differences in personality result from the relatively low SES of blacks.*

Another illustration has to do with the black family. Here it is useful to make a distinction between family structure and family functioning. Most of the studies dealing with the relation between family and personality among blacks focus on the effects of a

---

* Most studies follow one of two procedures. One is to compare blacks and whites on a given personality variable without controlling for SES (e.g., Baugham and Dahlstrom 8). The other is to match the two racial groups on SES before making a comparison (e.g., Biller 1968). In either event, they fail to make the racial comparison *both before and after the control.* (Exceptions are Rosen 5 and Lott and Lott 1963.) Thus they cannot ascertain whether holding SES constant reduces racial differences and therefore to what degree SES mediates black-white differences in personality.

Some authors argue that to discern modal personality patterns of blacks, one should control for, or match on, SES before comparing blacks with whites. Failure to do this, the argument runs, leads to a confounding of race with SES. I disagree. This position is based on the assumption that we should focus on the effects of minority group status on personality apart from the effects of SES. In my view, however, the lower SES of blacks is part and parcel of their minority group status. If blacks have lower levels of income and education, it is due in large part to the direct and indirect effects of discrimination. Therefore racial differences in SES should be thought of as a possible intervening variable in the causal chain leading from minority group status to personality. Instead of starting out by controlling for SES, researchers should make racial comparisons without a control and then afterwards determine the degree to which racial differences in SES account for racial differences in personality.

structural variable, namely the absence of the father. With the exception of Rainwater's study, the second selection in this anthology, few studies try to link the modal personality characteristics of blacks with the way black families function. One study suggests that, compared to white parents, black parents are more likely to punish their children physically (Gold 1958). It has been conjectured that this type of discipline contributes to the tendency of blacks to direct their aggressions "outward" (e.g., in verbal attacks on others) rather than "inward" (e.g., in depression). But no study has really tested this conjecture.

This discussion suggests a great need for research on the intervening mechanisms accounting for the differences between the modal personalities of black and white Americans. Are the differences explained entirely by the lower SES of blacks? Or only partly? Or not at all? How do the structure and functioning of black families affect the modal personality patterns of blacks? These are the kinds of questions that scholarship on black personality should try to answer.

To talk about the effects of discrimination and minority group status on personality is not to imply that all blacks react to these conditions in the same way. There is reason to believe that different segments of the black population vary in their modal personality patterns. Lower-class blacks and middle-class blacks, for example, don't exhibit the same qualities. Rosen (5) found that among lower-class respondents, blacks had the lowest need Achievement scores of any ethnic group. But among the higher-status respondents, the blacks scored very high compared to other ethnic groups. Although lower-class and middle-class blacks are both subject to discrimination, their modal personalities are different.

Blacks of different ages, moreover, may react differently to minority group status. The research on some variables has been done primarily on minors. This, for example, seems to be true of studies of racial differences in self-esteem. Scholars (e.g., Kardiner and Ovesey 1951) once assumed that, because blacks are treated as inferior, their self-esteem would be damaged. But as we shall see (Rosenberg 4), the findings on self-esteem are actually mixed, many studies failing to show that blacks have the low self-esteem that the investigators expected. Perhaps the reason for this inconsistency in the findings is that the researchers have confined their studies to black minors, who are sheltered from many of the harsh and demeaning experiences they will meet later on as adults. In judging his worth, an individual is most likely to compare his achievements with the achievements and the standards of his immediate associates. Because children's social networks are often segregated along lines of race, ethnicity, and class, the immediate associates of a black child are likely to have social characteristics very similar to his own. Consequently, black children are often unaware that their performances and accomplishments don't measure up to white standards. It is therefore not surprising that black children often have the same levels of self-esteem as white children. Black adults, on the other hand, are more exposed to, and more painfully aware of, the greater prestige and the greater economic success of whites. Thus the relatively low self-esteem that the classic authors attributed to blacks may indeed obtain— but only for adults, not children.

The intent of this anthology is to present selections illustrating the range of themes dealt with in the social scientific literature on black personality. The book is limited to non-intellective personality factors. The topics of intelligence and cognitive development have been omitted since they cannot, in my view, be adequately covered in one or two selections; they require a volume in themselves.

In introducing each selection, I have provided a summary of the relevant research findings, a discussion of the weaknesses of the research in a given area, and an examination of concepts and ideas that provide some perspective on the selection. A fault of some discussions of black personality is that they imply that there is a neat, commonly agreed upon body of knowledge in this area. This is not so. The data sometimes contain methodological weaknesses, and the findings are not always consistent. In the commentaries, I have noted the problematic character of our knowledge of many topics.

The commentary that precedes each selection notes other basic readings, which are fully cited in the comprehensive list of references (pp. 315–30). Readers interested in following up a particular topic should consult the selected bibliography (pp. 307–14).

The selections themselves are grouped in three sections. Part I of the anthology sketches the social and historical backdrop necessary for understanding the personality characteristics of American blacks. Included is a thumbnail description of those social trends and conditions that have characterized the situation of blacks in the twentieth century—segregation, discrimination, urbanization, poverty, and organized protest activity. Also discussed are the structure and functioning of the lower-class urban black family as the context within which personality development takes place.

Part II delineates some major characteristics of the modal personality of blacks. Most of the selections present data on racial differences in personality characteristics. Dealt with here are variables such as racial identification, self-esteem, need Achievement, alienation, and sex-role orientation.

Part III focuses on the behavioral expressions of the personality patterns of blacks. What, for example, are the personality correlates of academic performance and of militancy on civil rights? What are the psychological processes underlying violent crimes, "soul" rhetoric, riots, and mass protest? In presenting selections dealing with such questions, I do not intend to suggest that personality factors alone can account for any given form of behavior. Mass demonstrations, for example, are a response to the failure of American society to deal adequately with issues such as civil rights and poverty. Nonetheless, personality factors do play some role in behavior. More specifically, they are important in illuminating the psychological processes by which social conditions affect behavior and in delineating the personality characteristics of those engaging in various kinds of behavior. Studies of personality, then, can contribute to our understanding of the actions and reactions of blacks in American society.

BLACK PSYCHE

Part I: The Social and Historical Backdrop

COMMENTARY to
THE SITUATION OF BLACKS IN AMERICAN SOCIETY

To understand the modal personality characteristics of any group, we have to look at the social conditions that are shared by most, or at least many, members of that group and that set them apart from most other people. For black Americans, these conditions, which are discussed in the following selection, are: (1) discrimination and segregation, (2) poverty, (3) the matrifocal family,* (4) conditions of ghetto living, (5) the civil rights struggle and the resulting sense of relative deprivation, and (6) the resurgence of black nationalism in the last decade. Let us discuss each of these features.

What psychological bearing do discrimination and segregation have? For one thing, they signify low prestige in the society. They provide the mechanisms by which people can look down upon members of a minority group and make them objects of disparagement. In general, minority groups accept the evaluation that the larger society makes of them. Blacks are no exception. Thus, at least until recently, young black children have indicated on projective tests a low sense of identification with their racial group (Morland *3*).

Discrimination, furthermore, means that blacks are not rewarded on the basis of their accomplishments, but on the basis of their race. Blacks, for example, have historically been paid less than whites for the same effort and competence. This inequity is, to a large extent, responsible, one suspects, for the comparatively low levels of achievement motivation typically displayed by blacks (Rosen *5*). It is probably also responsible in part for the more frequent belief among blacks than among whites that the individual's own efforts and actions exert little influence on what happens to him (Coleman and others *13*; Gurin and others *14*).

Another salient characteristic of the situation facing American

---

* The matrifocal, or mother-centered, family is analyzed at length in the selection by Rainwater (*2*).

blacks—in large measure a direct and indirect effect of discrimination—is poverty. In 1970, 34 percent of Negro persons had incomes below the poverty line, compared to only 10 percent of whites (U.S. Bureau of Labor Statistics and U.S. Bureau of the Census 1971, p. 35). Poverty is a prime cause for the dominance of the mother in the black family (Rainwater 2). Although there is disagreement about the effects of such dominance (Hannerz 7), some authors have argued that it impedes proper sex-role development among black males.

In large part a product of poverty and residential segregation, ghetto living involves high crime rates, exploitation by neighborhood merchants, and anomie. The latter features contribute to the alienation that blacks commonly feel (Middleton 6). This alienation, in turn, partially accounts for the frustration and anger that some authors suggest are common among blacks (Berkowitz 11; Solomon and others 12).

On the positive side, residential concentration in the ghettoes of our cities has given blacks a measure of political power, as indicated by the rising number of black public officials (U.S. Bureau of Labor Statistics and U.S. Bureau of the Census 1971, pp. 142-43). This rise has to some extent reduced feelings of powerlessness, as have the victories of the civil rights movement. Nonetheless, many blacks remain disillusioned. The civil rights struggles have failed to accomplish what most blacks had hoped they would. And although the conditions of blacks have improved, the improvement has not kept pace with the increase in aspirations. A consequence has been severe frustration and, resulting from this, intense anger and aggressive feeling (Berkowitz 11; Solomon and others 12).

The most recent trend in the black community has been the strong resurgence of black nationalism—of the sentiment that blacks should take pride in their race, that "black is beautiful." Though hard evidence is lacking, this nationalism probably has encouraged the masses of blacks to identify with their racial group more than they have previously (Morland 3). Black nationalism may also have another effect. Individuals measure their own worth largely in terms of how successful they are in living up to standards set by their culture (Rosenberg 4). Black nationalism is possibly being accompanied by changes in cultural values and a rejection by blacks of the "success" ethic of the mainstream American culture. If so, changes are probably taking place in the criteria by which blacks gauge their sense of self-esteem (Hannerz *10*).

These features of the black social situation in America provide the backdrop necessary for understanding the modal personality patterns of this racial group. Though not of course exhaustive, the discussion here illustrates the ways in which social conditions shared by many blacks affect the psyche and contribute to the modal personality tendencies analyzed in the selections of this anthology.

The Situation of Blacks in American Society

NATIONAL ADVISORY COMMISSION ON CIVIL DISORDERS

As Southern white governments returned to power, beginning with Virginia in 1869 and ending with Louisiana in 1877, the process of relegating the Negro to a subordinate place in American life was accelerated. Disfranchisement was the first step. Negroes who defied the Klan and tried to vote faced an array of deceptions and obstacles: Polling places were changed at the last minute without notice to Negroes, severe time limitations were imposed on marking complicated ballots, votes cast incorrectly in a maze of ballot boxes were nullified. The suffrage provisions of state constitutions were rewritten to disfranchise Negroes who could not read, understand or interpret the Constitution. Some state constitutions permitted those who failed the tests to vote if their ancestors had been eligible to vote on January 1, 1860—a date when no Negro could vote anywhere in the South.

In 1896, there were 130,344 Negroes registered in Louisiana. In 1900, after the state rewrote the suffrage provisions of its constitutions, only 5,320 remained on the registrations books. Essentially the same thing happened in the other states of the former Confederacy.

SEGREGATION BY LAW

When the Supreme Court in 1883 declared the Civil Rights Act of 1875 unconstitutional, Southern states began to enact laws to

* Excerpted from pages 100, 105-13, 1, and 5-7 of *Report* by the National Advisory Commission on Civil Disorders published by the U. S. Government Printing Office, Washington, D. C., 1968.

segregate the races. In 1896, the Supreme Court in *Plessy v. Ferguson* approved "separate but equal" facilities; it was then that segregation became an established fact, by law as well as by custom. Negroes and whites were separated on public carriers and in all places of public accommodation, including hospitals and churches. In courthouses, whites and Negroes took oaths on separate Bibles. In most communities, whites were separated from Negroes in cemeteries.

Segregation invariably meant discrimination. On trains all Negroes, including those holding first-class tickets, were allotted seats in the baggage car. Negroes in public buildings had to use freight elevators and toilet facilities reserved for janitors. Schools for Negro children were at best a weak imitation of those for whites as states spent ten times more to educate white youngsters than Negroes. Discrimination in wages became the rule, whether between Negro and white teachers of similar training and experience or between common laborers on the same job.

Some Northern states enacted civil rights laws in the 1880s, but Negroes in fact were treated little differently in the North than in the South. As Negroes moved north in substantial numbers toward the end of the century, they discovered that equality of treatment did not exist in Massachusetts, New York, or Illinois. They were crowded by local ordinances into sections of the city where housing and public services were generally substandard. Overt discrimination in employment was a general practice and job opportunities apart from menial tasks were few. Most labor unions excluded Negroes from membership—or granted membership in separate and powerless Jim Crow locals. Yet when Negroes secured employment during strikes, labor leaders castigated them for undermining the principles of trade unionism. And when Negroes sought to move into the mainstream of community life by seeking membership in the organizations around them—educational, cultural, and religious—they were invariably rebuffed.

By the twentieth century, the Negro was at the bottom of American society. Disfranchised, Negroes throughout the country were excluded by employers and labor unions from white-collar jobs and skilled trades. Jim Crow laws and farm tenancy characterized Negro existence in the South. About one hundred lynchings occurred every year in the 1880s and 1890s; there were one hundred sixty-one lynchings in 1892. As increasing numbers of Negroes migrated to Northern cities, race riots became commonplace. Northern whites, even many former abolitionists, began to accept the white South's views on race relations.

That Northern whites would resort to violence was made clear in anti-Negro riots in New York City, 1900; Springfield, Ohio, 1904; Greensburg, Indiana, 1906; and Springfield, Illinois, 1908.

The Springfield, Illinois, riot lasted three days. It was initiated by a white woman's charge of rape by a Negro, inflamed by newspapers, and intensified by crowds of whites gathered around the jail demanding that the Negro, arrested and imprisoned, be lynched. When the sheriff transferred the accused and another Negro to a jail in a nearby town, rioters headed for the Negro section and attacked homes and businesses owned by or catering to Negroes. White owners who showed handkerchiefs in their windows averted harm to their stores. One Negro was summarily lynched, others were dragged from houses and streetcars and beaten. By the time National Guardsmen could reach the scene, six persons were dead—four whites and two Negroes. Property damage was extensive. Many Negroes left Springfield, hoping to find better conditions elsewhere, especially in Chicago.

THE POSTWAR PERIOD

White opinion in some quarters of America had begun to shift to a more sympathetic regard for Negroes during the New Deal, and the [Second World] War had accelerated that movement. Thoughtful whites had been painfully aware of the contradiction in opposing Nazi racial philosophy with racially segregated military units. In the postwar years, American racial attitudes became more liberal as new nonwhite nations emerged in Asia and Africa and took increasing responsibilities in international councils.

Against this background, the growing size of the Northern Negro vote made civil rights a major issue in national elections and, ultimately, in 1957, led to the establishment of the Federal Civil Rights Commission, which had the power to investigate discriminatory conditions throughout the country and to recommend corrective measures to the President. Northern and Western states outlawed discrimination in employment, housing and public accommodations, while the NAACP, in successive court victories, won judgments against racially restrictive covenants in housing, segregation in interstate transportation and discrimination in publicly-owned recreation facilities. The NAACP helped register voters, and in 1954, *Brown* v. *Board of Education* became the triumphant climax of the NAACP's campaign against educational segregation in the public schools of the South.

CORE, which had been conducting demonstrations in the Border states, its major focus on public accommodations, began experimenting with direct-action techniques to open employment opportunities. In 1947, in conjunction with the Fellowship of Reconciliation, CORE conducted a "Journey of Reconciliation"—what would later be called a "Freedom Ride"—in the states of the upper South to test compliance with the Supreme Court decision outlawing segregation on interstate buses. The resistance met by riders in some areas and the sentencing of two of them to thirty days on a North Carolina road gang dramatized the gap between American democratic theory and practice.

The Montgomery, Alabama, bus boycott of 1955-56 captured the imagination of the nation and of the Negro community in particular, and led to the growing use of direct-action techniques. It catapulted into national prominence the Reverend Martin Luther King, Jr., who, like the founders of CORE, held to a Gandhian belief in the principles of pacifism.

Even before a court decision obtained by NAACP attorneys in November, 1956, desegregated the Montgomery buses, a similar movement had started in Tallahassee, Florida. Afterward, another one developed in Birmingham, Alabama. In 1957, the Tuskegee Negroes undertook a three-year boycott of local merchants after the state legislature gerrymandered nearly all of the Negro voters outside of the town's boundaries. In response to a lawsuit filed by the NAACP, the Supreme Court ruled the Tuskegee gerrymander illegal.

These events were widely heralded. The "new Negro" had now emerged in the South—militant, no longer fearful of white hoodlums or mobs and ready to use his collective strength to achieve his ends. In this mood, King established the Southern Christian Leadership Conference in 1957 to coordinate direct-action activities in Southern cities.

Nonviolent direct action attained popularity not only because of the effectiveness of King's leadership, but because the older techniques of legal and legislative action had had limited success. Impressive as the advances in the fifteen years after World War II were, in spite of state laws and Supreme Court decisions, something was still clearly wrong. Negroes remained disfranchised in most of the South, though in the twelve years following the outlawing of the white primary in 1944, the number of Negroes registered in Southern states had risen from about 250,000 to nearly a million and a quarter. Supreme Court decisions desegregating transportation facilities were still being largely ignored in the South. Discrimination in employment and housing continued, not only in the South but also in Northern states with model civil rights laws. The Negro unemployment rate steadily moved upward after 1954. The South reacted to the Supreme Court's decision on school desegregation by attempting to outlaw the NAACP, intimidating civil rights leaders, calling for "massive resistance" to the Court's decision, curtailing Negro voter registration and forming White Citizens' Councils.

REVOLUTION OF RISING EXPECTATIONS

At the same time, Negro attitudes were changing. In what has been described as a "revolution in expectations," Negroes were gaining a new sense of self-respect and a new self-image as a result of the civil rights movement and their own advancement. King and others were demonstrating that nonviolent action could succeed in the South. New laws and court decisions and the increasing support of white public opinion gave American Negroes a new confidence in the future.

Negroes no longer felt that they had to accept the humiliations of second-class citizenship. Ironically, it was the very successes in the legislatures and the courts that, more perhaps than any other single factor, led to intensified Negro expectations and resulting dissatisfaction with the limitations of legal and legislative programs. Increasing Negro impatience accounted for the rising tempo of nonviolent direct action in the late 1950s, culminating in the student sit-ins of 1960 and the inauguration of what is popularly known as the "Civil Rights Revolution" or the "Negro Revolt."

Many believe that the Montgomery boycott ushered in this Negro Revolt, and there is no doubt that, in its importance, by projecting the image of King and his techniques, it had great importance. But the decisive break with traditional techniques came with the college student sit-ins that swept the South in the winter and spring of 1960. In dozens of communities in the upper South, the Atlantic coastal states and Texas, student demonstrations secured the desegregation of lunch counters in drug and variety stores. Arrests were numbered in the thousands, and brutality was evident in scores of communities. In the Deep South, the campaign ended in failure, even in instances where hundreds had been arrested, as in Montgomery, Orangeburg, South Carolina, and Baton Rouge. But the youth had captured the imagination of the Negro community and to a remarkable extent of the whole nation.

STUDENT INVOLVEMENT

The Negro protest movement would never be the same again. The Southern college students shook the power structure of the Negro community, made direct action temporarily preeminent as a civil rights tactic, speeded up the process of social change in race relations, and ultimately turned the Negro protest organizations toward a deep concern with the economic and social problems of the masses.

Involved in this was a gradual shift in both tactics and goals: from legal to direct action, from middle and upper class to mass action, from attempts to guarantee the Negro's constitutional rights to efforts to secure economic policies giving him equality of opportunity, from appeals to the sense of fair play of white Americans to demands based upon power in the black ghetto.

The successes of the student movement threatened existing Negro leadership and precipitated a spirited rivalry among civil rights organizations. The NAACP and SCLC associated themselves with the student movement. The organizing meeting of the Student Nonviolent Coordinating Committee (SNCC) at Raleigh, North Carolina, in April, 1960, was called by Martin Luther King, but within a year the youth considered King too cautious and broke with him.

The NAACP now decided to make direct action a major part of its strategy and organized and reactivated college and youth chapters in the Southern and Border states.

CORE, still unknown to the general public, installed James Farmer as national director in January, 1961, and that spring joined the front rank of civil rights organizations with the famous Freedom Ride to Alabama and Mississippi that dramatized the persistence of segregated public transportation. A bus-burning resulted in Alabama. Hundreds of demonstrators spent a month or more in Mississippi prisons. Finally, a new order from the Interstate Commerce Commission desegregating all interstate transportation facilities received partial compliance.

ORGANIZATIONAL DIFFERENCES

Disagreement over strategy and tactics inevitably became intertwined with personal and organizational rivalries. Each civil rights group felt the need for proper credit in order to obtain the prestige and financial contributions necessary to maintain and expand its own programs. The local and national, individual and organizational clashes stimulated competition and activity that further accelerated the pace of social change.

Yet there were differences in style. CORE was the most interracial. SCLC appeared to be the most deliberate. SNCC staff workers lived on subsistence allowances and seemed to regard going to jail as a way of life. The NAACP continued the most varied programs, retaining a highly effective lobby at the national capital and engaging in direct-action campaigns. The National Urban League under the leadership of Whitney M. Young, Jr., appointed executive director in 1961, became more outspoken and talked more firmly to businessmen who had previously been treated with utmost tact and caution.

The role of whites in the protest movement gradually changed. Instead of occupying positions of leadership, they found themselves relegated to the role of followers. Whites were likely to be suspect in the activist organizations. Negroes had come to feel less dependent on whites, more confident of their own power, and they demanded that their leaders be black. The NAACP had long since acquired Negro leadership but continued to welcome white liberal support. SCLC and SNCC were from the start Negro-led and Negro-dominated. CORE became predominantly Negro as it expanded in 1962 and 1963; today all executives are Negro, and a constitutional amendment adopted in 1965 officially limited white leadership in the chapters.

A major factor intensifying the civil rights movement was widespread Negro unemployment and poverty; an important force in awakening Negro protest was the meteoric rise to national prominence of the Black Muslims, established around 1930. The organization reached the peak of its influence when more progress toward equal rights was being made than ever before in American history, while at the same time the poorest groups in the urban ghettos were stagnating.

The Black Muslims preached a vision of the doom of the white "devils" and the coming dominance of the black man, promised a utopian paradise of a separate territory within the United States for a Negro state, and offered a practical program of building Negro business through hard work, thrift and racial unity. To those willing to submit to the rigid discipline of the movement, the Black Muslims organization gave a sense of purpose and dignity.

"FREEDOM NOW!" AND CIVIL RIGHTS LAWS

As the direct-action tactics took more dramatic form, as the civil rights groups began to articulate the needs of the masses and draw some of them to their demonstrations, the protest movement in 1963 assumed a new note of urgency, a demand for complete "Freedom Now!" Direct action returned to the Northern cities, taking the form of massive protests against economic, housing and educational inequities, and a fresh wave of demonstrations swept the South from Cambridge, Maryland, to Birmingham, Alabama. Northern Negroes launched street demonstrations against discrimination in the building trade unions, and, the following winter, school boycotts against de facto segregation.

In the North, 1963 and 1964 brought the beginning of the waves of civil disorders in Northern urban centers. In the South, incidents occurred of brutal white resistance to the civil rights movement, beginning with the murders of Mississippi Negro leader Medgar Evers, and of four Negro schoolgirls in a church in Birmingham.

The massive anti-Negro resistance in Birmingham and numerous other Southern cities during the spring of 1963 compelled the nation to face the problem of race prejudice in the South. President Kennedy affirmed that racial discrimination was a moral issue and asked Congress for a major civil rights bill. But a major impetus for what was to be the Civil Rights Act of 1964 was the March on Washington in August, 1963.

Early in the year, A. Philip Randolph issued a call for a March on Washington to dramatize the need for jobs and to press for a federal commitment to job action. At about the same time, Protestant, Jewish and Catholic churches sought and obtained representation on the March committee. Although the AFL-CIO national council refused to endorse the March, a number of labor leaders and international unions participated.

Reversing an earlier stand, President Kennedy approved the March. A quarter of a million people, about twenty percent of them white, participated. It was more than a summation of the past years of struggle and aspiration. It symbolized certain new directions: a deeper concern for the economic problems of the masses, more involvement of white moderates and new demands from the most militant, who implied that only a revolutionary change in American institutions would permit Negroes to achieve the dignity of citizens.

President Kennedy had set the stage for the Civil Rights Act of 1964. After his death, President Johnson took forceful and effective action to secure its enactment. The law settled the public accommodations issue in the South's major cities. Its voting section, however, promised more than it could accomplish. Martin Luther King and SCLC dramatized the issue locally with demonstrations at Selma, Alabama, in the spring of 1965. Again the national government was forced to intervene, and a new and more effective voting law was passed.

FAILURES OF DIRECT ACTION

Birmingham had made direct action respectable; Selma, which drew thousands of white moderates from the North, made direct action fashionable. Yet as early as 1964, it was becoming evident that, like legal action, direct action was of limited usefulness.

In Deep South states like Mississippi and Alabama, direct action had failed to desegregate public accommodation in the sit-ins of 1960–61. A major reason was that Negroes lacked the leverage of the vote. The demonstrations of the early 1960s had been successful principally in places like Atlanta, Nashville, Durham, Winston-Salem, Louisville, Savannah, New Orleans, Charleston, and Dallas—where Negroes voted and could swing elections. Beginning in 1961, Robert Moses, of SNCC, with the cooperation of CORE and NAACP, established voter registration projects in the cities and county seats of Mississippi. He succeeded in registering only a handful of Negroes, but by 1964, he had generated enough support throughout the country to enable the Mississippi Freedom Democratic Party, which he had created, to challenge dramatically the seating of the official white delegates from the state at the Democratic National Convention.

In the black ghettos of the North, direct action also largely failed. Street demonstrations did compel employers, from supermarkets to banks, to add Negroes to their work force in Northern and Western cities, and even in some Southern cities where the

Negroes had considerable buying power. However, separate and inferior schools, slum housing, and police hostility proved invulnerable to direct attack.

NEW DIRECTIONS

Although Negroes were being hired in increasing numbers, mass unemployment and underemployment remained. As economist Vivian Henderson pointed out in his testimony before the Commission:

> No one can deny that all Negroes have benefited from civil rights laws and desegregation in public life in one way or another. The fact is, however, that the masses of Negroes have not experienced tangible benefits in a significant way. This is so in education and housing. It is critically so in the area of jobs and economic security. Expectations of Negro masses for equal job opportunity programs have fallen far short of fulfillment.
>
> Negroes have made gains. . . . There have been important gains. But . . . the masses of Negroes have been virtually untouched by those gains.

Faced with the intransigence of the Deep South and the inadequacy of direct action to solve the problems of the slum-dwellers, Negro protest organizations began to diverge. The momentum toward unity, apparent in 1963, was lost. At the very time that white support for the protest movement was rising markedly, militant Negroes felt increasingly isolated from the American scene. On two things, however, all segments of the protest movement agreed: (1) Future civil rights activity would have to focus on economic and social discrimination in the urban ghettos; and (2) while demonstrations would still have a place, the major weapon would have to be the political potential of the black masses.

By the middle of the decade, many militant Negro members of SNCC and CORE began to turn away from American society and the "middle-class way of life." Cynical about the liberals and the leaders of organized labor, they regarded compromise, even as a temporary tactical device, as anathema. They talked more of "revolutionary" changes in the social structure and of retaliatory violence, and increasingly rejected white assistance. They insisted that Negro power alone could compel the white "ruling class" to make concessions. Yet they also spoke of an alliance of Negroes and unorganized lower class whites to overthrow the "power structure" of capitalists, politicians, and bureaucratic labor leaders who exploited the poor of both races by dividing them through an appeal to race prejudice.

At the same time that their activities declined, other issues, particularly Vietnam, diverted the attention of this country, and of some Negro leaders, from the issue of equality. In civil rights organizations, reduced financing made it increasingly difficult to support staff personnel. Most important was the increasing frustration of expectations that affected the direct-action advocates of the early 1960s—the sense of futility growing out of the feeling that progress had turned out to be "tokenism," that the compromises of the white community were sedatives rather than solutions and that the current methods of Negro protest were doing little for the masses of the race.

As frustration grew, the ideology and rhetoric of a number of civil rights activists became angrier. One man more than any other —a black man who grew up believing whites had murdered his father—became a spokesman for this anger: Malcolm X, who perhaps best embodied the belief that racism was so deeply ingrained in white America that appeals to conscience would bring no fundamental change.

"BLACK POWER"

In this setting, the rhetoric of Black Power developed. The precipitating occasion was the Meredith March from Memphis to Jackson in June, 1966, but the slogan expressed tendencies that had been present for a long time and had been gaining strength in the Negro community.

Black Power first articulated a mood rather than a program: disillusionment and alienation from white America and independence, race pride, and self-respect, or "black consciousness."

Having become a household phrase, the term generated intense discussion of its real meaning, and a broad spectrum of ideologies and programmatic proposals emerged.

In politics, Black Power meant independent action—Negro control of the political power of the black ghettos and its use to improve economic and social conditions. It could take the form of organizing a black political party or controlling the political machinery within the ghetto without the guidance or support of white politicians. Where predominantly Negro areas lacked Negroes in elective office, whether in the rural Black Belt of the South or in the urban centers, Black Power advocates sought the election of Negroes by voter registration campaigns, by getting out the vote, and by working for redrawing electoral districts. The basic belief was that only a well-organized and cohesive bloc of Negro voters could provide for the needs of the black masses. Even some Negro politicians allied to the major political parties adopted the term "Black Power" to describe their interest in the Negro vote.

In economic terms, Black Power meant creating independent, self-sufficient Negro business enterprise, not only by encouraging Negro entrepreneurs but also by forming Negro cooperatives in the ghettos and in the predominantly black rural counties of the South. In the area of education, Black Power called for local community control of the public schools in the black ghettos.

Throughout, the emphasis was on self-help, racial unity, and, among the most militant, retaliatory violence, the latter ranging from the legal right of self-defense to attempts to justify looting and arson in ghetto riots, guerrilla warfare, and armed rebellion.

Phrases like "Black Power," "Black Consciousness," and "Black is Beautiful," enjoyed an extensive currency in the Negro community, even within the NAACP and among relatively conservative politicians, but particularly among young intellectuals and Afro-American student groups on predominantly white college campuses. Expressed in its most extreme form by small, often local, fringe groups, the Black Power ideology became associated with SNCC and CORE.

Generally regarded today as the most militant among the important Negro protest organizations, they have developed different interpretations of the Black Power doctrine. SNCC calls for totally independent political action outside the established political parties, as with the Black Panther Party in Lowndes County, Alabama; rejects the political alliances with other groups until Negroes have themselves built a substantial base of independent political power; applauds the idea of guerrilla warfare; and regards riots as rebellions.

CORE has been more flexible. Approving the SNCC strategy, it also advocates working within the Democratic Party, forming alliances with other groups and, while seeking to justify riots as the natural explosion of an oppressed people against intolerable conditions, advocates violence only in self-defense. Both groups favor cooperatives, but CORE has seemed more inclined toward job-training programs and developing a Negro entrepreneurial class, based upon the market within the black ghettos.

THE MEANING

By 1967, whites could point to the demise of slavery, the decline of illiteracy among Negroes, the legal protection provided by the constitutional amendments and civil rights legislation, and the growing size of the Negro middle class. Whites would call it Negro progress, from slavery to freedom and toward equality.

Negroes could point to the doctrine of white supremacy, its persistence after emancipation and its influence on the definition of the place of Negroes in American life. They could point to their long fight for full citizenship when they had active opposition from most of the white population and little or no support from the Government. They could see progress toward equality accompanied by bitter resistance. Perhaps most of all, they could feel the persistent, pervasive racism that kept them in inferior segregated schools, restricted them to ghettos, barred them from fair employment, provided double standards in courts of justice, inflicted bodily harm on their children and blighted their lives with a sense of hopelessness and despair.

In all of this and in the context of professed ideals, Negroes would find more retrogression than progress, more rejection than acceptance.

Until the middle of the twentieth century, the course of Negro protest movements in the United States, except for slave revolts, was based in the cities of the North, where Negroes enjoyed sufficient freedom to mount a sustained protest. It was in the cities, North and South, that Negroes had their greatest independence and mobility. It was natural, therefore, for black protest movements to be urban-based—and, until the last dozen years or so, limited to the North. As Negroes migrated from the South, the mounting strength of their votes in northern cities became a vital element in drawing the Federal Government into the defense of the civil rights of Southern Negroes. While rural Negroes today face great racial problems, the major unsolved questions that touch the core of Negro life stem from discrimination embedded in urban housing, employment, and education.

Over the years the character of Negro protest has changed. Originally, it was a white liberal and Negro upper class movement aimed at securing the constitutional rights of Negroes through propaganda, law suits, and legislation. In recent years, the emphasis in tactics shifted first to direct action and then—among the most militant—to the rhetoric of "Black Power." The role of white liberals declined as Negroes came to direct the struggle. At the same time, the Negro protest movement became more of a mass movement, with increasing participation from the working classes. As these changes were occurring, and while substantial progress was being made to secure constitutional rights for the Negroes, the goals of the movement were broadened. Protest groups now demand special efforts to overcome the Negro's poverty and cultural deprivation—conditions that cannot be erased simply by ensuring constitutional rights.

THE BASIC CAUSES

The summer of 1967 again brought racial disorder to American cities, and with them shock, fear, and bewilderment to the Nation.

In addressing the question "Why did it happen?" we shift our focus to the factors within the society at large that created a mood of violence among many urban Negroes.

Race prejudice has shaped our history decisively; it now threatens to affect our future.

White racism is essentially responsible for the explosive mixture which has been accumulating in our cities since the end of World War II. Among the ingredients of this mixture are:

—Pervasive discrimination and segregation in employment, education, and housing, which have resulted in the continuing exclusion of great numbers of Negroes from the benefits of economic progress.

—Black in-migration and white exodus, which have produced the massive and growing concentrations of impoverished Negroes in our major cities, creating a growing crisis of deteriorating facilities and services and unmet human needs.

—The black ghettos, where segregation and poverty converge on the young to destroy opportunity and enforce failure. Crime, drug addiction, dependency on welfare, and bitterness and resentment against society in general and white society in particular are the result.

At the same time, most whites and some Negroes outside the ghetto have prospered to a degree unparalleled in the history of civilization. Through television and other media, this affluence has been flaunted before the eyes of the Negro poor and the jobless ghetto youth.

Yet these facts alone cannot be said to have caused the disorders. Recently, other powerful ingredients have begun to catalyze the mixture:

—Frustrated hopes are the residue of the unfulfilled expectations aroused by the great judicial and legislative victories of the civil rights movement and the dramatic struggle for equal rights in the South.

—A climate that tends toward approval and encouragement of violence as a form of protest has been created by white terrorism directed against nonviolent protest; by the open defiance of law and Federal authority by state and local officials resisting desegregation; and by some protest groups engaging in civil disobedience who turn their backs

on nonviolence, go beyond the constitutionally protected rights of peti-
tion and free assembly, and resort to violence to attempt to compel
alteration of laws and policies with which they disagree.

—The frustrations of powerlessness have led some Negroes to the conviction that there is no effective alternative to violence as a means of
achieving redress of grievances, and of "moving the system." These
frustrations are reflected in alienation and hostility toward the institutions of law and government and the white society which controls
them, and in the reach toward racial consciousness and solidarity reflected in the slogan "Black Power."

—A new mood has sprung up among Negroes, particularly among the
young, in which self-esteem and enhanced racial pride are replacing
apathy and submission to "the system."

—The police are not merely a "spark" factor. To some Negroes police
have come to symbolize white power, white racism, and white repres-
sion. And the fact is that many police do reflect and express these
white attitudes. The atmosphere of hostility and cynicism is reinforced
by a widespread belief among Negroes in the existence of police brutality and in a "double standard" of justice and protection—one for
Negroes and one for whites.

THE FORMATION OF THE RACIAL GHETTOS*

Throughout the twentieth century the Negro population of the
United States has been moving steadily from rural areas to urban
and from South to North and West. In 1910, ninety-one percent
of the Nation's 9.8 million Negroes lived in the South and only
twenty-seven percent of American Negroes lived in cities of 2,500
persons or more. Between 1910 and 1966 the total Negro population more than doubled, reaching 21.5 million, and the number
living in metropolitan areas rose more than fivefold (from 2.6
million to 14.8 million). The number outside the South rose
elevenfold (from 885,000 to 9.7 million).

Negro migration from the South has resulted from the expectation of thousands of new and highly paid jobs for unskilled

* The term "ghetto" as used in this Report refers to an area within a city characterized
by poverty and acute social disorganization and inhabited by members of a racial or
ethnic group under conditions of involuntary segregation.

workers in the North and the shift to mechanized farming in the South. However, the Negro migration is small when compared to earlier waves of European immigrants. Even between 1960 and 1966, there were 1.8 million immigrants from abroad compared to the 613,000 Negroes who arrived in the North and West from the South.

As a result of the growing number of Negroes in urban areas, natural increase has replaced migration as the primary source of Negro population increase in the cities. Nevertheless, Negro migration from the South will continue unless economic conditions there change dramatically.

Basic data concerning Negro urbanization trends indicate that:

—Almost all Negro population growth (ninety-eight percent from 1950 to 1966) is occurring within metropolitan areas, primarily within central cities.*

—The vast majority of white population growth (seventy-eight percent from 1960 to 1966) is occurring in suburban portions of metropolitan areas. Since 1960, white central city population has declined by 1.3 million.

—As a result, central cities are becoming more heavily Negro while the suburban fringes around them remain almost entirely white.

—The twelve largest central cities now contain over two-thirds of the Negro population outside the South, and almost one-third of the Negro total in the United States.

Within the cities, Negroes have been excluded from white residential areas through discriminatory practices. Just as significant is the withdrawal of white families from, or their refusal to enter, neighborhoods where Negroes are moving or already residing. About twenty percent of the urban population of the United States changes residence every year. The refusal of whites to move into "changing" areas when vacancies occur means that most vacancies eventually are occupied by Negroes.

The result, according to a recent study, is that in 1960 the

---

* A "central city" is the largest city of a standard metropolitan statistical area, that is, a metropolitan area containing at least one city of 50,000 or more inhabitants.

average sergregation index for two hundred seven of the largest U.S. cities was 86.2. In other words, to create an unsegregated population distribution, an average of over 86 percent of all Negroes would have to change their place of residence within the city.

UNEMPLOYMENT, FAMILY STRUCTURE, AND SOCIAL DISORGANIZATION

Although there have been gains in Negro income nationally, and a decline in the number of Negroes below the "poverty level," the condition of Negroes in the central city remains in a state of crisis. Between 2 and 2.5 million Negroes—sixteen to twenty percent of the total Negro population of all central cities—live in squalor and deprivation in ghetto neighborhoods.

Employment is a key problem. It not only controls the present for the Negro American but, in a most profound way, it is creating the future as well. Yet, despite continuing economic growth and declining national unemployment rates, the unemployment rate for Negroes in 1967 was more than double that for whites.

Equally important is the undesirable nature of many jobs open to Negroes and other minorities. Negro men are more than three times as likely as white men to be in low-paying, unskilled, or service jobs. This concentration of male Negro employment at the lowest end of the occupational scale is the single most important cause of poverty among Negroes.

In one study of low-income neighborhoods, the "sub-employment rate," including both unemployment and under-employment, was about thirty-three percent, or 8.8 times greater than the overall unemployment rate for all U.S. workers.

Employment problems, aggravated by the constant arrival of new unemployed migrants, many of them from depressed rural areas, create persistent poverty in the ghetto. In 1966, about 11.9 percent of the Nation's whites and 40.6 percent of its nonwhites were below the poverty level defined by the Social Security Administration (in 1966, $3,335 per year for an urban family of four). Over 40 percent of the nonwhites below the poverty level live in the central cities.

Employment problems have drastic social impact in the ghetto. Men who are chronically unemployed or employed in the lowest status jobs are often unable or unwilling to remain with their families. The handicap imposed on children growing up without fathers in an atmosphere of deprivation is increased as mothers are forced to work to provide support.

The culture of poverty that results from unemployment and family breakup generates a system of ruthless, exploitative relationships within the ghetto. Prostitution, dope addiction, and crime create an environmental "jungle" characterized by personal insecurity and tension. Children growing up under such conditions are likely participants in civil disorder.

CONDITIONS OF LIFE IN THE RACIAL GHETTO

A striking difference in environment from that of white, middle-class Americans profoundly influences the lives of residents of the ghetto.

Crime rates, consistently higher than in other areas, create a pronounced sense of insecurity. For example, in one city one low-income Negro district had thirty-five times as many serious crimes against persons as a high-income white district. Unless drastic steps are taken, the crime problems in poverty areas are likely to continue to multiply as the growing youth and rapid urbanization of the population outstrip police resources.

Poor health and sanitation conditions in the ghetto result in higher mortality rates, a higher incidence of major diseases, and lower availability and utilization of medical services. The infant mortality rate for nonwhite babies under the age of one month is fifty-eight percent higher than for whites; for one to twelve months it is almost three times as high. The level of sanitation in the ghetto is far below that in high-income areas. Garbage collection is often inadequate. Of an estimated fourteen thousand cases of rat bite in the United States in 1965, most were in ghetto neighborhoods.

Ghetto residents believe they are exploited by local merchants; and evidence substantiates some of these beliefs. A study conducted in one city by the Federal Trade Commission showed that higher prices were charged for goods sold in ghetto stores than in other areas.

Lack of knowledge regarding credit purchasing creates special pitfalls for the disadvantaged. In many states, garnishment practices compound these difficulties by allowing creditors to deprive individuals of their wages without hearing or trial.

COMPARING THE IMMIGRANT AND NEGRO EXPERIENCE

Why have so many Negroes, unlike the European immigrants, been unable to escape from the ghetto and from poverty?

We believe the following factors play a part:

—The maturing economy. When the European immigrants arrived, they gained an economic foothold by providing the unskilled labor needed by industry. Unlike the immigrant, the Negro migrant found little opportunity in the city. The economy, by then matured, had little use for the unskilled labor he had to offer.

—The disability of race. The structure of discrimination has stringently narrowed opportunities for the Negro and restricted his prospects. European immigrants suffered from discrimination, but never so pervasively.

—Entry into the political system. The immigrants usually settled in rapidly growing cities with powerful and expanding political machines, which traded economic advantages for political support. Ward-level grievance machinery, as well as personal representation, enabled the immigrant to make his voice heard and his power felt.

By the time the Negro arrived, these political machines were no longer so powerful or so well equipped to provide jobs or other favors, and in many cases were unwilling to share their remaining influence with Negroes.

—Cultural factors. Coming from societies with a low standard of living and at a time when job aspirations were low, the immigrants sensed little deprivation in being forced to take the less desirable and poorer paying jobs. Their large and cohesive families contributed to total income. Their vision of the future—one that led to a life outside of the ghetto—provided the incentive necessary to endure the present.

Although Negro men worked as hard as the immigrants, they were unable to support their families. The entrepreneurial opportunities had vanished. As a result of slavery and long periods of unemployment, the Negro family structure had become matriarchal; the males played a secondary and marginal family role—one which offered little compensation for their hard and unrewarding labor. Above all, segregation denied Negroes access to good jobs and the opportunity to leave the ghetto. For them, the future seemed to lead only to a dead end.

Today, whites tend to exaggerate how well and quickly they escaped from poverty. The fact is that immigrants who came from rural backgrounds, as many Negroes do, are only now, after three generations, finally beginning to move into the middle class.

By contrast, Negroes began concentrating in the city less than two generations ago, and under much less favorable conditions. Although some Negroes have escaped poverty, few have been able to escape the urban ghetto.

COMMENTARY on
CRUCIBLE OF IDENTITY

Personality develops, to a large extent, in the intimate setting of the family. It is shaped both subtly and not-so-subtly by parents' treatment of the child and by the general tone of family relations. Yet it is a central theme of this reader that the major influences on the modal personality characteristics of blacks are discrimination and poverty—influences which are outside the family. How can we reconcile these two ideas? The answer lies in the influence that the larger social structure exerts on the patterns of family life. If discrimination and poverty influence personality, their influence is largely indirect and mediated by the family. That is to say, they affect the structure and functioning of the family, which in turn influence the developing personalities of children.

Racial differences in family structure have been well documented. The feature of the black family that has received the most attention has been its mother-centered structure, often the result of divorce, desertion, or separation. In 1971, 29 percent of non-white families lacked a father, compared to only 9 percent of white families. In the last few decades, moreover, the rate of father absence among blacks has increased while the rate among whites has remained constant (U.S. Bureau of Labor Statistics and U.S. Bureau of the Census 1971, p. 107). The matrifocal, or mother-centered, family is not evenly distributed among all segments of the black population. As Rainwater demonstrates in the following selection, it is most common among poor urban blacks. Indeed, the head of the family for the majority of poor blacks is female, and the majority of poor black children live in fatherless households (U.S. Bureau of Labor Statistics and U.S. Bureau of the Census 1971, pp. 109 and 111). Note that these data refer to only one point in time. The cumulative rate is probably greater. That is, a much higher proportion of black youngsters probably experience family life without a father figure sometime in the first eighteen years of their lives.

The mother-centered structure is a product of several factors. In part it is a legacy of the slavery period in American history, when marriage among slaves was not recognized and family members were often separated from each other in the course of being sold. More important, however, has been the migration of blacks from the rural south to the urban north. Migration has removed blacks from the social controls that serve to protect family life. But the most damaging present-day influences on black family life are discrimination and poverty. Because of both the direct and indirect effects of discrimination, black males are at a marked disadvantage in getting and holding well-paying jobs. Thus many black fathers have a hard time supporting their wives and children. This places severe strains on family life and eventually leads to the breakup of many low-income black families (Liebow 1967; Bernard 1966, pp. 19-23; U.S. Department of Labor 1965, chapter 3).

The stress on the mother-centered pattern of many black families is the hallmark of the controversial report by Moynihan for the U.S. Department of Labor (1965). This report has been under fire on a number of counts.* For one thing, the critics argue that Moynihan exaggerates racial differences in family structure. When presenting data on the proportion of households in which the father is absent, for example, Moynihan fails to control statistically for income. The effect is spuriously to inflate the gap between blacks and whites in rates of father absence since blacks tend to be poorer than whites and poor families are more likely to be matrifocal than middle-income families. Second, Moynihan argues that the absence of the father is a factor in several "pathological" phenomena, such as school failure, delinquency, and drug addiction, which have high rates among blacks. The critics interpret Moynihan as placing moral blame for these pathologies on defects in the black family. This assignment of blame, they argue, detracts from the role that white racism plays in the "tangle of pathology." Third, in focusing on family instability, Moynihan ignores the intactness of the overwhelming majority of black families and supplies verbal ammunition that racists may use in their propaganda. Finally, the critics argue that

---

* Selections containing criticisms of the Moynihan report have been reprinted in Rainwater and Yancy (1967, chapters 16 and 17).

Moynihan ignores the strengths of the black family. Black households, for example, are more likely than white households to include extended kin, such as grandmothers and aunts. This extended kinship has been one feature of the black family that has enabled it to cope with the problems and strains of living imposed on blacks by white society.

In the debate on the black family, Rainwater clearly sides with Moynihan inasmuch as his selection focuses on the mother-centered structure. But this structure is only a starting point in Rainwater's analysis. He is more concerned with the stages in the life of the family and with the flavor of family life among poor urban blacks. It is in the context of the family, Rainwater's analysis suggests, that many of the personality characteristics dealt with in Parts II and III of this reader develop. These characteristics operate as disabilities insofar as they hinder efforts to achieve a more gratifying way of life. The family, however, is not in any moral sense at fault. On the contrary, the fault lies with what Rainwater calls "white cupidity" and with the horrendous conditions that many blacks live under as a result of this cupidity.

Crucible of Identity

THE NEGRO LOWER-CLASS FAMILY

LEE RAINWATER*

As long as Negroes have been in America, their marital and family patterns have been subjects of curiosity and amusement, moral indignation and self-congratulation, puzzlement and frustration, concern and guilt, on the part of white Americans.† As some Negroes have moved into middle-class status, or acquired standards of American common-man respectability, they too have shared these attitudes toward the private behavior of their fellows, sometimes with a moral punitiveness to rival that of whites, but at other times with a hard-headed interest in causes and remedies rather than moral evaluation. Moralism permeated the subject of Negro sexual, marital, and family behavior in the polemics of slavery apologists and abolitionists as much as in the Northern and Southern civil rights controversies of today. Yet, as long as the dialectic of good or bad, guilty or innocent, overshadows a

* Reprinted by permission from *Daedalus*, Journal of the American Academy of Arts and Sciences, Boston: Mass., vol. 95, number 1, pp. 172–216, 1966; and by the author.

† Although this paper is not a formal report of the Pruitt-Igoe research, all of the illustrations of family behavior given in the text are drawn from interviews and observations that are part of that study. The study deals with the residents of the Pruitt-Igoe housing projects in St. Louis. Some 10,000 people live in these projects which comprise forty-three eleven-story buildings near the downtown area of St. Louis. Over half of the households have female heads, and for over half of the households the principal income comes from public assistance of one kind or another. The research has been in the field for a little over two years. It is a broad community study which thus far has relied

concern with who, why, and what can be, it is unlikely that realistic and effective social planning to correct the clearly desperate situation of poor Negro families can begin.

This paper is concerned with a description and analysis of slum Negro family patterns as these reflect and sustain Negroes' adaptations to the economic, social, and personal situation into which they are born and in which they must live. As such it deals with facts of lower-class life that are usually forgotten or ignored in polite discussion. We have chosen not to ignore these facts in the belief that to do so can lead only to assumptions which would frustrate efforts at social reconstruction, to strategies that are unrealistic in the light of the actual day-to-day reality of slum Negro life. Further, this analysis will deal with family patterns which interfere with the efforts slum Negroes make to attain a stable way of life as working- or middle-class individuals and with the effects such failure in turn has on family life. To be sure, many Negro families live *in* the slum ghetto, but are not *of* its culture (though even they, and particularly their children, can be deeply affected by what happens there). However, it is the individuals who succumb to the distinctive family life style of the slum who experience the greatest weight of deprivation and who have the greatest difficulty responding to the few self-improvement resources that make their way into the ghetto. In short, we propose to explore in depth the family's role in the "tangle of pathology" which characterizes the ghetto.

The social reality in which Negroes have had to make their lives during the 450 years of their existence in the western hemisphere has been one of victimization "in the sense that a system of social

principally on methods of participant observation and open-ended interviewing. Data on families come from repeated interviews and observations with a small group of families. The field workers are identified as graduate students at Washington University who have no connection with the housing authority or other officials, but are simply interested in learning about how families in the project live. This very intensive study of families yields a wealth of information (over 10,000 pages of interview and observation reports) which obviously cannot be analyzed within the limits of one article. In this article I have limited myself to outlining a typical family stage sequence and discussing some of the psychosocial implications of growing up in families characterized by this sequence. In addition, I have tried to limit myself to findings which other literature on Negro family life suggests are not limited to the residents of the housing projects we are studying.

relations operates in such a way as to deprive them of a chance to share in the more desirable material and non-material products of a society which is dependent, in part, upon their labor and loyalty." In making this observation, St. Clair Drake goes on to note that Negroes are victimized also because "they do not have the same degree of access which others have to the attributes needed for rising in the general class system—money, education, 'contacts,' and 'know-how' (Drake, 1965). The victimization process started with slavery; for 350 years thereafter Negroes worked out as best they could adaptations to the slave status. After emancipation, the cultural mechanisms which Negroes had developed for living the life of victim continued to be serviceable as the victimization process was maintained first under the myths of white supremacy and black inferiority, later by the doctrines of gradualism which covered the fact of no improvement in position, and finally by the modern Northern system of ghettoization and indifference.

Yet the implicit paradigm of much of the research on Negro Americans has been an overly simplistic one concentrating on two terms of an argument:

$$\text{White cupidity} \longrightarrow \text{Negro suffering}$$

As an intellectual shorthand, and even more as a civil rights slogan, this simple model is both justified and essential. But, as a guide to greater understanding of the Negro situation as human adaptation to human situations, the paradigm is totally inadequate because it fails to specify fully enough the *process* by which Negroes adapt to their situations as they do, and the limitations one kind of adaptation places on possibilities for subsequent adaptations. A reassessment of previous social research, combined with examination of current social research on Negro ghetto communities, suggests a more complex, but hopefully more veridical model:

White cupidity

creates

Structural Conditions Highly Inimical to Basic Social Adaptation (low-income availability, poor education, poor services, stigmatization)

to which Negroes adapt

by

Social and Personal Responses which serve to sustain the individual in
his punishing world but also generate aggressiveness toward the self and
others

which results in

Suffering directly inflicted by Negroes on themselves and on others.

In short, whites, by their greater power, create situations in which
Negroes do the dirty work of caste victimization for them.

It is the central thesis of this paper that the caste-facilitated
infliction of suffering by Negroes on other Negroes and on themselves appears most poignantly within the confines of the family,
and that the victimization process as it operates in families prepares and toughens its members to function in the ghetto world, at
the same time that it seriously interferes with their ability to
operate in any other world. This, however, is very different from
arguing that "the family is to blame" for the deprived situation
ghetto Negroes suffer; rather we are looking at the logical outcome
of the operation of the widely ramified and interconnecting caste
system. In the end we will argue that only palliative results can be
expected from attempts to treat directly the disordered family
patterns to be described. Only a change in the original "inputs" of
the caste system, the structural conditions inimical to basic social
adaptation, can change family forms.

THE AUTONOMY OF THE SLUM GHETTO

Just as the deprivations and depredations practiced by white
society have had their effect on the personalities and social life of
Negroes, so also has the separation from the ongoing social life of
the white community had its effect. In a curious way, Negroes
have had considerable freedom to fashion their own adaptation
within their separate world. The larger society provides them with
few resources but also with minimal interference in the Negro
community on matters which did not seem to affect white interests. Because Negroes learned early that there were a great many
things they could not depend upon whites to provide, they
developed their own solutions to recurrent human issues. These
solutions can often be seen to combine, along with the predomi-
nance of elements from white culture, elements that are distinctive

to the Negro group. Even more distinctive is the *configuration* which emerges from those elements Negroes share with whites and those which are different.

For our purposes, however, the most important thing about the freedom which whites have allowed Negroes within their own world is that it has required them to work out their own ways of making it from day to day, from birth to death. The subculture that Negroes have created may be imperfect but it has been viable for centuries; it behooves both white and Negro leaders and intellectuals to seek to understand it even as they hope to change it.*

Negroes have created, again particularly within the lower-class slum group, a range of institutions to structure the tasks of living a victimized life and to minimize the pain it inevitably produces. In the slum ghetto these institutions include prominently those of the social network—the extended kinship system and the "street system" of buddies and broads which tie (although tenuously and unpredictably) the "members" to each other—and the institutions of entertainment (music, dance, folk tales) by which they instruct, explain, and accept themselves. Other institutions function to provide escape from the society of the victimized: the church (Hereafter!) and the civil rights movement (Now!).

THE FUNCTIONAL AUTONOMY
OF THE NEGRO FAMILY

The history of the Negro family has been ably documented by historians and sociologists (Stampp 1956; Franklin 1956; Tannenbaum 1946; Frazier 1939; and Herskovits 1941). In slavery, conjugal and family ties were reluctantly and ambivalently recognized by the slave holders, were often violated by them, but proved necessary to the slave system. This necessity stemmed both

---

* See Gouldner (1958), for a discussion of functional autonomy and dependence of structural elements in social systems. We are suggesting here that lower-class groups have a relatively high degree of functional autonomy *vis a vis* the total social system because that system does little to meet their needs. In general the fewer the rewards a society offers members of a particular group in the society, the more autonomous will that group prove to be with reference to the norms of the society. Only by constructing an elaborate repressive machinery, as in concentration camps, can the effect be otherwise.

from the profitable offspring of slave sexual unions and the necessity for their nurture, and from the fact that the slaves' efforts to
sustain patterns of sexual and parental relations mollified the men
and women whose labor could not simply be commanded. From
nature's promptings, the thinning memories of African heritage,
and the example and guilt-ridden permission of the slave holders,
slaves constructed a partial family system and sets of relations that
generated conjugal and familial sentiments. The slave holder's
recognition in advertisements for runaway slaves of marital and
family sentiments as motivations for absconding provides one
indication that strong family ties were possible, though perhaps
not common, in the slave quarter. The mother-centered family
with its emphasis on the primacy of the mother-child relation and
only tenuous ties to a man, then, is the legacy of adaptation
worked out by Negroes during slavery.

After emancipation this family design often also served well to
cope with the social disorganization of Negro life in the late nine-
teenth century. Matrifocal families, ambivalence about the desirability of marriage, ready acceptance of illegitimacy, all sustained
some kind of family life in situations which made it difficult to
maintain a full nuclear family. Yet in the hundred years since
emancipation, Negroes in rural areas have been able to maintain
full nuclear families almost as well as similarly situated whites. As
we will see, it is the move to the city that results in the very high
proportion of mother-headed households. In the rural system the
man continues to have important functions; it is difficult for a
woman to make a crop by herself, or even with the help of other
women. In the city, however, the woman can earn wages just as a
man can, and she can receive welfare payments more easily than
he can. In rural areas, although there may be high illegitimacy
rates and high rates of marital disruption, men and women have an
interest in getting together; families are headed by a husband-wife
pair much more often than in the city. That pair may be much less
stable than in the more prosperous segments of Negro and white
communities but it is more likely to exist among rural Negroes
than among urban ones.

In the United States, unlike the Caribbean, early marriage

confers a kind of permanent respectable status upon a woman which she can use to deny any subsequent accusations of immorality or promiscuity once the marriage is broken and she becomes sexually involved in visiting or common-law relations. The relevant effective status for many Negro women is that of "having been married" rather than "being married"; having the right to be called "Mrs." rather than currently being Mrs. Someone-in-Particular.

For Negro lower-class women, then, first marriage has the same kind of importance as having a first child. Both indicate that the girl has become a woman but neither one that this is the last such activity in which she will engage. It seems very likely that only a minority of Negro women in the urban slum go through their child-rearing years with only one man around the house.

Among the Negro urban poor, then, a great many women have the experience of heading a family for part of their mature lives, and a great many children spend some part of their formative years in a household without a father-mother pair. From Table 1 we see that in 1960, forty-seven percent of the Negro poor urban families with children had a female head. Unfortunately cumulative statistics are hard to come by; but, given this very high level for a cross-sectional sample (and taking into account the fact that the median age of the children in these families is about six years), it seems very likely that as many as two-thirds of Negro urban poor children will not live in families headed by a man

TABLE 1

PROPORTION OF FEMALE HEADS FOR FAMILIES WITH CHILDREN
BY RACE, INCOME, AND URBAN–RURAL CATEGORIES

Negroes	Rural	Urban	Total
Negroes			
under $3000	18%	47%	36%
$3000 and over	5	8	7
TOTAL	14	23	21
Whites			
under $3000	12%	38%	22%
$3000 and over	2	4	3
TOTAL	4	7	6

Source: U.S. Census: 1960, PC (1) D.U.S. Volume, Table 225; State Volume, Table 140.

and a woman throughout the first eighteen years of their lives.

One of the other distinctive characteristics of Negro families, both poor and not so poor, is the fact that Negro households have a much higher proportion of relatives outside the mother-father-children triangle than is the case with whites. For example, in St. Louis Negro families average 0.8 other relatives per household compared to only 0.4 for white families. In the case of the more prosperous Negro families this is likely to mean that an older relative lives in the home providing baby-sitting services while both the husband and wife work and thus further their climb toward stable working- or middle-class status. In the poor Negro families it is much more likely that the household is headed by an older relative who brings under her wings a daughter and that daughter's children. It is important to note that the three-generation household with the grandmother at the head exists only when there is no husband present. Thus, despite the high proportion of female-headed households in this group and despite the high proportion of households that contain other relatives, we find that almost all married couples in the St. Louis Negro slum community have their own household. In other words, when a couple marries it establishes its own household; when that couple breaks up the mother either maintains that household or moves back to her parents or grandparents.

Finally we should note that Negro slum families have more children than do either white slum families or stable working- and middle-class Negro families. Mobile Negro families limit their fertility sharply in the interest of bringing the advantages of mobility more fully to the few children that they do have. Since the Negro slum family is both more likely to have the father absent and more likely to have more children in the family, the mother has a more demanding task with fewer resources at her disposal. When we examine the patterns of life of the stem family we shall see that even the presence of several mothers does not necessarily lighten the work load for the principal mother in charge.

THE FORMATION AND MAINTENANCE OF FAMILIES

We will outline below the several stages and forms of Negro

lower-class family life. At many points these family forms and the
interpersonal relations that exist within them will be seen to have
characteristics in common with the life styles of white lower-class
families.* At other points there are differences, or the Negro pattern will be seen to be more sharply divergent from the family life
of stable working- and middle-class couples.

GOING TOGETHER

The initial steps toward mating and family formation in the
Negro slum take place in a context of highly developed boys' and
girls' peer groups. Boys and young men participating in the
street system of peer-group activity are much caught up in games
of furthering and enhancing their status as significant persons.
These games are played out in small and large gatherings through
various kinds of verbal contests that go under the names of
"sounding," "signifying," and "working game." Very much a part
of a boy's or man's status in this group is his ability to win
women. The man who has several women "up tight," who is successful in "pimping off" women for sexual favors and material
benefits, is much admired. In sharp contrast to white lower-class
groups, there is little tendency for males to separate girls into
"good" and "bad" categories.† Observations of groups of Negro
youths suggest that girls and women are much more readily referred to as "that bitch" or "that whore" than they are by their
names, and this seems to be a universal tendency carrying no
connotation that "that bitch" is morally inferior to or different
from other women. Thus, all women are essentially the same, all
women are legitimate targets, and no girl or woman is expected to
be virginal except for reason of lack of opportunity or immaturity.
From their participation in the peer group and according to standards legitimated by the total Negro slum culture, Negro boys and

*For discussions of white lower-class families, see Rainwater, Colemen, and Handel
(1959); Rainwater (1964a); Gans (1962); Cohen and Hodges (1963); Miller (1964); and
Komarovsky (1964). Discussions of Negro slum life can be found in Drake and Cayton
(1962); and Clark (1965); and of Negro community life in small-town and rural settings
in Davis, Gardner, and Gardner (1944); and Lewis (1955).

† Discussions of white lower-class attitudes towards sex may be found in Green (1971);
Whyte (1943b); and Rainwater (1964b).

young men are propelled in the direction of girls to test their "strength" as seducers. They are mercilessly rated by both their peers and the opposite sex in their ability to "talk" to girls; a young man will go to great lengths to avoid the reputation of having a "weak" line (Hammond 1965; and Reiss 1964).

The girls share these definitions of the nature of heterosexual relations; they take for granted that almost any male they deal with will try to seduce them and that given sufficient inducement (social not monetary) they may wish to go along with his line. Although girls have a great deal of ambivalence about participating in sexual relations, this ambivalence is minimally moral and has much more to do with a desire not to be taken advantage of or get in trouble. Girls develop defenses against the exploitative orientations of men by devaluing the significance of sexual relations ("he really didn't do anything bad to me"), and as time goes on by developing their own appreciation of the intrinsic rewards of sexual intercourse.

The informal social relations of slum Negroes begin in adolescence to be highly sexualized. Although parents have many qualms about boys and, particularly, girls entering into this system, they seldom feel there is much they can do to prevent their children's sexual involvement. They usually confine themselves to counseling somewhat hopelessly against girls becoming pregnant or boys being forced into situations where they might have to marry a girl they do not want to marry.

Girls are propelled toward boys and men in order to demonstrate their maturity and attractiveness; in the process they are constantly exposed to pressures for seduction, to boys "rapping" to them. An active girl will "go with" quite a number of boys, but she will generally try to restrict the number with whom she has intercourse to the few to whom she is attracted or (as happens not infrequently) to those whose threats' of physical violence she cannot avoid. For their part, the boys move rapidly from girl to girl seeking to have intercourse with as many as they can and thus build up their "reps." The activity of seduction is itself highly cathected; there is gratification in simply "talking to" a girl as long as the boy can feel that he has acquitted himself well.

At sixteen Joan Bemias enjoys spending time with three or four very close girl friends. She tells us they follow this routine when the girls want to go out and none of the boys they have been seeing lately is available: "Every time we get ready to go someplace we look through all the telephone numbers of boys we'd have and we call them and talk so sweet to them that they'd come on around. All of them had cars you see. (I: What do you do to keep all these fellows interested?) Well nothing. We don't have to make love with all of them. Let's see, Joe, J. B., Albert, and Paul, out of all of them I've been going out with I've only had sex with four boys, that's all." She goes on to say that she and her girl friends resist boys by being unresponsive to their lines and by breaking off relations with them on the ground that they're going out with other girls. It is also clear from her comments that the girl friends support each other in resisting the boys when they are out together in groups.

Joan has had a relationship with a boy which has lasted six months, but she has managed to hold the frequency of intercourse down to four times. Initially she managed to hold this particular boy off for a month but eventually gave in.

BECOMING PREGNANT

It is clear that the contest elements in relationships between men and women continue even in relationships that become quite steady. Despite the girls' ambivalence about sexual relations and their manifold efforts to reduce its frequency, the operation of chance often eventuates in their becoming pregnant. This was the case of Joan. With this we reach the second stage in the formation of families, that of premarital pregnancy. (We are outlining an ideal-typical sequence and not, of course, implying that all girls in the Negro slum culture become pregnant before they marry but only that a great many of them do.)

Joan was caught despite the fact that she was considerably more sophisticated about contraception than most girls or young women in the group (her mother had both instructed her in contraceptive techniques and constantly warned her to take precautions). No one was particularly surprised at her pregnancy although she, her boy friend, her mother, and others regarded it as

*See the discussion of aleatory processes leading to premarital fatherhood in Short and Strodtbeck (1965).

unfortunate. For girls in the Negro slum, pregnancy before marriage is expected in much the same way that parents expect their
children to catch mumps or chicken pox; if they are lucky it will
not happen but if it happens people are not too surprised and
everyone knows what to do about it. It was quickly decided that
Joan and the baby would stay at home. It seems clear from the
preparations that Joan's mother is making that she expects to have
the main responsibility for caring for the infant. Joan seems quite
indifferent to the baby; she shows little interest in mothering the
child although she is not particularly adverse to the idea so long as
the baby does not interfere too much with her continued participation in her peer group.

In general, when a girl becomes pregnant while still living at
home it seems taken for granted that she will continue to live
there and that her parents will take a major responsibility for
rearing the children. Since there are usually siblings who can help
out and even siblings who will be playmates for the child, the
addition of a third generation to the household does not seem to
place a great stress on relationships within the family. It seems
common for the first pregnancy to have a liberating influence on
the mother once the child is born in that she becomes socially and
sexually more active than she was before. She no longer has to be
concerned with preserving her status as a single girl. Since her
mother is usually willing to take care of the child for a few years,
the unwed mother has an opportunity to go out with girl friends
and with men and thus become more deeply involved in the peer-
group society of her culture. As she has more children and perhaps
marries she will find it necessary to settle down and spend more
time around the house fulfilling the functions of a mother herself.

It would seem that for girls pregnancy is the real measure of
maturity, the dividing line between adolescence and womanhood.
Perhaps because of this, as well as because of the ready resources
for child care, girls in the Negro slum community show much less
concern about pregnancy than do girls in the white lower-class
community and are less motivated to marry the fathers of their
children. When a girl becomes pregnant the question of marriage
certainly arises and is considered, but the girl often decides that

she would rather not marry the man either because she does not want to settle down yet or because she does not think he would make a good husband.

It is in the easy attitudes toward premarital pregnancy that the matrifocal character of the Negro lower-class family appears most clearly. In order to have and raise a family it is simply not necessary, though it may be desirable, to have a man around the house. While the AFDC program may make it easier to maintain such attitudes in the urban situation, this pattern existed long before the program was initiated and continues in families where support comes from other sources.

GETTING MARRIED

As noted earlier, despite the high degree of premarital sexual activity and the rather high proportion of premarital pregnancies, most lower-class Negro men and women eventually do marry and stay together for a shorter or longer period of time. Marriage is an intimidating prospect and is approached ambivalently by both parties. For the girl it means giving up a familiar and comfortable home that, unlike some other lower-class subcultures, places few real restrictions on her behavior. (While marriage can appear to be an escape from interpersonal difficulties at home, these difficulties seldom seem to revolve around effective restrictions placed on her behavior by her parents.) The girl also has good reason to be suspicious of the likelihood that men will be able to perform stably in the role of husband and provider; she is reluctant to be tied down by a man who will not prove to be worth it.

From the man's point of view the fickleness of women makes marriage problematic. It is one thing to have a girl friend step out on you, but it is quite another to have a wife do so. Whereas premarital sexual relations and fatherhood carry almost no connotation of responsibility for the welfare of the partner, marriage is supposed to mean that a man behaves more responsibly, becoming a provider for his wife and children even though he may not be expected to give up all the gratifications of participation in the street system.

For all of these reasons both boys and girls tend to have rather negative views of marriage as well as a low expectation that marriage will prove a stable and gratifying existence. When marriage does take place it tends to represent a tentative commitment on the part of both parties with a strong tendency to seek greater commitment on the part of the partner than on one's own part. Marriage is regarded as a fragile arrangement held together primarily by affectional ties rather than instrumental concerns.

Marriage as a way out of an unpleasant situation can be seen in the case of one of our informants, Janet Cowan:

Janet has been going with two men, one of them married and the other single. The married man's wife took exception to their relationship and killed her husband. Within a week Janet and her single boy friend, Howard, were married. One way out of the turmoil the murder of her married boy friend had stimulated (they lived in the same building) was to choose marriage as a way of "settling down." However, after marrying the new couple seemed to have little idea how to set themselves up as a family. Janet was reluctant to leave her parents' home because her parents cared for her two illegitimate children. Howard was unemployed and therefore unacceptable in his parent-in-law's home, nor were his own parents willing to have his wife move in with them. Howard was also reluctant to give up another girl friend in another part of town. Although both he and his wife maintained that it was all right for a couple to step out on each other so long as the other partner did not know about it, they were both jealous if they suspected anything of this kind. In the end they gave up on the idea of marriage and went their separate ways.

HUSBAND-WIFE RELATIONS

Characteristic of both the Negro and white lower class is a high degree of conjugal role segregation (Rainwater 1964a, pp. 28–60). That is, husbands and wives tend to think of themselves as having very separate kinds of functioning in the instrumental organization of family life, and also as pursuing recreational and outside interests separately. The husband is expected to be a provider; he resists assuming functions around the home so long as he feels he is doing his proper job of bringing home a pay check. He feels he has the right to indulge himself in little ways if he is successful at his task. The wife is expected to care for the home and children and make her husband feel welcome and comfortable. Much that is distinctive to Negro family life stems from the fact that husbands often are not stable providers. Even when a particular man is, his wife's conception of men in general is such that she is pessimistic about the likelihood that he will continue to do well in this area. A great many Negro wives work to supplement the family income. When this is so the separate incomes earned by husband and wife tend to be treated not as "family" income but as the individual property of the two persons involved. If their wives work, husbands are likely to feel that they are entitled to retain a larger share of the income they provide; the wives, in turn, feel that the husbands have no right to benefit from the purchases they make out of their own money. There is, then, "my money" and "your money." In this situation the husband may come to feel that the wife should support the children out of her income and that he can retain all of his income for himself.

While white lower-class wives often are very intimidated by their husbands, Negro lower-class wives come to feel that they have a right to give as good as they get. If the husband indulges himself, they have the right to indulge themselves. If the husband steps out on his wife, she has the right to step out on him. The commitment of husbands and wives to each other seems often a highly instrumental one after the "honeymoon" period. Many wives feel they owe the husband nothing once he fails to perform his provider role. If the husband is unemployed the wife increasingly refuses to perform her usual duties for him. For example, one woman, after mentioning that her husband had cooked four eggs for himself, commented, "I cook for him when he's working but right now he's unemployed; he can cook for himself." It is important, however, to understand that the man's status in the home depends not so much on whether he is working as on whether he brings money into the home. Thus, in several of the families we have studied in which the husband receives disability payments his status is as well-recognized as in families in which the husband is working.*

* Yancey (n.d.). The effects of unemployment on the family have been discussed by Bakke (1940); Komarovsky (1960); and Koos (1946). What seems distinctive to the Negro slum culture is the short time lapse between the husband's loss of a job and his wife's considering him superfluous.

Because of the high degree of conjugal role segregation, both white and Negro lower-class families tend to be matrifocal in comparison to middle-class families. They are matrifocal in the sense that the wife makes most of the decisions that keep the family going and has the greatest sense of responsibility to the family. In white as well as in Negro lower-class families women tend to look to their female relatives for support and counsel, and to treat their husbands as essentially uninterested in the day-to-day problems of family living.* In the Negro lower-class family these tendencies are all considerably exaggerated so that the matrifocality is much clearer than in white lower-class families.

MARITAL BREAKUP

The precipitating causes of marital disruption seem to fall mainly into economic or sexual categories. The husband has little credit with his wife to tide him over periods of unemployment. Wives seem very willing to withdraw commitment from husbands who are not bringing money into the house. They take the point of view that he has no right to take up space around the house, to use its facilities, or to demand loyalty from her. Even where the wife is not inclined to press these claims, the husband tends to be touchy because he knows that such definitions are usual in his group, and he may, therefore, prove difficult for even a well-meaning wife to deal with. If husbands do not work they tend to play around. Since they continue to maintain some contact with their peer groups, whenever they have time on their hands they move back into the world of the street system and are likely to get involved in activities which pose a threat to their family relationships.

Drink is a great enemy of the lower-class housewife, both white and Negro. Lower-class wives fear their husband's drinking because it costs money, because the husband may become violent and take out his frustrations on his wife, and because drinking may lead to sexual involvements with other women (Rainwater 1964a).

The combination of economic problems and sexual difficulties

*See particularly Komarovsky's discussion of "barriers to marital communication," (chapter 7), and "confidants outside of marriage" (chapter 9, 1964).

can be seen in the case of the following couple in their early twenties:

> When the field worker first came to know them, the Wilsons seemed to be working hard to establish a stable family life. The couple had been married about three years and had a two-year-old son. Their apartment was very sparsely furnished but also very clean. Within six weeks the couple had acquired several rooms of inexpensive furniture and obviously had gone to a great deal of effort to make a liveable home. Husband and wife worked on different shifts so that the husband could take care of the child while the wife worked. They looked forward to saving enough money to move out of the housing project into a more desirable neighborhood. Six weeks later, however, the husband had lost his job. He and his wife were in great conflict. She made him feel unwelcome at home and he strongly suspected her of going out with other men. A short time later they had separated. It is impossible to disentangle the various factors involved in this separation into a sequence of cause and effect, but we can see something of the impact of the total complex.

> First Mr. Wilson loses his job: "I went to work one day and the man told me that I would have to work until 1:00. I asked him if there would be any extra pay for working overtime and he said no. I asked him why and he said, 'If you don't like it you can kiss my ass.' He said that to me. I said, 'Why do I have to do all that?' He said, 'Because I said so.' I wanted to jam (fight) him but I said to myself I don't want to be that ignorant, I don't want to be as ignorant as he is, so I just cut out and left. Later his father called me (it was a family firm) and asked why I left and I told him. He said, 'If you don't want to go along with my son then you're fired.' I said O.K. They had another Negro man come in to help me part time before they fired me. I think they were trying to have him work full time because he worked for them before. He has seven kids and he takes their shit."

> The field worker observed that things were not as hard as they could be because his wife had a job, to which he replied, "Yeah, I know, that's just where the trouble is. My wife has become independent since she began working. If I don't get a job pretty soon I'll go crazy. We have a lot of little arguments about nothing since she got so independent." He went on to say that his wife had become a completely different person recently; she was hard to talk to because she felt that now that she was

working and he was not there was nothing that he could tell her. On her last pay day his wife did not return home for three days; when she did she had only seven cents left from her pay check. He said that he loved his wife very much and had begged her to quit fooling around. He is pretty sure that she is having an affair with the man with whom she rides to work. To make matters worse his wife's sister counsels her that she does not have to stay home with him as long as he is out of work. Finally the wife moved most of their furniture out of the apartment so that he came home to find an empty apartment. He moved back to his parents' home (also in the housing project).

The gains and losses in marriage and in the post-marital state often seem quite comparable. Once they have had the experience of marriage, many women in the Negro slum culture see little to recommend it in the future, important as the first marriage may have been in establishing their maturity and respectability.

THE HOUSE OF MOTHERS

As we have seen, perhaps a majority of mothers in the Negro slum community spend at least part of their mature life as mothers heading a family. The Negro mother may be a working mother or she may be an AFDC mother, but in either case she has the problems of maintaining a household, socializing her children, and achieving for herself some sense of membership in relations with other women and with men. As is apparent from the earlier discussion, she often receives her training in how to run such a household by observing her own mother manage without a husband. Similarly she often learns how to run a three-generation household because she herself brought a third generation into her home with her first, premarital, pregnancy.

Because men are not expected to be much help around the house, having to be head of the household is not particularly intimidating to the Negro mother if she can feel some security about income. She knows it is a hard, hopeless, and often thankless task, but she also knows that it is possible. The maternal household in the slum is generally run with a minimum of organization. The children quickly learn to fend for themselves, to go to the store, to make small purchases, to bring change home, to watch after themselves when the mother has to be out of the home, to amuse themselves, to set their own schedules of sleeping, eating, and going to school. Housekeeping practices may be poor, furniture takes a terrific beating from the children, and emergencies constantly arise. The Negro mother in this situation copes by not setting too high standards for herself, by letting things take their course. Life is most difficult when there are babies and pre-school children around because then the mother is confined to the home. If she is a grandmother and the children are her daughter's, she is often confined since it is taken as a matter of course that the mother has the right to continue her outside activities and that the grandmother has the duty to be responsible for the child.

In this culture there is little of the sense of the awesome responsibility of caring for children that is characteristic of the working and middle class. There is not the deep psychological involvement with babies which has been observed with the working-class mother (Rainwater, Colemen and Handel 1959). The baby's needs are cared for on a catch-as-catch-can basis. If there are other children around and they happen to like babies, the baby can be over-stimulated; if this is not the case, the baby is left alone a good deal of the time. As quickly as he can move around he learns to fend for himself.

Negro lower-class mothers often indicate that they try very hard to keep their young children at home and away from the streets; they often seem to make the children virtual prisoners in the home. As the children grow and go to school they inevitably do become involved in peer-group activities. The mother gradually gives up, feeling that once the child is lost to this pernicious outside world there is little she can do to continue to control him and direct his development. She will try to limit the types of activities that go on in the home and to restrict the kinds of friends that her children can bring into the home, but even this she must give up as time goes on, as the children become older and less attentive to her direction.

The lack of control that mothers have over much that goes on in their households is most dramatically apparent in the fact that their older children seem to have the right to come home at any time once they have moved and to stay in the home without contributing to its maintenance. Though the mother may be resentful about being taken advantage of, she does not feel she can turn her children away. For example, sixty-five-year-old Mrs. Washington plays hostess for weeks or months at a time to her forty-year-old daughter and her small children, and to her twenty-three-year-old granddaughter and her children. When these daughters come home with their families the grandmother is expected to take care of the young children and must argue with her daughter and granddaughter to receive contributions to the daily household ration of food and liquor. Or, a twenty-year-old son comes home from the Air Force and feels he has the right to live at home without working and to run up an eighty-dollar long-distance telephone bill.

BOY FRIENDS, NOT HUSBANDS

The older mothers, surrounded by their own children and grandchildren, are not able to move freely in the outside world, to participate in the high life which they enjoyed when younger and more foot-loose. They are disillusioned with marriage as providing any more secure economic base than they can achieve on their own. They see marriage as involving just another responsibility without a concomitant reward—"It's the greatest thing in the world to come home in the afternoon and not have some curly headed twot in the house yellin' at me and askin' me where supper is, where I've been, what I've been doin', and who I've been seein'." In this situation the woman is tempted to form relationships with men that are not so demanding as marriage but still provide companionship and an opportunity for occasional sexual gratification.

There seem to be two kinds of boy friends. Some boy friends "pimp" off mothers; they extract payment in food or money for their companionship. This leads to the custom sometimes called "Mother's Day," the tenth of the month when the AFDC checks come (cf. Schwartz and Henderson 1964). On this day one can observe an influx of men into the neighborhood, and much partying. But there is another kind of boy friend, perhaps more numerous than the first, who instead of being paid for his services pays for the right to be a pseudo family member. He may be the father of one of the woman's children and for this reason makes a steady contribution to the family's support, or he may simply be a man whose company the mother enjoys and who makes reasonable gifts to the family for the time he spends with them (and perhaps implicitly for the sexual favors he receives). While the boy friend does not assume fatherly authority within the family, he often is known and liked by the children.

Even when the boy friend contributes ten or twenty dollars a month to the family he is in a certain sense getting a bargain. If he is a well-accepted boy friend he spends considerable time around the house, has a chance to relax in an atmosphere less competitive than that of his peer group, is fed and cared for by the woman, yet has no responsibilities which he cannot renounce when he wishes. When women have stable relationships of this kind with boy friends they often consider marrying them but are reluctant to take such a step. Even the well-liked boy friend has some shortcomings—one woman said of her boy friend:

> "Well he works; I know that. He seems to be a nice person, kind hearted. He believes in survival for me and my family. He don't much mind sharing with my youngsters. If I ask him for a helping hand he don't seem to mind that. The only part I dislike is his drinking."

The woman in this situation has worked out a reasonably stable adaptation to the problems of her life; she is fearful of upsetting this adaptation by marrying again. It seems easier to take the "sweet" part of the relationship with a man without the complexities that marriage might involve.

It is in this kind of world that boys and girls in the Negro slum community learn their sex roles. It is not just, or even mainly, that fathers are often absent but that the male role models around boys are ones which emphasize expressive, affectional techniques for making one's way in the world. The female role models available to girls emphasize an exaggerated self-sufficiency (from the point of view of the middle class) and the danger of allowing oneself to be dependent on men for anything that is crucial. By the time she is mature, the woman learns that she is most secure when she herself manages the family affairs and when she dominates her men. The man learns that he exposes himself to the least risk of

failure when he does not assume a husband's and father's responsibilities but instead counts on his ability to court women and to
ingratiate himself with them.

IDENTITY PROCESSES IN THE FAMILY

Household groups function for cultures in carrying out the
initial phases of socialization and personality formation. It is in
the family that the child learns the most primitive categories of
existence and experience, and that he develops his most deeply
held beliefs about the world and about himself.* From the child's
point of view, the household *is* the world; his experiences as he
moves out of it into the larger world are always interpreted in
terms of his particular experience within the home. The painful
experiences which a child in the Negro slum culture has are, therefore, interpreted as in some sense a reflection of this family world.
The impact of the system of victimization is transmitted through
the family; the child cannot be expected to have the sophistication
an outside observer has for seeing exactly where the villains are.
From the child's point of view, if he is hungry it is his parents'
fault; if he experiences frustrations in the streets or in the school it
is his parents' fault; if that world seems incomprehensible to him it
is his parents' fault; if people are aggressive or destructive toward
each other it is his parents' fault, not that of a system of race
relations. In another culture this might not be the case; if a sub-
culture could exist which provided comfort and security within its
limited world and the individual experienced frustration only
when he moved out into the larger society, the family might not
be thought so much to blame. The effect of the caste system,
however, is to bring home through a chain of cause and effect all
of the victimization processes, and to bring them home in such a
way that it is often very difficult even for adults in the system to

* Talcott Parsons concludes his discussion of child socialization, the development of an
"internalized family system" and internalized role differentiation by observing, "The
internalization of the family collectivity as an object and its values should not be lost
sight of. This is crucial with respect to . . . the assumption of representative roles outside
the family on behalf of it. Here it is the child's family membership which is decisive, and
thus his acting in a role in terms of its values for 'such as he'" Parsons and Bales (1955,
p. 113).

see the connection between the pain they feel at the moment and the structured patterns of the caste system.

Let us take as a central question that of identity formation within the Negro slum family. We are concerned with the question of who the individual believes himself to be and to be becoming. For Erikson, identity means a sense of continuity and social sameness which bridges what the individual *"was* as a child and what he is *about to become* and also reconciles his *conception of himself* and his community's recognition of him." Thus identity is a "self-realization coupled with a mutual recognition" (Erikson 1959). In the early childhood years identity is family-bound since the child's identity is his identity *vis-à-vis* other members of the family. Later he incorporates into his sense of who he is and is becoming his experiences outside the family, but always influenced by the interpretations and evaluations of those experiences that the family gives. As the child tries on identities, *announces* them, the family sits as judge of his pretensions. Family members are both the most important judges and the most critical ones, since who he is allowed to become affects them in their own identity strivings more crucially than it affects anyone else. The child seeks a sense of valid identity, a sense of being a particular person with a satisfactory degree of congruence between who he feels he is, who he announces himself to be, and where he feels his society places him.* He is uncomfortable when he experiences disjunction between his own needs and the kinds of needs legitimated by those around him, or when he feels a disjunction between his sense of himself and the image of himself that others play back to him.†

TELL IT LIKE IT IS

When families become involved in important quarrels the psychosocial underpinnings of family life are laid bare. One such

---

*For a discussion of the dynamics of the individual's *announcements* and the society's *placements* in the formation of identity, see Stone (1962, pp. 86–118).

†The importance of identity for social behavior is discussed in detail in Goodenough (1963, pp. 176–251); and in Rainwater (1966a). The images of self and of other family members is a crucial vairable in Hess and Handel's psychosocial analysis of family life (1959, esp. pp. 6–11).

quarrel in a family we have been studying brings together in one place many of the themes that seem to dominate identity problems in Negro slum culture. The incident illustrates in a particularly forceful and dramatic way family processes which our field work, and some other contemporary studies of slum family life, suggest unfold more subtly in a great many families at the lower-class level. The family involved, the Johnsons, is certainly not the most disorganized one we have studied; in some respects their way of life represents a realistic adaptation to the hard living of a family nineteen years on AFDC with a monthly income of $202 for nine people. The two oldest daughters, Mary Jane (eighteen years old) and Esther (sixteen) are pregnant; Mary Jane has one illegitimate child. The adolescent sons, Bob and Richard, are much involved in the social and sexual activities of their peer group. The three other children, ranging in age from twelve to fourteen, are apparently also moving into this kind of peer-group society.

> When the argument started Bob and Esther were alone in the apartment with Mary Jane's baby. Esther took exception to Bob's playing with the baby because she had been left in charge; the argument quickly progressed to a fight in which Bob cuffed Esther around, and she tried to cut him with a knife. The police were called and subdued Bob with their nightsticks. At this point the rest of the family and the field worker arrived. As the argument continued, these themes relevant to the analysis which follows appeared:
>
> 1) The sisters said that Bob was not their brother (he is a half-brother to Esther, and Mary Jane's full brother). Indeed, they said their mother "didn't have no husband. These kids don't even know who their daddies are." The mother defended herself by saying that she had one legal husband, and one common-law husband, no more.
>
> 2) The sisters said that their fathers had never done anything for them, nor had their mother. She retorted that she had raised them "to the age of womanhood" and now would care for their babies.
>
> 3) Esther continued to threaten to cut Bob if she got a chance (a month later they fought again, and she did cut Bob, who required twenty-one stitches).
>
> 4) The sisters accused their mother of favoring their lazy brothers and asked her to put them out of the house. She retorted that the girls

were as lazy, that they made no contribution to maintaining the household, could not get their boy friends to marry them or support their children, that all the support came from her AFDC check. Mary Jane retorted that "the baby has a check of her own."

5) The girls threatened to leave the house if their mother refused to put their brothers out. They said they could force their boy friends to support them by taking them to court, and Esther threatened to cut her boy friend's throat if he did not co-operate.

6) Mrs. Johnson said the girls could leave if they wished but that she would keep their babies; "I'll not have it, not knowing who's taking care of them."

7) When her thirteen-year-old sister laughed at all of this, Esther told her not to laugh because she, too, would be pregnant within a year.

8) When Bob laughed, Esther attacked him and his brother by saying that both were not man enough to make babies, as she and her sister had been able to do.

9) As the field worker left, Mrs. Johnson sought his sympathy. "You see, Joe, how hard it is for me to bring up a family. . . . They sit around and talk to me like I'm some kind of a dog and not their mother."

10) Finally, it is important to note for the analysis which follows that the following labels—"black-assed," "black bastard," "bitch," and other profane terms—were liberally used by Esther and Mary Jane, and rather less liberally by their mother, to refer to each other, to the girls' boy friends, to Bob, and to the thirteen-year-old daughter.

Several of the themes outlined previously appear forcefully in the course of this argument. In the last year and a half the mother has become a grandmother and expects shortly to add two more grandchildren to her household. She takes it for granted that it is her responsibility to care for the grandchildren and that she has the right to decide what will be done with the children since her own daughters are not fully responsible. She makes this very clear to them when they threaten to move out, a threat which they do not really wish to make good nor could they if they wished to.

However, only as an act of will is Mrs. Johnson able to make this a family. She must constantly cope with the tendency of her adolescent children to disrupt the family group and to deny that they are in fact a family—"He ain't no brother of mine"; "The baby has a check of her own." Though we do not know exactly what processes communicate these facts to the children it is clear that in growing up they have learned to regard themselves as not fully part of a solidary collectivity. During the quarrel this message was reinforced for the twelve-, thirteen-, and fourteen-year-old daughters by the four-way argument among their older sisters, older brother, and their mother.

The argument represents vicious unmasking of the individual members' pretenses to being competent individuals.* The efforts of the two girls to present themselves as masters of their own fate are unmasked by the mother. The girls in turn unmask the pretensions of the mother and of their two brothers. When the thirteen-year-old daughter expresses some amusement they turn on her, telling her that it won't be long before she too becomes pregnant. Each member of the family in turn is told that he can expect to be no more than a victim of his world, but that this is somehow inevitably his own fault.

In this argument masculinity is consistently demeaned. Bob has no right to play with his niece, the boys are not really masculine because at fifteen and sixteen years they have yet to father children, their own fathers were no-goods who failed to do anything for their family. These notions probably come originally from the mother, who enjoys recounting the story of having her common-law husband imprisoned for nonsupport, but this comes back to haunt her as her daughers accuse her of being no better than they in ability to force support and nurturance from a man. In contrast, the girls came off somewhat better than the boys, although they must accept the label of stupid girls because they have similarly failed and inconveniently become pregnant in the first place. At least they can and have had children and therefore have some meaningful connection with the ongoing substance of life. There is something important and dramatic in which they participate, while the boys, despite their sexual activity, "can't get no babies."

In most societies, as children grow and are formed by their elders into suitable members of the society they gain increasingly a sense of competence and ability to master the behavioral environment their particular world presents. But in Negro slum culture

*See the discussion of "masking" and "unmasking" in relation to disorganization and re-equilibration in families by Spiegel (1960, pp. 375–77).

growing up involves an ever-increasing appreciation of one's short-comings, of the impossibility of finding a self-sufficient and gratifying way of living.* It is in the family first and most devastatingly that one learns these lessons. As the child's sense of frustration builds he too can strike out and unmask the pretensions of others. The result is a peculiar strength and a pervasive weakness. The strength involves the ability to tolerate and defend against degrading verbal and physical aggressions from others and not to give up completely. The weakness involves the inability to embark hopefully on any course of action that might make things better, particularly action which involves cooperating and trusting attitudes toward others. Family members become potential enemies to each other, as the frequency of observing the police being called in to settle family quarrels brings home all too dramatically.

The conceptions parents have of their children are such that they are constantly alert as the child matures to evidence that he is as bad as everyone else. That is, in lower-class culture human nature is conceived of as essentially bad, destructive, immoral.† This is the nature of things. Therefore any one child must be inherently bad unless his parents are very lucky indeed. If the mother can keep the child insulated from the outside world, she feels she may be able to prevent his inherent badness from coming out. She feels that once he is let out into the larger world the badness will come to the fore since that is his nature. This means that in the identity development of the child he is constantly exposed to identity labeling by his parents as a bad person. Since as he grows up he does not experience his world as particularly gratifying, it is very easy for him to conclude that this lack of gratification is due to the fact that something is wrong with him. This, in turn, can readily be assimilated to the definitions of being a bad person offered him by those with whom he lives.‡ In this

---

* See the discussion of self-identity and self-esteem in Pettigrew (1964, pp. 6–11).

† Rainwater, Coleman, and Handel (1959, pp. 44–51). See also the discussion of the greater level of "anomie" and mistrust among lower-class people in Mizruchi (1954). Unpublished research by the author indicates that for one urban lower-class sample (Chicago) Negroes scored about 50 percent higher on Srole's anomie scale than did comparable whites.

‡For a discussion of the child's propensity from a very early age for speculation and developing explanations, see Silverberg (1953, pp. 81ff.).

way the Negro slum child learns his culture's conception of being-in-the-world, a conception that emphasizes inherent evil in a chaotic, hostile, destructive world.

BLACKNESS

To a certain extent these same processes operate in white lower-class groups, but added for the Negro is the reality of blackness. "Black-assed" is not an empty pejorative adjective. In the Negro slum culture several distinctive appellations are used to refer to oneself and others. One involves the terms, "black" or "nigger." Black is generally a negative way of naming, but nigger can be either negative or positive, depending upon the context. It is important to note that, at least in the urban North, the initial development of racial identity in these terms has very little directly to do with relations with whites. A child experiences these identity placements in the context of the family and in the neighborhood peer group; he probably very seldom hears the same terms used by whites (unlike the situation in the South). In this way, one of the effects of ghettoization is to mask the ultimate enemy so that the understanding of the fact of victimization by a caste system comes as a late acquisition laid over conceptions of self and of other Negroes derived from intimate, and to the child often traumatic, experience within the ghetto community. If, in addition, the child attends a ghetto school where his Negro teachers either overtly or by implication reinforce his community's negative conceptions of what it means to be black, then the child has little opportunity to develop a more realistic image of himself and other Negroes as being damaged by whites and not by themselves. In such a situation, an intelligent man like Mr. Wilson (quoted on pp. 50–51) can say with all sincerity that he does not feel most Negroes are ready for integration—only under the experience of certain kinds of intense personal threat coupled with exposure to an ideology that places the responsibility on whites did he begin to see through the direct evidence of his daily experience.

To those living in the heart of a ghetto, black comes to mean not just "stay back," but also membership in a community of persons who think poorly of each other, who attack and manipulate each other, who give each other small comfort in a desperate world. Black comes to stand for a sense of identity as no better than these destructive others. The individual feels that he must embrace an unattractive self in order to function at all.

We can hypothesize that in those families that manage to avoid the destructive identity imputations of "black" and that manage to maintain solidarity against such assaults from the world around, it is possible for children to grow up with a sense of both Negro and personal identity that allows them to socialize themselves in an anticipatory way for participation in the larger society.* This broader sense of identity, however, will remain a brittle one as long as the individual is vulnerable to attack from within the Negro community as "nothing but a nigger like everybody else" or from the white community as "just a nigger." We can hypothesize further that the vicious unmasking of essential identity as black described above is least likely to occur within families where the parents have some stable sense of security, and where they therefore have less need to protect themselves by disavowing responsibility for their children's behavior and denying the children their patrimony as products of a particular family rather than of an immoral nature and an evil community.

In sum, we are suggesting that Negro slum children as they grow up in their families and in their neighborhoods are exposed to a set of experiences—and a rhetoric which conceptualizes them—that brings home to the child an understanding of his essence as a weak and debased person who can expect only partial gratification of his needs, and who must seek even this level of gratification by less than straight-forward means.

STRATEGIES FOR LIVING

In every society complex processes of socialization inculcate in their members strategies for gratifying the needs with which they are born and those which the society itself generates. Inextricably linked to these strategies, both cause and effect of them, are the

*See Ellison's autobiographical descriptions of growing up on Oklahoma City, 1964.

existential propositions which members of a culture entertain about the nature of their world and of effective action within the world as it is defined for them. In most of American society two grand strategies seem to attract the allegiance of its members and guide their day-to-day actions. I have called these strategies those of *the good life* and of *career success* (Rainwater 1966a). A good life strategy involves efforts to get along with others and not to rock the boat, a comfortable familism grounded on a stable work career for husbands in which they perform adequately at the modest jobs that enable them to be good providers. The strategy of career success is the choice of ambitious men and women who see life as providing opportunities to move from a lower to a higher status, to "accomplish something," to achieve greater than ordinary material well-being, prestige, and social recognition. Both of these strategies are predicated on the assumption that the world is inherently rewarding if one behaves properly and does his part. The rewards of the world may come easily or only at the cost of great effort, but at least they are there.

In the white and particularly in the Negro slum worlds little in the experience that individuals have as they grow up sustains a belief in a rewarding world. The strategies that seem appropriate are not those of a good, family-based life or of a career, but rather *strategies for survival*.

Much of what has been said above can be summarized as encouraging three kinds of survival strategies. One is the strategy of the *expressive life style* which I have described elsewhere as an effort to make yourself interesting and attractive to others so that you are better able to manipulate their behavior along lines that will provide some immediate gratification (Rainwater 1966a). Negro slum culture provides many examples of techniques for seduction, or persuading others to give you what you want in situations where you have very little that is tangible to offer in return. In order to get what you want you learn to "work game," a strategy which requires a high development of a certain kind of verbal facility, a sophisticated manipulation of promise and interim reward. When the expressive strategy fails or when it is unavailable there is, of course, the great temptation to adopt a *violent strategy* in which you force others to give you what you need once you fail to win it by verbal or other symbolic means.* Finally, and increasingly as members of the Negro slum culture grow older, there is the *depressive strategy* in which goals are increasingly constricted to the bare necessities for survival (not as a social being but simply as an organism).† This is the strategy of "I don't bother anybody and I hope nobody's gonna bother me; I'm simply going through the motions to keep body (but not soul) together." Most lower-class people follow mixed strategies, as Walter Miller (1958) has observed, alternating among the excitement of the expressive style, the desperation of the violent style, and the deadness of the depressed style. Some members of the Negro slum world experiment from time to time with mixed strategies that also incorporate the stable working-class model of the good American life, but this latter strategy is exceedingly vulnerable to the threats of unemployment or a less than adequate pay check, on the one hand, and the seduction and violence of the slum world around them, on the other.

* Short and Strodtbeck (1965, pp. 248-64) see violent behavior in juvenile gangs as a kind of last resort strategy in situations where the actor feels he has no other choice.

† Wiltse (1963) speaks of a "pseudo depression syndrome" as characteristic of many AFDC mothers.

Part II: The Characteristics of the Modal Personality

COMMENTARY on
*RACE AWARENESS AMONG AMERICAN AND
HONG KONG CHINESE CHILDREN*

There is a long tradition of research on the attitudes of black children toward their own race.* A common technique in this research is to show a youngster white and black dolls, or pictures of white and black children, and then to ask questions such as: "Which children would you prefer to play with?" "Which doll has the nice color?" "Which doll is bad?" In response to such questions, the majority of black children almost invariably prefer the white dolls or children and reject the dolls or children of their own race.†

Many studies have shown that as the black child grows older, this tendency to reject his own racial group declines. Grossack (1956), for example, found that blacks of college age have more pride in their race than black children do. Nonetheless the rejection of black identity is not confined to children. Black men, for instance, tend to use white standards of physical appearance in judging the beauty of black women (Martin 1964).‡

In the following selection, Morland replicates the findings that other investigators have obtained on the racial preferences of black children. But he goes beyond these findings by comparing white and black children in the United States with Chinese children in Hong Kong. The data suggest that the Chinese children are far less

* Among the investigations in this tradition are Clark and Clark (1947); Stevenson and Stewart (1958); Morland (1962, 1963, 1966, 3); Gregor and McPherson (1966a); and Asher and Allen (1969). For an able review and synthesis of the literature, see Proshansky and Newton (1968).

† The literature on racial preferences also deals with the ability of young children to differentiate between white and black persons. The main finding of this research is that this ability "first appears at roughly age three in both Negro and white children. . . . This ability increases steadily until approximately age six or seven, when all children are able to make these identifications accurately" (Proshansky and Newton 1968, p. 184).

‡ For other studies suggesting negative attitudes toward their own race among older blacks, see Bayton, Austin and Burke (1965); Middleton and Morland (1959); and Johnson (1957).

likely than the blacks in the United States to have negative attitudes toward their racial group. Why? Although Hong Kong is a multi-racial society and the Chinese belong to a non-white ethnic group, there is little, if any, discrimination against them. Unlike the blacks in American society, the Chinese in Hong Kong are, in status, equal with—not subordinate to—the whites. Thus if a black child looks down on his racial group, it seems to be in large part because his society, as we saw in Part I, looks down on it.

This interpretation is corroborated by data from other societies. The blacks in Nigeria who control and dominate the country, are less likely than American blacks to adopt white standards of physical beauty. Nigerians appear to attach greater value to Negroid features (Martin 1964). On the other hand, in South Africa— which, as one of the most virulently racist societies on the globe, systematically degrades the black man—black children exhibit a marked aversion toward their racial group (Gregor and McPherson 1966b). Data from several societies thus suggest that the attitudes of nonwhites toward their racial group are mainly determined by the treatment they receive from the society. If the society discriminates against and degrades the group, many nonwhites will feel ashamed of their race. If the society accords the racial group dignity and equality of treatment, nonwhites will take pride in their racial identity.

In recent years, blacks in the United States have reversed their traditional acquiescence in the white man's disparagement of their race and have increasingly begun to take pride in being black (Derbyshire and Brody 1964; Kirkhart 1963; Grossack 1956, 1957; Hoetker and Siegel 1970).* The sixties saw an immense rise in black consciousness and black pride, as epitomized in the slogan "black is beautiful" (e.g., Hannerz 10). What will be the effects of this new mood on the racial preferences of children? Will the concern with, and discussion of, black identity among Negro adults alter the racial preferences of young children?

The assumption currently being made by many writers is that increased racial consciousness has given blacks a psychological

---

* Only one study suggests a contrary tendency toward an increasing rejection of black identity (Asher and Allen 1969).

boost. Actually there is little empirical research testing this assumption. We know that those who take pride in their blackness tend to be more militant and more active in civil rights activities (Marx 9; Maliver 1965; Noel 1964). But beyond that point, our knowledge is skimpy. The commonly accepted assertion that high self-esteem accompanies positive racial identification, for example, is open to question and requires more empirical study than it has received (Trent 1957; Butts 1963; Rosenberg and Simmons 1971). What difference does it make in the day-to-day life of a black if he has pride in his race? Does such pride encourage a greater sense of control over his personal life? Does it reduce his frustrations and alienation? Does it help his work at school or on the job? As yet we really don't know the answers to such questions. In view of their importance and of their policy implications, we desperately need research designed to find some of the answers.

Race Awareness among American and Hong Kong Chinese Children

J. KENNETH MORLAND*

The awareness of race in young children has been studied in several societies, including the United States, New Zealand, South Africa, and England. These studies have differed somewhat in the types of measuring instruments used and in the aspects of race awareness considered. However, each of them has shown that the pattern of race awareness is related to the structure of race relations and to the social norms underlying the structure. Specifically, from the studies in at least three of the societies, the following general finding relating race awareness to social structure has emerged: *In a multiracial society in which there is a dominant and a subordinate race, young children of the subordinate race tend to prefer and identify with members of the dominant race, while children of the dominant race tend to prefer and identify with members of their own race.*

Evidence in the United States for this generalization has come from research showing that American Negro children of preschool age prefer and identify with Caucasians and that American Caucasian children also prefer and identify with Caucasians. Among these studies are those of Clark and Clark (1947), who used dolls; Goodman (1946, 1964), who used drawings, puzzles, and direct observation; Stevenson and Steward (1958), who used doll assembly, figure discrimination, and incomplete stories; Williams

* Excerpted from the *American Journal of Sociology*, vol. 75 (November 1969), pp. 360–74, by permission from the University of Chicago Press, Chicago: Illinois, and of the author. Copyright 1971 by the University of Chicago. All rights reserved.

and Robertson (1967), who employed a color-meaning picture series with an adaptation of a semantic differential test; and Morland (1958, 1962, 1963a, 1963b, 1966), who used sets of photographs. One American study takes partial exception to these rather consistent findings. Greenwald and Oppenheim (1968), using a modification of the Clark doll test, raised a question about the validity of one measure of Negro self-identification; however, they tended to support previous findings about racial preference and did not challenge other findings on American Negro self-identification. In New Zealand, Vaughan has compared the responses of Caucasian and Maori children through the use of pictures and dolls and has found that the Maori were significantly less likely to favor their own race than the Caucasians were to favor theirs (Vaughan 1963a; 1963b; 1964a; 1964b). Research in South Africa was done by Gregor and McPherson (1966) with the Clark doll test. They found that Bantu children tended to prefer and identify with Caucasian dolls and that South African Caucasian children also tended to prefer and identify with Caucasian dolls. In England, research by Pushkin with Caucasian and Negro children, using line drawings and doll play, found that ethnic attitudes were related to social characteristics of areas in London. However, the article in which this was reported (Jahoda, Veness, and Pushkin 1966) gave only preliminary conclusions on this research.

Two elaborations of the generalization relating race awareness to social structure are present in the research cited above. The data from South Africa show that as far as numbers are concerned the dominant race need not be as large as the subordinate, for Caucasians, the dominant race, make up only about one-fourth of the population. There are also indications from Vaughan's (1963a, pp. 100–102) research in New Zealand and from my research in this country (Morland 1962, pp. 279–80) that young children learn to prefer and identify with the dominant race before they develop the ability to employ racial terms accurately in differentiating between the races. This can be interpreted to mean that these attitudes are learned indirectly, rather than through direct instruction that employs the names of the races.

A STUDY OF HONG KONG CHINESE CHILDREN

One way to test the generalization about the relationship between race awareness and the presence of dominant and subordinate races would be to study the nature of race awareness in a multi-racial setting in which no race was clearly dominant. Such a study could, incidentally, act as a check on the normative theory of racial prejudice, about which more will be said later. It could be assumed that in this sort of setting there would be a different pattern of race awareness from that cited above, since the social structure in regard to race relations and the norms supporting that structure would be different. I sought to test this assumption by measuring the race awareness of young Chinese children in Hong Kong in the spring of 1967 and comparing the findings with those I obtained in the United States.*

THE HONG KONG SETTING

The British acquired the island of Hong Kong in 1842, when it was inhabited by only a few fishermen. To the island was added the peninsula of Kowloon in 1860 and the New Territories in 1898, completing the almost 400 square miles that compose the Colony today. The population has increased to nearly 4 million, 98 percent of whom are Chinese. The others in the population are mostly British, but there are also Americans, Asiatic Indians, and a variety of other nationalities present. Approximately 500,000 tourists, most of whom are Caucasian, visit Hong Kong each year. In the Hong Kong setting neither the Chinese nor the Caucasian race (represented mainly by the British) is dominant. The British hold top government posts, it is true, and they head a number of important businesses. Also, most of the foreigners in Hong Kong are relatively affluent. However, the Chinese are also prominent in business, education, government, social life (including the most prestigious clubs), and a number of them are very wealthy. Also, the Chinese reputedly have deep pride in their nation and in their

* A year's residence in Hong Kong was made possible by a grant under the Mutual Educational and Cultural Exchange Act of 1961 (Fulbright-Hays Act) and a sabbatical leave from Randolph-Macon Woman's College. The Chinese University of Hong Kong, at which I taught, offered valuable assistance with the research project.

cultural heritage, a pride evidently shared by the Chinese in Hong Kong. The most appropriate description of the social structure of the Colony is one in which the Caucasians and Chinese might be said to hold parallel positions. The Colony is officially bilingual; there is no racially based exclusion of any sort; all schools in which English is the chief mode of communication are "integrated"; one of the two television channels is English, the other Chinese; the more than ninety movie theaters show a wide variety of Chinese, British, and American films; there are three English-language newspapers and a dozen or so papers in the Chinese language.

MEASURING INSTRUMENT

In order to provide a valid comparison of the race awareness of Hong Kong Chinese children with American children, the equivalent of the author's photograph-interview test used in the United States was constructed. Six photographs of Caucasians and Negroes used in the United States were matched with six photographs of Chinese and Caucasians. These photographs were made by professional photographers in Hong Kong, and the models as well as the final pictures were selected by the author and his nineteen Chinese students in a social anthropology class at the Chinese University of Hong Kong. The six photographs depicted: (1) four Chinese children, two boys and two girls, sitting around a table, drawing pictures; (2) four Caucasian children, two boys and two girls of the same age and size as the Chinese models, at the same table drawing pictures; (3) four men, two Caucasian and two Chinese, drinking tea; (4) six women, three Caucasian and three Chinese, drinking tea; (5) four girls, two Caucasian and two Chinese, playing with dolls; (6) four boys, two Chinese and two Caucasian, playing with toys.

The set of English questions used in the picture-interview with the American children was translated into Chinese through the following procedure. The author's nineteen Chinese students, all of whom had studied English for at least eight years, first made separate and independent translations, from which they worked out a consensus of the most accurate Chinese translation. The author then had this Chinese version of the interview checked for accuracy by a Chinese faculty colleague who knew English well.

THE SUBJECTS

Responses were obtained from three hundred nineteen Chinese children of ages four, five, and six in four schools. All of the children of these ages who were present on the days of testing were interviewed, the only selection being on the basis of age. Two of the schools were for privileged children and two for poor families living in resettlement flats built by the government. This difference in socioeconomic level made it possible to analyze the responses by socioeconomic status to see if such status was related to race awareness. There is, of course, no claim that these three hundred nineteen children are representative of all Chinese children of these ages in Hong Kong. However, since all of them were born in the Colony, it can be assumed that their awareness of race is derived from the socialization process generally experienced by the Chinese children of Hong Kong. The picture-interviews were conducted in March and April 1967 by twelve of my Chinese students who had been trained by me.

A COMPARISON OF HONG KONG AND AMERICAN CHILDREN

In order to compare the race awareness of children in the Hong Kong and U.S. settings, three racial groupings were formed: American Caucasian, American Negro, and Hong Kong Chinese. One hundred and fifty children in each grouping were matched by age,* and in the two American groupings the number of children from the North and from the South was the same.† These

---

* The age distribution for each grouping was: sixty-six four-year-olds, fifty-seven five-year-olds, and twenty-seven six-year-olds. Age was controlled in the comparison, for studies of race awareness have generally found it to be significantly related to most aspects of race awareness.

† In comparing race awareness in northern and southern American children in an earlier report I found that Negro subjects differed significantly by region on one of seven measures and that Caucasian subjects differed significantly by region on two of seven measures Morland (1966). Hence this control of region was introduced. It might be added that southern subjects differed significantly by race on six of seven measures and that northern subjects differed by race on four of seven measures.

American children had been tested by me and my students during 1964, 1965, and 1966 in Hartford, Bloomfield, and East Granby, Connecticut, and in Lynchburg and Prince Edward County, Virginia.

The set of photographs and the questions asked about them were designed to measure racial acceptance, racial preference, and racial self-identification. The results of each of these measures will be presented in turn.

RACIAL ACCEPTANCE

To find the willingness of the subjects to play with children of their own race and those of the other race, each was given three chances to say if he would like to play with groups and with individuals of both races: in Pictures 1 and 2 (groups), Picture 5 (girls), and Picture 6 (boys). Color and race were not mentioned in these questions, which asked, "Would you like to play with these children [or with this child]?" followed by "Why?" or "Why not?" The responses of a subject were scored as "Acceptance" if he indicated a majority of times that he would like to play with those in question, "Nonacceptance" if he said most frequently he would not like to play with them for any reason other than racial, and "Rejection" if he said most often he did not want to play with them because of their race. Almost all of the subjects in the three groupings accepted members of their own race, with no significant difference among the three, as can be seen in Table 1.

TABLE 1
ACCEPTANCE OF OWN RACE BY AMERICAN CAUCASIAN, AMERICAN NEGRO, AND HONG KONG CHINESE CHILDREN

Racial Grouping (N *for Each = 150*)	*Acceptance of Own Race* (%)	*Nonacceptance of Own Race* (%)	*Rejection of Own Race* (%)
American Caucasian	95.3	4.7	0.0
American Negro	89.3	10.7	0.0
Hong Kong Chinese	89.3	10.7	0.0

These results show that this form of racial self-acceptance is evidently not related to the differences in the social structures of Hong Kong and the United States. However, Table 2 indicates that American Negro acceptance of the dominant race was higher than American Caucasian acceptance of members of the parallel race. On the other hand, the Chinese and the Caucasian children did not differ significantly. It is to be noted that the great majority of children in both of the sociocultural settings accepted children of the other race, with very few of them rejecting those of other races explicitly because of race.*

TABLE 2

ACCEPTANCE OF OTHER RACE BY AMERICAN CAUCASIAN, AMERICAN NEGRO, AND HONG KONG CHINESE CHILDREN*

Racial Grouping (N for Each = 150)	Acceptance of Other Race (%)	Nonacceptance of Other Race (%)	Rejection of Other Race (%)
American Caucasian	81.3	14.7	4.0
American Negro†	95.3	4.7	0.0
Hong Kong Chinese	75.3	23.3	1.3

* "Other Race" for Caucasian is Negro; for Negro is Caucasian; for Chinese is Caucasian.
† Significantly different from other two groupings at .001 level, by x^2 test, with "Nonacceptance" and "Rejection" combined.

RACIAL PREFERENCE

Immediately following the questions about acceptance of one's own and of the other race, the subjects were asked to indicate a preference between the two races. Again the interviewer did not

* Categorizing answers as either "Rejection" or "Nonacceptance" was based on the response to the question, "Why not?" asked after the subject had indicated that he did not want to play with the children or the child depicted. The responses of two Chinese who said they did not want to play with the Caucasians in the pictures, "because I do not like Western children," were categorized as "Rejection." However, the responses of two Chinese that they did not want to play with the Caucasian children, "because I do not know their language," were categorized as "Nonacceptance." Obviously, such categorization poses difficulties, although it is nonetheless important.

mention race or color, but pointed to the picture and asked, "Would you rather play with these children [this child], or with those [that one]?" He was asked to choose between groups of the two races (Pictures 1 and 2), among girls of the two races (Picture 5), and among boys of the two races (Picture 6). Replies were scored as "Prefer Own Race," "Prefer Other Race," or "Preference Not Clear," depending on the most frequent answer. Table 3 shows that all three groupings differed significantly. However, a majority of the Caucasian and Chinese children preferred their own race, while a majority of Negro children preferred the other race.

TABLE 3

RACIAL PREFERENCE OF AMERICAN CAUCASIAN, AMERICAN NEGRO, AND HONG KONG CHINESE CHILDREN*

Racial Grouping (N for Each = 150)	Prefer Own Race (%)	Prefer Other Race (%)	Preference Not Clear (%)
American Caucasian†	82.0	12.0	6.0
American Negro†	28.0	53.3	18.7
Hong Kong Chinese†	65.3	25.3	9.3

* American children chose between Caucasian and Negro; Hong Kong children chose between Caucasian and Chinese.

† Significantly different from each of other two groupings at the .001 level, by the $x2$ test.

The preference of the Negro respondents can be interpreted to mean that as members of the subordinate race they reflect the bias for Caucasians that characterizes American society.* A plausible interpretation of the difference between the American Caucasian and Hong Kong Chinese subjects is that race differences carry more importance for status in a multiracial society that has dominant and subordinate races than they do in a society in which races have parallel positions. It is to be noted that in both societies preference for one race did not mean rejection or nonacceptance of the other race (including one's own race) when no choice was

* I have elaborated on this interpretation elsewhere (Morland 1958, p. 137; 1963b, p. 240). Vaughan makes a similar interpretation for the New Zealand children (1963b, p. 69).

involved. As was shown earlier (Tables 1 and 2), the great majority of respondents accepted both their own and the other race.*

RACIAL SELF-IDENTIFICATION

In learning racial categories recognized by his society, a child not only learns this in regard to others but also in regard to himself. To measure aspects of racial self-identification, subjects were asked which children in the pictures they look most like and which children they would rather be. Table 4 summarizes the responses to the first question, and Table 5 summarizes responses to the second. In both types of self-identification, American Caucasian subjects clearly identified with their own race. In contrast, the American Negro children tended to identify with Caucasians. About the same proportion of Negro subjects said they looked like Caucasians in the pictures as said they looked like Negroes in the pictures, and almost two-thirds of the Negro

TABLE 4

RESPONSES OF AMERICAN CAUCASIAN, AMERICAN NEGRO, AND HONG KONG CHINESE TO THE QUESTION, "WHICH CHILD DO YOU LOOK MOST LIKE?"*

Racial Grouping (N for Each = 150)	Most Like Child of Own Race (%)	Most Like Child of Other Race (%)	Not Sure, or Did Not Know (%)
American Caucasian†	76.7	12.0	11.3
American Negro†	46.7	45.3	8.0
Hong Kong Chinese†	36.0	14.0	50.0

* American children chose between Caucasian and Negro; Hong Kong children chose between Caucasian and Chinese.

† Significantly different from each of the other two groupings at the .001 level, by the x^2 test.

* Some studies which have not measured acceptance of one's own and of other races when no choice was involved have assumed that preference for one race implied rejection of the other (e.g., Clark and Clark 1947, p. 175). The results of tables 1, 2, and 3 above also suggest that the type of question which forces the respondent to characterize one of the dolls or pictures in an unfavorable way (e.g., in the Clark doll test, saying "Give me the doll that looks bad") might be rephrased, by asking *if* one of the dolls actually looks bad. Such rephrasing was done by Greenwald and Oppenheim (1968, pp. 49–50).

TABLE 5

RESPONSES OF AMERICAN CAUCASIAN, AMERICAN NEGRO,
AND HONG KONG CHINESE CHILDREN TO THE QUESTION,
"WHICH CHILD WOULD YOU RATHER BE?"*

Racial Grouping (N for Each = 150)	Rather Be Child of Own Race (%)	Rather Be Child of Other Race (%)	Not Sure, or Did Not Know (%)
American Caucasian†	76.7	14.7	8.7
American Negro†	33.3	62.0	4.7
Hong Kong Chinese†	54.0	28.0	18.0

* American children chose between Caucasian and Negro; Hong Kong children chose between Caucasian and Chinese.

† Significantly different from other two groupings at .001 level, by x^2 test.

respondents said they would rather be one of the Caucasians than one of the Negro children. The Hong Kong data are not so consistent. Although more than twice as many Chinese children said they looked more like the Chinese than like the Caucasian children in the pictures, exactly one-half of them were not sure or insisted that they looked no more like one than they did the other. On the other hand, over one-half of the Chinese subjects said they would rather be one of the Chinese than one of the Caucasian children.

Differences between the American Negro and Caucasian responses can again be explained in terms of the effects of the privileged position of Caucasians in the society and the consequent identification, probably unconscious, of the Negro subjects with the dominant race.

RACIAL RECOGNITION ABILITY

Additional understanding of variations in racial self-identification among the American and Chinese subjects can be gained by looking at the results of the measure of racial recognition ability. After the subjects had been shown each of the pictures and were asked questions that did not mention race in any way, they were shown the pictures again and asked to identify the race of those depicted. The American children were asked, for each picture, if they saw a white person to point to him, and if they saw a colored person or a Negro to point to him.* For the Hong Kong subjects, the terms used to test recognition ability were "Chinese" and "Westerner."† A child was scored "High" if he answered correctly each time or if he missed not more than twice; he was scored "Low" if he missed more than twice.‡ As a rule, a child obviously either knew the terms and was correct each time or he did not know what they meant and missed consistently.

It can be seen from Table 6 that American Caucasian children demonstrated a significantly higher racial recognition ability than either the American Negro or Hong Kong Chinese children and that the Negro and Chinese children made similar scores on recognition ability. However, replies to an additional question, asked at the end of the interview about the race to which the subject himself belonged, showed quite different results for the American Negro and the Hong Kong Chinese children. Table 7 compares the replies of those who scored "High" in recognition ability, since it can be assumed that only these children knew the meaning of the racial terms employed. Almost all of the Hong Kong Chinese who scored "High" replied that they were Chinese, and almost all of the American Caucasians who scored "High" said that they were white. However, only about two-thirds of the Negro subjects scoring "High" said that they were members of their own race, and one-fourth said that they were white. These results show that the American sociocultural milieu makes it difficult for a Negro child to accept his racial identity, probably because of his unconscious desire to be identified with the privileged race. However, children of the dominant race in America and of a parallel race in Hong Kong are similar in learning and in accepting their racial designation. It might be added that the acknowledgment of racial

* The term "colored" was used first, and if the respondent knew this term, "Negro" was not used. But if he did not know "colored," he was asked to point to a Negro in the picture. "Colored" was found to be better known than "Negro" from preliminary testing.

† The term "Westerner" was decided upon after pretesting Chinese children. If the respondent did not know "Westerner," the interviewer then used the term *yang kuei-tse*, which means "foreign devil" or "foreigner." The latter is evidently more often employed by lower than by upper status Chinese.

‡ This cutting point was derived from an earlier study of mine in which the validity and reliability of racial recognition were tested (Morland 1958, p. 134).

TABLE 6

RACIAL RECOGNITION ABILITY OF AMERICAN CAUCASIAN, AMERICAN NEGRO, AND HONG KONG CHINESE CHILDREN*

Racial Grouping (N for Each = 150)	High Ability (%)	Low Ability (%)
American Caucasian†	70.7	29.3
American Negro	49.3	50.7
Hong Kong Chinese	48.7	51.3

* American children are measured on their ability to point out "white" and "colored" (or "Negro") persons; Hong Kong children on their ability to point out "Chinese" and "Western" (or "foreign") persons.

† Significantly different from the other two groups at the .001 level, by x^2 test.

TABLE 7

RESPONSES OF AMERICAN CAUCASIAN, AMERICAN NEGRO, AND HONG KONG CHINESE CHILDREN OF HIGH RACIAL RECOGNITION ABILITY TO THE QUESTION ASKING TO WHAT RACE THEY BELONGED*

Racial Grouping of Children of High Recognition Ability	Member of Own Race (%)	Member of Other Race (%)	Reply Not Clear (%)
American Caucasian (N = 106)	97.2	1.9	0.9
American Negro† (N = 74)	68.9	25.7	5.4
Hong Kong Chinese (N = 73)	97.3	2.7	0.0

* American children were asked, "Are you white, or are you colored [or are you a Negro] ?"; Hong Kong children were asked, "Are you a Chinese, or are you a Westerner [or are you a foreigner] ?"

† Significantly different from the other two groupings at the .001 level, by the x^2 test, with "Member of Other Race" and "Reply Not Clear" combined.

membership was not easy for the American Negro subjects. When asked to what race they belonged, a number of Negro children answered reluctantly and with obvious discomfort.* On the other

* An example of this is the reaction of a five-year-old Negro girl of high recognition ability in Hartford, Connecticut. When asked, "Are you white or are you colored?" she at first responded, "I'm colored." But, then, with strong feeling, she added: "No I'm not. I'm white. I wanna be *big!* Similar reactions of American Negro children have been reported by Clark and Clark (1947, p. 178); Goodman (1946, p. 626); and Trager and Yarrow (1952, p. 143). Consequences of this difficulty in the acceptance of racial identity by Negro children have been discussed by Ausubel and Ausubel (1963) and by Meeks (1967).

hand, the American Caucasian and Hong Kong Chinese subjects gave their racial membership readily and with ease.

CONCLUSIONS

This comparison of American and Hong Kong Chinese children upholds the assumption that race awareness varies with the social structure, for it reveals a different pattern of race awareness in a society with dominant and subordinate races from that in a society with parallel races. The findings show that Hong Kong Chinese children differed significantly from both the American Caucasian and American Negro children on racial preference and on two measures of racial self-identification. The Hong Kong children, unlike the American Negro children, preferred and identified with members of their own race. In this way they were like the American Caucasian children, who also preferred and identified with their own race.

The study of race awareness among the Hong Kong Chinese children questions an interpretation of the research cited at the beginning of this paper that shows that members of the subordinate race tend to prefer and identify with members of the dominant race. This interpretation is derived from findings on the connotation of color in several societies in which the color "white" has a highly favorable evaluation, while the colors "black" and "brown" have unfavorable evaluations. Such evaluations have been found in the United States (among Negroes as well as among Caucasians), in Germany, in Denmark, in India, and in Hong Kong.* Thus, the preference for and identification with the lighter-skinned dominant race by the darker-skinned subordinate race in the United States, South Africa, and New Zealand cited earlier in this paper, might be the result, not of social structure, but of a universal human bias for that which is "light" as opposed to that which is "dark." The Hong Kong data on race awareness

---

* See, especially, the work of Williams (1964; 1966); Williams and Carter (1967), and Williams, Morland, and Underwood (in press). I have collected data on color connotations among Hong Kong Chinese and Asiatic Indian students. In these societies, of ten colors evaluated, "white" had the most favorable and "black" the least favorable rating.

cast doubt on such an interpretation, for the Chinese children preferred and identified with the darker of the two races in the pictures, that is, with their own rather than with the Caucasian race.

The findings of this study can be interpreted as lending support to the normative theory of racial prejudice. This theory holds that such prejudice is a function of the norms of a society. As Westie has put it: "Prejudice is built into the culture in the form of normative precepts—that is, notions of 'ought to be'—which define the ways in which members of the group ought to behave in relation to members of selected outgroups" (1964, pp. 583–84). While the racial preference and identification reported reflect more of a racial bias than a racial prejudice (Morland 1962, p. 279), it is highly probable that such preference and identification are incipient in prejudice and underlie it. And, pertinent to the normative theory, this comparison of Hong Kong and American children has shown that the patterning of race awareness is indeed different when the social structure and the norms supporting that structure are different. In turn, the normative theory helps to explain the findings of the research. If we take it for granted that children begin early in life to see differences in persons around them, the theory leads us to believe that they will consider these differences important only if their society makes them the basis of categorization and calls for a particular kind of response to those in the category. Thus, in a multiracial society, we assume that children can see variations in skin color, hair form, and the like. However, it is the society which determines how much attention is to be paid to these variations and whether or not certain groupings are to be recognized on the basis of selected characteristics. Furthermore, it can be assumed that it is in the socialization process that children learn not only what physical traits are used as a basis of classification but also what attitudes are to be held toward those in the classification.

There are several limitations to this comparison of American and Hong Kong children that point toward the need for further research. First, only one of the parallel races in Hong Kong was tested. The major reason for not testing Caucasian children was that their families are, for the most part, temporary residents of Hong Kong, assigned for specified periods of time and granted leaves to return to their "home" in England, the United States, Canada, or some other nation. While the Caucasian population of Hong Kong forms a continuous parallel race to the Chinese in one sense, the personnel of the Caucasian representation constantly changes, and, most important for the validity of comparison, the Caucasian children undergo the socialization process in their parents' home country as well as in Hong Kong. Additional testing of the generalization is needed in other sociocultural settings in which more than one race is present. Significant investigations could be made, for example, in societies in which members of the Negro race are dominant or at least are not subordinate. Such countries as Kenya, Liberia, Sierra Leone, and Zambia would provide fruitful sociocultural settings for research.

Second, the terms "dominant," "subordinate," and "parallel" are qualitative concepts that need to be more precisely defined and measured. If this were done, differences in the degree of dominance and subordination could then be related to differences in race awareness. Also, some consideration of the degree of "visibility" of different races should be made. It is possible to account for at least part of the difference in the race awareness of American Caucasian and Hong Kong Chinese children through the greater contrast between the skin color of American Caucasian and American Negro than between the skin color of Chinese and Caucasian. Of course, it is to be remembered that this apparently greater visibility did not affect the responses of the American Negro subjects, at least as far as preferring and identifying with Caucasians were concerned. Present explorations of this factor of visibility are being made by me and my students by measuring the level of race awareness of American Caucasian children through the use of pictures of Chinese and Caucasians, and by comparing the results with those obtained from pictures of Negroes and Caucasians. Also, the level of awareness of American Negro children is presently being measured by using pictures of all three racial groupings in the same test.

In order to ascertain the extent to which the socialization

process involved in acquiring race awareness is deliberate and the extent to which it is nondeliberate, racial recognition ability could be related to racial preference and identification.* Of special interest would be a study of American Negro children who do not identify with and who do not show preference for the dominant race. Has there been deliberate teaching about racial identity in their homes? Studies could also be made of the effectiveness of current attempts to bring about pride in race through such slogans as "Black Is Beautiful" and through the development of "Black Power."† Implicit in the findings of the present research is the assumption that if the American social structure changes so that Negroes are no longer in a subordinate position, the racial preference and racial self-identification of Negro children will change. This assumption could be tested by studies conducted over the next several years.

* This was done in a limited way by me in earlier research (1958; 1962; 1963b). Indications were that the process is nondeliberate, for children tended to learn the patterned types of racial preference and identification before they learned racial designations.

† A recent study by Floyd (1969), using my picture test with black preschool children in Philadelphia, compared the race awareness of the children of parents who differed in the strength of their belief in "Black Pride," "Black Power," etc. Floyd found that the only significant relationship between scores on the parent belief scale and the responses of their children to the picture test was: "the stronger the parent support of 'Black Power,' 'Black Pride,' and the 'Black Revolution' in general, the more the child wants to be white" (Floyd 1969, pp. 48–49).

COMMENTARY on
SOCIETY AND THE ADOLESCENT SELF-IMAGE

A person's attitude toward himself is a reflection of the attitudes others have toward him and of the way in which others treat him. At least this is a cardinal assumption usually made in social psychology. Given the discriminatory and degrading treatment that blacks have received, and their historically low status in American society, a corrolary of this assumption is that blacks are likely to have low self-esteem.

Such assertions about self-esteem also derive from another line of reasoning. Most theorists assume that one's race is an important element in how he thinks and feels about himself. If the data of Morland (3) and other investigators are correct in indicating that black youngsters have negative attitudes toward their race, it would follow that blacks disapprove of a critical aspect of their self-image. Hence they should have low self-esteem.*

Although this theorizing all sounds very convincing, we had best be skeptical. That blacks are lacking in self-acceptance seems so obvious that every armchair theorist assents to it. Nevertheless it is not supported by the evidence. When we look at studies statistically comparing the races on measures that seem specifically to measure self-esteem, we discover that the findings are mixed. Granted, some studies do corroborate the proposition that blacks have relatively low self-esteem (Deutsch 1960; Keller 1963; Grossack 1957a; Lang and Henderson 1968; Williams and Byars 1968). But about half of the studies do not (Coleman and others *14*; Rosenberg *5*; Baughman and Dahlstrom 1968, p. 433; Gibby and Gabler 1967; Carpenter and Busse 1969; Rosenberg and Simmons 1971). In fact, they suggest either that the level of self-esteem among blacks does not differ significantly from that of whites or that it is actually higher than that of whites.†

* For the different versions of the above arguments, see Clark (1965, pp. 63–69); Kardiner and Ovesey (1951, pp. 302–05); Liebow (1967); Pettigrew (1964, pp. 6–11); and Rainwater (5).

† For a discussion and review of the evidence that challenges the view that blacks are likely to have low self-esteem, see McCarthy and Yancey (1971).

Those studies disputing the traditional theorizing are exemplified by the selection reprinted here. Rosenberg compares adolescents from fourteen ethnic and racial groups and finds that although the self-esteem of blacks is less than that of whites, the difference is small. The author then critically examines the hypothesis that a person's self-esteem is influenced by the prestige of his ethnic group. In speculating on why the data fail to support the hypothesis, Rosenberg points out that an individual may refuse to accept as part of his self-image society's ranking of his ethnic group. In addition, other factors (for example, an individual's own accomplishments) may weigh more heavily than the prestige of his ethnic group in determining how a person feels about himself.

Race, Ethnicity, and Self-Esteem

MORRIS ROSENBERG*

This study takes as its point of departure the assumption that the self-image is central to the subjective life of the individual, largely determining his thoughts, feelings, and behavior. At first glance this topic would appear to be a purely private, personal, and idiosyncratic phenomenon. And yet it is equally plain that the individual's self-picture is not purely non-objective art, reflecting the impulses and inspiration of the creator, but is rather a more or less clear portrait based upon the information provided by his social experience.

It is the nature and influence of this social experience that I have been especially interested in understanding. The child is raised in a family, whether broken or intact; he may have brothers or sisters, in varying combinations; he has parents who have certain feelings toward him. From this ferment of social interaction a self-picture begins to emerge. This family lives in a neighborhood, belongs to a social class, usually identifies with a religious group, derives from a national background. These social groupings impose on the child a characteristic style of life, set of values, and system of beliefs and ideals which covertly, imperceptibly, unintentionally, but no less powerfully, provide the bases for self-judgment. With a different background the child would *be* different and would see himself differently.

* Selections from Morris Rosenberg, *Society and the Adolescent Self-Image* (Princeton University Press, 1965; Princeton Paperback, 1968), pp. vii-viii, 16-18, 30-33, 53-63, 302–304, with deletions and modifications. Reprinted by permission of Princeton University Press, and of the author.

THE MEANING OF SELF-ESTEEM

Self-esteem is a positive or negative attitude toward a particular object, namely, the self. But self-esteem has two quite different connotations. One connotation of high self-esteem is that the person thinks he is "very good"; a very different connotation is that he thinks he is "good enough." It is thus possible for a person to consider himself superior to most others but to feel inadequate in terms of certain standards he has set for himself. Conversely, an adolescent may consider himself an average person but be quite contented with the self he observes. In one sense a person's self-esteem may be high whereas in the other sense it may be medium or low.

High self-esteem, as reflected in our scale items, expresses the feeling that one is "good enough." The individual simply feels that he is a person of worth; he respects himself for what he is, but he does not stand in awe of himself nor does he expect others to stand in awe of him. He does *not* necessarily consider himself superior to others.

One might consider using the term "self-acceptance" to describe these people, since this term implies that the individual knows what he is, is aware of his virtues and deficiencies, and accepts what he sees without regret. But our high self-esteem students do not simply accept themselves for what they are; they also want to grow, to improve, to overcome their deficiencies. They respect the self they observe, but they note imperfections and inadequacies, and hope, usually with confident anticipation of success, that they will overcome these deficiencies.

One might also consider applying the term self-satisfaction to describe these people, were this term not too loaded with the connotation of smugness.

When we speak of high self-esteem, then, we shall simply mean that the individual respects himself, considers himself worthy; he does not necessarily consider himself better than others, but he definitely does not consider himself worse; he does not feel that he is the ultimate in perfection but, on the contrary, recognizes his limitations and expects to grow and improve.

Low self-esteem, on the other hand, implies self-rejection, self-dissatisfaction, self-contempt. The individual lacks respect for the self he observes. The self-picture is disagreeable, and he wishes it were otherwise.

The measure of self-esteem employed in this study is a ten-item Guttman scale which has satisfactory reproducibility and scalability. We explicitly attempted to select items which openly and directly dealt with the dimension under consideration. Respondents were asked to strongly agree, agree, disagree, or strongly disagree with the following items:

—On the whole, I am satisfied with myself.
—At times I think I am no good at all.
—I feel that I have a number of good qualities.
—I am able to do things as well as most other people.
—I feel I do not have much to be proud of.
—I certainly feel useless at times.
—I feel that I am a person of worth, at least on an equal plane with others.
—I wish I could have more respect for myself.
—All in all, I am inclined to feel that I am a failure.
—I take a positive attitude toward myself.

"Positive" and "negative" items were presented alternately in order to reduce the effect of respondent set. While the reader may question one or another item, there is little doubt that the items generally deal with a favorable or unfavorable attitude toward oneself.

Practical considerations required the utilization of a measure which was easy and economical to administer. This scale is internally reliable and unidimensional and appears to have face validity. If the scale actually measures low self-esteem, then we would expect those with low scores to appear depressed to others and to express feelings of discouragement and unhappiness; to manifest symptoms of "neuroticism" or anxiety; to hold a low sociometric status in the group; to be described as commanding less respect than others and to feel that others have little respect for them. The evidence supports these expectations.

THE SAMPLE

A major purpose of this study was to learn how different social experiences, stemming from membership in groups characterized by different values, perspectives, or conditions of existence, would bear upon levels of self-esteem and upon self-values. The population selected for study was the student body attending public high schools in New York State. Various social classes, races, religious groups, rural and urban communities, and nationality groups are all well represented in this state. Broad geographical range was sacrificed by the selection of a single state, but a wide range of other social characteristics did appear in our sample.

The sample consists of ten high schools selected by random procedures from the roster of public high schools in New York State. High schools were stratified by size of community, and the ultimate selection was made by means of a Table of Random Numbers. Since the sampling unit was the high school rather than the individual, the adequacy with which the sample represents the population of students cannot be determined. A further limitation of the sample lies in the fact that it omits students in parochial or private secular schools, adolescents who have dropped out of school before reaching their junior or senior years, and students absent from school on the day the questionnaires were administered. The sample, then, consists of 5,024 high school juniors and seniors from ten randomly selected public high schools present on the day of administration.

Within the classrooms, teachers distributed three questionnaire forms alternately to their students and read instructions to them. Each student completed one questionnaire form. The questionnaires were anonymous. In response to two questions added at the end of the questionnaires, the great majority of students said that they found the questionnaires interesting to fill out and that they had little difficulty answering the questions.

ETHNIC AND RACIAL GROUP CHARACTERISTICS

The oft-quoted description of American society as a "melting pot" is intended to convey the idea that a variety of national groupings, characterized by distinctively different subcultures, in the course of time come to lose their distinctive cultural characteristics and increasingly come to assume cultural elements in common. And yet nationality may be the major basis of cultural differentiation, and national groupings in American society may represent the most distinctive subcultures in the broader society.

Today, however, it is less easy to distinguish such national groupings than it was in the early decades of this century. Almost all our respondents are American-born, and most of their parents are as well. In many cases the father is of one national origin, the mother of another. Or either parent may be of mixed national origin. In the present analysis we have identified the ethnic or racial origins of those students whose parents had the same single national, religious or racial background.

Table 1 presents the distribution of self-esteem among fourteen ethnic and racial groups (including mixed categories of "others"). The question may immediately be raised whether the ethnic differences in self-esteem are not simple reflections of social class differences. In order to check this possibility, we have computed standardized self-esteem distributions for each of these groups, i.e., the self-esteem which would appear if the social class positions of all groups were equal.

Our procedure was as follows: We first placed our fourteen ethnic groups in a rank order based upon the proportion in each group with high self-esteem. After standardizing each group on social class, we rank-ordered these groups on the basis of the standardized figures. The Spearman Rank Correlation Coefficient between the original and the standardized groups is .97. This would suggest that if the social class distributions of these groups were the same, the general pattern appearing in the table would remain virtually unchanged.

Since the observed results do not appear to be a reflection of social class, it is worth calling attention to several points in the table.

1) First, it may be noted that there is no indication that the distribution of self-acceptance in a group is related to the social

prestige of that group in American society. In the table, we see that Negroes, who are exposed to the most intense, humiliating, and crippling forms of discrimination in virtually every institutional area, do not have particularly low self-esteem. The self-esteem of these youngsters is slightly below that of whites—39 percent of the Negroes and 45 percent of the whites had high self-esteem—but it is not nearly as low as one might expect if general societal status were an important determinant of self-esteem.*

At the same time adolescents of English or Welsh descent, who are certainly the heart of the Old Yankee stock and whose pride is buttressed by a long tradition and an historical location in an established position, are also slightly lower in self-esteem than other groups. For the other groups, the distribution of self-esteem within the group shows no striking similarity to the prestige rank accorded them in the broader society. For example, we have compared the Bogardus attitudes toward ethnic groups (1959, p. 441), based on data collected in 1956, with the proportion of corresponding ethnic groups (represented by twenty-five or more cases) with high self-esteem. The Spearman Rank Correlation coefficient is .04, indicating virtually no correlation.

Having said this, a number of qualifications must immediately be introduced: First, there are a large number of ethnic groups— e.g., Scandinavians, French, Yugoslavians—which are not sufficiently represented in our sample. It may be that if the full range of ethnic groups were adequately represented, the results would lead to a different over-all conclusion; even among those ethnic groups which are represented, the number of cases is often considerably less than would be desired; and although the high schools

---

* Has a small pocket of well-to-do, successful, and educated Negroes chanced to fall in our sample? Our data suggest that this is not so. [The data show] that Negroes in our sample are considerably more likely to come from the lowest classes and to have poorly educated parents, and are less likely to be taking academic course programs and to come from small towns. The social characteristics of these Negroes are thus generally in accord with expectations. Of course, we know nothing about the Negroes who have dropped out of school before the junior year. There is nothing in these data, however, to suggest that these Negroes are socially atypical of those who have remained in school at least until near the end of the junior year.

TABLE 1

ETHNIC OR RACIAL GROUP AND SELF–ESTEEM

| | Self-Esteem | | | | |
Catholics	High	Medium	Low	Total percent	(Number)
German Catholics	48%	27	25	100	(64)
Italian Catholics	45%	25	30	100	(643)
Irish Catholics	39%	25	36	100	(120)
Spanish-Portuguese Catholics	28%	32	40	100	(25)
Polish Catholics	28%	28	45	100	(65)
All other Catholics*	44%	26	30	100	(998)
Jews					
German Jews	62%	19	19	100	(21)
Russian Jews	59%	21	21	100	(63)
Polish Jews	51%	20	29	100	(35)
All other Jews*	52%	24	24	100	(474)
Protestants					
German Protestants	53%	21	26	100	(150)
English-Welsh Protestants	39%	24	37	100	(122)
Negro Protestants	39%	28	34	100	(80)
All other Protestants*	43%	25	32	100	(1375)

* Includes those of mixed national origin, i.e., either (1) father and mother are of different national origins, or (2) father or mother is of mixed national origin.

in our study were selected on the basis of strictly random procedures, the small number of high schools studied introduces the possibility of sampling error. We may, then, repeat the statement that our data provide no indication of a linear relationship between an ethnic group's prestige rank and the distribution of self-esteem in the group, but view this generalization in the light of the above mentioned statistical considerations.

2) The second point is that various ethnic groups do differ substantially in their distribution of self-esteem.* The most

* We have restricted our comparisons to those groups represented by twenty-five or more cases (with the exception of German Jews).

conspicuous groups in our study are the Germans and the Poles. It may be noted that, within each religious group, Germans are more likely to have high self-esteem than others. German Catholics are more likely to have high self-esteem than other Catholics, German Jews than other Jews, and German Protestants than other Protestants. On the other hand, in the two religious groups in which adolescents of Polish origin are represented, the group self-esteem is lowest. Polish Catholics are more likely to have low self-esteem than other Catholics, and Polish Jews are more likely to have low self-esteem than other Jews.

We thus see that national origin is associated with self-esteem. The most striking differences, for which an adequate number of cases are available, appear between the Russian Jews and the Polish Catholics. Fifty-nine percent of the former, but only 27 percent of the latter, had high self-esteem; conversely, the Polish Catholics were over twice as likely as the Russian Jews to have low self-esteem (45 percent to 21 percent).

DISCUSSION

In considering the relationship of broad social group memberships to self-esteem, one is likely to be guided in a general way by one of two hypotheses:

THE STRATIFICATION HYPOTHESIS

Many studies have shown that, in American society, religious groups, races, nationality groups, and, of course, social classes differ in social prestige. If the respect accorded the individual by others is influenced by the prestige rank of the group, then we might expect an association between group social esteem and individual self-esteem. As Cartwright (1950, p. 440) expresses the point: "The groups to which a person belongs serve as primary determiners of his self-esteem. To a considerable extent, *personal* feelings of worth depend on the social evaluation of the *groups* with which a person is identified. Self-hatred and feelings of worthlessness tend to arise from membership in underprivileged or outcast groups."

THE SUBCULTURAL HYPOTHESIS

According to this approach, members of broad social groups—classes, religions, nationalities, races—are seen as sharing certain interests, attitudes, values, or other aspects of styles of life. These groups, for example, might differ in the way they raised their children. If child-rearing practices has a bearing upon self-esteem, then this differential treatment might create differences in levels of self-acceptance.

Of course, differences in prestige may have an influence on styles of life and group styles of life may influence social prestige. Nevertheless, at a given point in time, one may ask: Do group differences in self-esteem appear to be closely associated with social prestige in the broader society or do they appear to stem from differences in group thoughts, customs, practices or characteristic life experiences?

As an over-all pattern, our data do not lend strong support to the stratification hypothesis. We have seen that the social prestige of a nationality or religious group is generally unrelated to the self-acceptance of its members. As far as social class is concerned, students from higher social classes are more likely than those from lower social classes to have high self-esteem, but the differences are not large, they are not the same for boys and girls, and they appear to be due in part to certain kinds of parent-child relationships. It seems likely that, among adolescents, subcultural norms, or other characteristic aspects of experience deriving from cultural factors, are more important than general social prestige as determinants of self-esteem.

It is important, however, to emphasize that the members of our sample are adolescents, not adults, and that their class, nationality, and religious statuses are ascribed, not achieved. In other words, in the adult world, differential occupational achievement, dominance or submission, power or impotence, prestige or disesteem, may influence one's self-esteem, whereas in the adolescent world, the reflected glory deriving from the occupational achievement of one's father may be less important. Nor does this mean that achievement is unimportant for the adolescent. On the contrary, a successful school record or successful interpersonal relationships are, as we shall see, definitely related to self-esteem. But these reflect the adolescent's own achievements, whereas his class, religion, and nationality are assigned to him by society; he has nothing to do with it.

The second point is that the individual need not necessarily accept the social evaluation of his worth as his personal definition of his worth; on the contrary, there is a wide variety of "coping mechanisms" that may be adopted in order to save one's self-esteem in the face of social disprivilege. For one thing, members of an ethnic group will often rank their own group higher than others rank it. Secondly, group members may tend to react to the disesteem in which they are held by interpreting this as an expression of the selfishness or pathology of the discriminator rather than as inadequacy in themselves. Third, a group member may compare himself with the nationals of his country of origin (or even of his parents), over whom he has considerable material superiority, rather than the still more highly prestigious groups in his present country of residence. Fourth, group members living in socially homogeneous neighborhoods are likely to confine their other associations to people of the same class or ethnic background; hence their feelings of self-esteem may be based upon relative prestige within a class or ethnic group than between groups.

The third point is the following: When we deal with self-esteem, we are asking whether the individual considers himself adequate—a person of worth—not whether he considers himself superior to others. Implicated in such a feeling of adequacy is the relationship between one's standards and one's accomplishments; or, to quote the felicitous formula of William James (1950, p. 310):

$$\text{Self-Esteem} = \frac{\text{Success}}{\text{Pretensions}}$$

Thus, a person who has modest goals and fulfills these may consider himself a perfectly worthwhile person. He will not deem himself superior to others, but he will be relatively satisfied with himself; such self-satisfaction would, in our study, be reflected in a high self-esteem score. Differential occupational goals might have similar consequences for self-esteem. It is reasonable to assume that a middle-class youth will be at least as uncertain about his ability to become a doctor as a working-class youth is about his ability to become a plumber. Group-determined goals and standards, as well as accomplishments, must be considered in attempting to account for feelings of self-worth.

This point is highlighted by some data brought to my attention by my colleague, Dr. Melvin Ember. In his study of nursing personnel in a mental hospital, he found that among attendants, who are the lowest ranking nursing personnel, Negroes had *higher* self-esteem than whites, according to our scale. In this Middle Atlantic city, the job of attendant is a relatively good position for a Negro but a very poor position for a white. Self-esteem may be more a matter of one's position within one group than the rank of the group in relation to other groups.

The most striking differences in self-esteem appear, then, not when we consider the factor of prestige rank in the broader society, but when we consider specific groups which probably represent distinctive subcultures. Such groups tend to be characterized by distinctive styles of life; they possess characteristic conceptions of right or wrong; they share certain patterns of values and systems of aspirations; very likely they show distinctive kinds of family life; they may well share characteristic child-rearing values and practices; their degree of group acceptance and integration may vary; their perspectives of human nature and of the nature of the world may differ; and so on. Such groups might be upper-class Jews, lower-class Catholics, German Protestants, Italian Catholics, Russian Jews, Polish Catholics, etc. It is in the comparisons among such groups that the most distinctive differences in self-esteem appear.

COMMENTARY on
RACE, ETHNICITY, AND THE ACHIEVEMENT SYNDROME

Need Achievement is the motivation to succeed, to perform well in relation to a standard of excellence or in comparison with others. The person with high need Achievement makes intense efforts to accomplish a goal and to overcome the obstacles and difficulties that stand in the way of his reaching the goal. He is a striver.

The assessment of the strength of a person's motivation to achieve is based on projective techniques utilizing fantasy production. The most common procedure is to present the subject with a series of pictures and ask him to make up stories about them. The assumption is that the subject will project his needs, wishes, fears, etc. into his stories. The basic criterion for whether a story has achievement imagery or not is whether it contains any reference to the striving to meet a standard of excellence. The story, for example, might concern a young surgeon who is trying to develop skill in performing a critical operation. Need Achievement here is indicated by the physician's endeavoring to attain proficiency in a task. Using such criteria, psychologists have developed systematic procedures for scoring the level of need Achievement shown by the stories.

If two individuals are equally endowed with the aptitudes and innate potentials necessary for performing an activity, we would expect the one with the high need Achievement to perform better. Although the evidence is not entirely consistent, it does in general bear out this expectation, at least for males (Birney 1968, pp. 862–65, 881–84; Brown 1965, pp. 438–41; Byrne 1966, pp. 305–08). A number of studies, for example, show that need Achievement is correlated with academic performance. Those who score high on the need tend to get higher grade point averages in school and to complete more years of schooling. Need Achievement also seems a good basis on which to predict striving in the occupational world. The greater a person's motivation to achieve, the data suggest, the more likely he is to prefer a highly prestigious occupation and to be upwardly mobile.

It is in light of data such as these that Rosen's study (5) takes on significance. His main finding is that, on the average, blacks score lower on need Achievement than whites. Other investigators have obtained the same finding (Baughman and Dahlstrom 1968, chapter 12; Mingione 1965; Mussen 1953).* An important factor in the relatively low educational and occupational attainments of blacks, therefore, may be their low motivation to achieve.†

Assuming this conjecture is valid, it is nonetheless not justified to blame the blacks for their condition. On the contrary, achievement motivation seems to be only an intervening variable mediating the effects of poverty and minority group status. As Rosen points out, the level of achievement motivation is largely a function of achievement training. That is, it depends on the degree to which the parents have high expectations for the performances of their children and reward their children for meeting these expectations. In the day-to-day handling of children, parents are influenced by their perceptions of the adult world. With little hope that their children will one day be able to climb the social ladder, parents have little incentive to engage in achievement training. This interpretation is supported in part by Rosen's finding that, unlike most black youngsters, upper-status black children have extremely high need Achievement scores. The

---

* Two studies are exceptions. Mingione (1968) and Veroff et al. (1960) failed to find significant differences between blacks and whites on need Achievement. Mingione's results are open to questions because her study used a measure of doubtful validity. In contrast to the usual procedure of presenting pictures about which the subject makes up stories, she presented topic sentences. This unconventional technique produced measures of need Achievement that failed to correlate with school grades and with intelligence. The investigation by Veroff and his associates, which also showed no significant racial differences, differs from the other studies cited here in one important respect: the respondents were all adults. Whether this accounts for the exceptional findings of this study, however, is not clear.

† Featherman (1971) presents data conflicting with the hypothesis that ethnic differences in occupational achievement are due to differences in modal personality variables. However, need Achievement was not among the personality variables of his analysis. One suspects that the results of Featherman's study might have been different had this crucial variable been part of his analysis.

parents of these children presumably have more hope for the future of their offspring—and therefore engage in more achievement training—than do other black parents. One suspects, then, that to develop higher levels of need Achievement, blacks must enjoy greater equality of opportunity and suffer less discrimination.*

* Since Rosen's article was written, important advances have been made in the theory of achievement motivation. An exposition of these advances can be found in Atkinson and Feather (1966). According to current thinking, the degree to which a person strives for success in any given situation depends not only on his level of need Achievement but also on his estimate of how likely he is to be successful at the task and on the value he attaches to success in the task. For a discussion of the implications of these theoretical advances for the academic performance of blacks, see Katz (1967).

Race, Ethnicity, and the Achievement Syndrome

BERNARD C. ROSEN*

The upward mobility rates of many racial and ethnic groups in America have been markedly dissimilar when compared with one another and with some white Protestant groups. For example, among the "new immigration" groups which settled primarily in the Northeast, the Greeks and Jews have attained middle class status more rapidly than most of their fellow immigrants. In general, ethnic groups with Roman Catholic affiliation have moved up less rapidly than non-Catholic groups. And the vertical mobility of Negroes, even in the less repressive environment of the industrial Northeast, has been relatively slow (Warner and Srole 1945; Strodtbeck 1958a; Davie 1936).

The reasons offered to explain these differences vary with the group in question. Thus, differences in group mobility rates have sometimes been interpreted as a function of the immigrant's possession of certain skills which were valuable in a burgeoning industrial society. In this connection, there is some evidence that many Jews came to America with occupational skills better suited to urban living than did their fellow immigrants. Social mobility seems also to be related to the ability of ethnic and racial groups to organize effectively to protect and promote their interests. Both the Greeks and the Jews were quicker to develop effective community organizations than were other immigrants who had

* Reprinted from the *American Sociological Review*, vol. 24 (February 1959), pp. 47-60 by permission from the publisher, the American Sociological Association, and the author.

not previously faced the problem of adapting as minority groups. For the Jews, this situation grew out of their experiences with an often hostile gentile world; for the Greeks, out of their persecutions by the Turks. The repressiveness of the social structure or the willingness of the dominant groups to permit others to share in the fruits of a rich, expanding economy has also been given as an explanation of differential group mobility. This argument has merit in the case of Negroes, but it is less valid in a comparison of the Jews with Southern Italians or French-Canadians. Finally, it has been suggested that groups with experiences in small town or urban environments were more likely to possess the cultural values appropriate to achievement in American society than were ethnic and racial groups whose cultures had been formed in rural, peasant surroundings. Here, again, it has been noted that many Jews and a small but influential number of Levantine Greeks had come from small towns or cities, while most of the Roman Catholic immigrants from Eastern and Southern Europe (and Southern Negroes before their migration to the North) came from rural communities (cf. Glazer 1958; Warner and Srole 1945; Burgess 1913; Saloutos 1945; Kalijarvi 1942; Strodtbeck 1958b; and Myrdal 1944).

As valid as these explanations may be—and we believe they have merit—they overlook one important factor: *the individual's psychological and cultural orientation towards achievement;* by which we mean his psychological need to excel, his desire to enter the competitive race for social status, and his initial possession of or willingness to adopt the high valuation placed upon personal achievement and success which foreign observers from Tocqueville to Laski have considered an important factor in the remarkable mobility of individuals in American society.

Three components of this achievement orientation are particularly relevant for any study of social mobility. The first is a psychological factor, *achievement motivation,* which provides the internal impetus to excel in situations involving standards of excellence. The second and third components are cultural factors, one consisting of certain *value orientations* which implement achievement-motivated behavior, the other of culturally influenced *educational-vocational aspiration levels.* All three factors may affect status achievement; one moving the individual to excel, the others organizing and directing his behavior towards high status goals. This motive-value-aspiration complex has been called the *Achievement Syndrome* (Rosen 1956).

It is the basic hypothesis of this study that many racial and ethnic groups were not, and are not now, alike in their orientation toward achievement, particularly as it is expressed in the striving for status through social mobility, and that this difference in orientation has been an important factor contributing to the dissimilarities in their social mobility rates. Specifically, this paper examines the achievement motivation, values, and aspirations of members of six racial and ethnic groups. Four of these are "new immigration" ethnic groups with similar periods of residence in this country who faced approximately the same economic circumstances upon arrival: the French-Canadians, Southern Italians, Greeks, and East European Jews. The fifth is the Negro group in the Northeast, the section's largest "racial" division. The last, and in some ways the most heterogeneous, is the native-born white Protestant group. Contributing to the fact that these six groups have not been equally mobile, we suggest, are differences in the three components of the achievement syndrome: their incidence is highest among Jews, Greeks, and white Protestants, lower among Southern Italians and French-Canadians, and lowest among Negroes.

RESEARCH PROCEDURE

The date were collected from a purposive sample of 954 subjects residing in 62 communities in four Northeastern states: 51 in Connecticut, seven in New York, three in New Jersey, and one in Massachusetts. The subjects are 427 pairs of mothers and their sons; 62 pairs are French-Canadians, 74 are Italians, 47 are Greeks, 57 are Jews, 65 are Negroes, and 122 are white Protestants. Most subjects were located through the aid of local religious, ethnic, or service organizations, or through their residence in neighborhoods believed to be occupied by certain groups. The subject's group membership was determined ultimately by asking the mothers in personal interviews to designate their religion and land of national origin. The interviewers, all of whom were upper-classmen enrolled in two sociology classes, were instructed to draw respondents from various social strata.* The respondent's social class position was determined by a modified version of Hollingshead's Index of Social Position, which uses occupation and education of the main wage-earner, usually the father, as the principal criteria of status. Respondents were classified according to this index into one of five social classes, from the highest status group, Class I, to the lowest, Class V (Hollingshead and Redlich 1953). Most of the mothers and all of the sons are native-born, the sons ranging in age from eight to fourteen years (the mean age is about eleven years). There are no significant age differences between the various groups.

Two research instruments were a projective test to measure achievement motivation and a personal interview to obtain information on achievement value orientations and related phenomena. Achievement motivation has been defined by McClelland and his associates as a re-integration of affect aroused by cues in situations involving standards of excellence. Such standards usually are imparted to the individual by his parents, who impart the understanding that they expect him to perform well in relation to these standards of excellence, rewarding him for successful endeavor and punishing him for failure. In time he comes to have similar expectations of himself when exposed to situations involving standards of excellence and re-experiences the affect associated with his earlier efforts to meet these standards. The behavior of people with high achievement motivation is characterized by persistent striving and general competitiveness.

Using a Thematic Apperception Test, McClelland and his associates have developed a method of measuring the achievement motive that involves identifying and counting the frequency with which imagery about evaluated performance in competition with a

* The interviewers were trained by the writer; efforts were made to control for interviewer biases. It should be remembered that the sample is not random at any point in the selection process. Hence, the reader is cautioned to regard the data presented here as tentative and suggestive.

standard of excellence appears in the thoughts of a person when he tells a brief story under time pressure. This imagery now can be identified objectively and reliably. The test assumes that the more the individual shows indications of connections between evaluated performance and affect in his fantasy, the greater the degree to which achievement motivation is part of his personality (McClelland, et al 1953). This projective test, which involves showing the subject four ambiguous pictures and asking him to tell a story about each, was given privately and individually to the sons in their homes. Their imaginative responses to the pictures were scored by two judges; the Pearson product moment correlation between the two scorings was .86, an estimate of reliability similar to those reported in earlier studies using this measure.

Following the boys' testing, their mothers were interviewed privately. The interview guide included several standardized questions designed to indicate the mother's achievement value orientations, her educational and vocational aspirations for her son, and the degree to which she had trained him to be independent.

FINDINGS AND INTERPRETATION

ACHIEVEMENT MOTIVATION

Empirical studies have shown that achievement motivation is generated by (at least) two kinds of socialization practices: (1) *achievement training,* in which the parents, by imposing standards of excellence upon tasks, by setting high goals for their child, and by indicating their high evaluation of his competence to do a task well, communicate to him that they expect evidences of high achievement; (2) *independence training,* in which the parents indicate to the child that they expect him to be self-reliant and, at the same time, grant him relative autonomy in decision-making situations where he is given both freedom of action and responsibility for success or failure. Essentially, achievement training is concerned with getting the child to *do things well,* while independence training seeks to teach him to do things *on his own.* Although both kinds often occur together and each contributes to the development of achievement motivation, achievement training is the more important of the two (Winterbottom 1958; Rosen 1957).

Two bodies of information—ethnographic studies of the "old world" or non-American culture and recent empirical investigations of the training practices used by Americans of various ethnic backgrounds—strongly indicate that the six groups examined here, in the past and to some extent today, differ with respect to the degree to which their members typically emphasize achievement and independence training. Ethnic differences in these matters were first studied by McClelland, who noted that the linkage between independence training and achievement motivation established by recent empirical studies suggests an interesting parallel with Weber's classic description of the characterological consequences of the Protestant Reformation. Weber reasoned, first, concerning salvation, that an important aspect of the Protestant theological position was the shift from reliance on an institution (the Church) to a greater reliance upon self; it seemed reasonable to assume that Protestant parents who prepared their children for increased self-reliance in religious matters would also tend to stress the necessity for the child to be self-reliant in other aspects of his life. Secondly, Weber's description of the personality types produced by the Reformation is strikingly similar to the picture of the person with high achievement motivation; for example, the hard-working, thrifty Protestant working girl, the Protestant entrepreneur who "gets nothing out of his wealth for himself except the irrational sense of having done his job well" (McClelland 1955).

The hypothesis deduced from these observations was put to the test by McClelland, who questioned white Protestant, Irish-Catholic, Italian-Catholic, and Jewish mothers about their independence training practices. He found that Protestants and Jews favored earlier independence training than Irish and Italian Catholics (McClelland, et al 1955). These findings are supported and enlarged upon by data derived from questioning the 427 mothers in this study about their training practices. The mothers were asked, "At what age do you expect your son to do the following things?" and to note the appropriate items from the following list (taken from the Winterbottom [1958] index of training in independence and mastery):*

1. To be willing to try things on his own without depending on his mother for help.
2. To be active and energetic in climbing, jumping, and sports.
3. To try hard things for himself without asking for help.
4. To be able to lead other children and assert himself in children's groups.
5. To make his own friends among children of his own age.
6. To do well in school on his own.
7. To have interests and hobbies of his own. To be able to entertain himself.
8. To do well in competition with other children. To try hard to come out on top in games and sports.
9. To make decisions like choosing his own clothes or deciding to spend his money by himself.

An index of independence training was derived by summing the ages for each item and taking the mean figure. The data in Table 1 show that the Jews expect earliest evidence of self-reliance from their children (mean age 6.83 years), followed by the Protestants (6.87), Negroes (7.23), Greeks (7.67), French-Canadians (7.99), and Italians (8.03). Both primary sources of variation—ethnicity and social class—are significant at the .01 level.

Data on the relative emphasis which racial and ethnic groups place upon achievement *training* (that is, imposing standards of excellence upon tasks, setting high goals for the child to achieve, and communicating to him a feeling that his parents evaluate highly his task-competence) are much more difficult to obtain. Achievement training as such, in fact, is rarely treated in studies of ethnic socialization practices. Hence, inferences about achievement training were drawn primarily from ethnographic and

* Though primarily a measure of independence training, two items in this index—items 6 and 8—are considered measures of mastery training, a concept akin to our notion of achievement training. The failure to disentangle independence training from mastery (achievement) training has been responsible for some confusion in earlier studies of the origins of achievement motivation. (For an analysis of this confusion, see Rosen 1957.) The two components were kept in the index in order to maintain comparability between this study and the earlier work on ethnic groups by McClelland reported above.

TABLE 1

MEAN AGE OF INDEPENDENCE TRAINING BY
ETHNICITY AND SOCIAL CLASS

Ethnicity	Social Class*				
	I-II-III	IV	V	$\bar{x}$	N
French-Canadian	8.00	7.69	8.08	7.99	62
Italian	6.79	7.89	8.47	8.03	74
Greek	6.33	8.14	7.52	7.67	47
Jew	6.37	7.29	6.90	6.83	57
Negro	6.64	6.98	7.39	7.23	65
Protestant	5.82	7.44	7.03	6.87	122
$\bar{x}$	6.31	7.64	7.59		

Ethnicity: $F = 8.55$ $P < .01$
Social Class: $F = 21.48$ $P < .001$
Ethnicity X Class: $F = 6.25$ $P < .01$

* The three-class breakdown was used in an earlier phase of the analysis. An examination of the means of cells using a four-class breakdown revealed no change in pattern and did not warrant new computations.

historical materials, which are usually more informative about achievement as such than about relevant socialization practices.

The groups about which the most is known concerning achievement training, perhaps, are the Protestants, the Jews, and, to a lesser extent, the Greeks. These groups traditionally have stressed excellence and achievement. In the case of the Protestants, this tradition can be located in the Puritan Ethic with its concept of work as a "calling" and the exhortation that a job be done well. Of course, not all Protestants would be equally comfortable with this tradition; it is much more applicable, for example, to Presbyterians and Quakers than to Methodists and Baptists. Nonetheless, the generally longer residence of Protestants in this country makes it probable that they would tend to share the American belief that children should be encouraged to develop their talents and to set high goals, possibly a bit beyond their reach. The observation that Jews stress achievement training is commonplace. Zyborowski and Herzog (1952) note the strong tendency among *shtetyl* Jews to expect and to reward evidences of achievement even among very young children. The image of the Jewish mother as eager for her son to excel in competition and to set ever higher goals for himself is a familiar one in the literature of Jewish family life. Careful attention to standards of excellence in the Greek home is stressed by the parents: children know that a task which is shabbily performed will have to be re-done. In this country, the Greek is exhorted to be "a credit to his group." Failure to meet group norms is quickly perceived and where possible punished; while achievement receives the approbation of the entire Greek community.

Among the Southern Italians (the overwhelming majority of American-Italians are of Southern Italian extraction), French-Canadians, and Negroes the tradition seems to be quite different. More often than not they came from agrarian societies or regions in which opportunities for achievement were strictly curtailed by the social structure and where habits of resignation and fatalism in the face of social and environmental frustrations were psychologically functional. Under such conditions children were not typically exhorted to be achievers or urged to set their sights very high. Of course, children were expected to perform tasks, as they are in most societies, but such tasks were usually farm or self-caretaking chores, from which the notion of competition with standards of excellence is not excluded, but is not ordinarily stressed. As for communicating to the child a sense of confidence in his competence to do a task well, there is some evidence that in the father-dominant Italian and French-Canadian families, pronounced concern with the child's ability might be perceived as a threat to the father (Williams 1938; Miner 1939).

On the whole, the data indicate that Protestants, Jews, and Greeks place a greater emphasis on independence and achievement training than Southern Italians and French-Canadians. The data on the Negroes are conflicting: they often train children relatively early in self-reliance, but there is little evidence of much stress upon achievement training. No doubt the socialization practices of these groups have been modified somewhat by the acculturating influences of American society since their arrival in the

Northeast.* But ethnic cultures tend to survive even in the face of strong obliterating forces, and we believe that earlier differences between groups persist—a position supported by the present data on self-reliance training. Hence, the hypothesis that the racial and ethnic groups considered here differ with respect to achievement motivation. We predicted that, on the average, achievement motivation scores would be highest among the Jews, Greeks, and white Protestants, lower among the Italians and French-Canadians, and lowest among the Negroes. Table 2 shows that the data support these predictions, indicated by the following mean scores: Greeks 10.80, Jews 10.53, Protestants 10.11, Italians 9.65, French-Canadians 8.82, and Negroes 8.40.

TABLE 2

MEAN ACHIEVEMENT MOTIVATION SCORES
BY ETHNICITY AND SOCIAL CLASS

Ethnicity	I-II	III	IV	V	$\bar{x}$	N
			Social Class			
French-Canadian	10.00	10.64	8.78	7.75	8.82	62
Italian	8.86	12.81	7.54	10.20	9.65	74
Greek	9.17	12.13	10.40	8.75	10.80	47
Jew	10.05	10.41	10.94	11.20	10.53	57
Negro	11.36	9.00	8.23	6.72	8.40	65
Protestant	11.71	10.94	9.39	7.31	10.11	122
$\bar{x}$	10.55	11.26	9.01	8.32		

Ethnicity: $F = 1.23$ $P > .05$
Social Class: $F = 5.30$ $P < .005$
Ethnicity X Class: $F = 1.32$ $P > .05$

A series of "t" tests of significance between means (a one-tail test was used in cases where the direction of the difference had been predicted) was computed. The differences between Greeks, Jews, and Protestants are not statistically significant. The Italian score is significantly lower ($P < .05$) than the score for the Greeks,

* It does not necessarily follow that the impact of American culture has reduced the differences between groups. An argument can be made that for some groups life in America has accentuated differences by allowing certain characteristics of the groups to develop. We have in mind particularly the Greeks and Jews whose need to excel could find little avenue for expression through status striving in Europe.

but not for the Jews and Protestants. The largest differences are
between the French-Canadians and Negroes on the one hand and
the remaining groups on the other: the French-Canadian mean
score is significantly lower (P < .01) than those of all other groups
except Italians and Negroes; the mean score for all Negroes is
significantly lower (P < .01) than the scores for all other groups
except French-Canadians. A "Roman Catholic" score was
obtained by combining Italian and French-Canadian scores, and
scores for all non-Negro groups were combined to form a "White"
score. The differences between group means were tested for significance (by a one-tail "t" test) and it was found that the
"Catholic" score is significantly lower than the scores for Protestants, Greek Orthodox, and Jews (P < .01). The Negro mean score
is significantly lower than the combined score of all white groups
(P < .002).

A comparison of ethnic-racial differences does not tell the
whole story. There are also significant differences between the
social classes. In fact, analysis of Table 2 indicates that social class
accounts for more of the variance than ethnicity: the F ratio for
ethnicity is 1.23 (P < .05), for class 5.30 (P < .005). The small
number of cases in Classes I and II greatly increases the within-
group variance; when these two classes are combined with Class III
the variance is decreased and the F ratio for ethnicity increases
sharply to 2.13 (P < .06). Social class, however, remains more
significantly related to achievement motivation than ethnicity.
This finding is especially important in this study since the proportion of subjects in each class varies for the ethnic groups. There are
relatively more middle class than lower class subjects among the
Jews, Greeks, and Protestants than among Italians, French-
Canadians, and Negroes. To control for social class it was necessary to examine the differences between cells as well as between
columns and rows. A series of "t" tests of differences between the
means of cells revealed that for the most part the earlier pattern
established for total ethnic means persists, although in some
instances the differences between groups are decreased, in others
increased, and in a few cases the direction of the differences is
reversed. Neither ethnicity nor social class alone is sufficient to

predict an individual's score; both appear to contribute something to the variance between groups, but on the whole social class is a better predictor than ethnicity. Generally, a high status person from an ethnic group with a low mean achievement motivation score is more likely to have a high score than a low status person from a group with a high mean score. Thus, the mean score for Class I–II Negroes is higher than the score for Class IV–V white Protestants: the score for the former is 11.36, for the latter, 7.31; a "t" test revealed that the difference between these two means is significant at the .05 level, using a two-tail test. This relatively high score for Class I–II Negroes, the third highest for any cell in the table, indicates, perhaps, the strong motivation necessary for a Negro to achieve middle class status in a hostile environment. Generally, the scores for each group decrease as the class level declines, except for the Jews whose scores are inversely related to social status—a finding for which we can offer no explanation.

ACHIEVEMENT VALUE ORIENTATIONS

Achievement motivation is one part of the achievement syndrome; an equally important component is the achievement value orientation. Value orientations are defined as meaningful and affectively charged modes of organizing behavior—principles that guide human conduct. They establish criteria which influence the individual's preferences and goals. Achievement values and achievement motivation, while related, represent genuinely different components of the achievement syndrome, not only conceptually but also in their origins and, as we have shown elsewhere, in their social correlates (Rosen 1956). Value orientations, because of their conceptual content, are probably acquired in that stage of the child's cultural training when verbal communication of a fairly complex nature is possible. Achievement motivation or the need to excel, on the other hand, has its origins in parent-child interaction beginning early in the child's life when many of these relations are likely to be emotional and unverbalized. Analytically, then, the learning of achievement oriented values can be independent of the acquisition of the achievement motive, although empirically they often occur together.

Achievement values affect social mobility in that they focus the individual's attention on status improvement and help to shape his behavior so that achievement motivation can be translated into successful action. The achievement motive by itself is not a sufficient condition of social mobility: it provides internal impetus to excel, but it does not impel the individual to take the steps necessary for status achievement. Such steps in our society involve, among other things, a preparedness to plan, work hard, make sacrifices, and be physically mobile. Whether or not the individual will understand their importance and accept them will depend in part upon his values.

Three sets of values (a modification of Kluckhohn's [1950] scheme) were identified as elements of the achievement syndrome,* as follows:

1. Activistic-Passivistic Orientation concerns the extent to which the culture of a group encourages the individual to believe in the possibility of his manipulating the physical and social environment to his advantage. An activistic culture encourages the individual to believe that it is both possible and necessary for him to improve his status, whereas a passivistic culture promotes the acceptance of the notion that individual efforts to achieve mobility are relatively futile.

2. Individualistic-Collectivistic Orientation refers to the extent to which the individual is expected to subordinate his needs to the group. This study is specifically concerned with the degree to which the society expects the individual to maintain close physical proximity to his family of orientation, even at the risk of limiting vocational opportunities; and the degree to which the society emphasizes group incentives rather than personal rewards. The collectivistic society places a greater stress than the individualistic on group ties and group incentives.

3. Present-Future Orientation concerns the society's attitude toward time and its impact upon behavior. A present oriented society stresses the merit of living in the present, emphasizing immediate gratifications; a future oriented society encourages the belief that planning and present sacrifices are worthwhile, or morally obligatory, in order to insure future gains.

* For the most part, the value orientations examined in this study, their description, and the items used to index them, are identical with those which appear in Rosen (1956).

Examination of ethnographic and historical materials on the cultures of the six ethnic groups revealed important differences in value orientation—differences antedating their arrival in the Northeast. The cultures of white Protestants, Jews, and Greeks stand out as considerably more individualistic, activistic, and future-oriented than those of the Southern Italians, French-Canadians, and Negroes. Several forces—religious, economic, and national—seem to have long influenced the Protestants in this direction, including, first, the Puritan Ethic with its stress upon individualism and work; then the impact of the liberal economic ethic (Weber's "Spirit of Capitalism") emphasizing competitive activity and achievement; and finally, the challenge of the frontier, with its consequent growth of a national feeling of optimism and manifest destiny. All of these factors tended very early to create a highly activistic, individualistic, future-oriented culture—the picture of American culture held by foreign observers since Tocqueville. (For a history of the development of the liberal economic ethic and its manifestation on the American scene, see Randall 1926; Galbraith 1958.)

The Jews, who for centuries had lived in more or less hostile environments, have learned that it is not only possible to manipulate their environment to insure survival but even to prosper in it. Jewish tradition stresses the possibility of the individual rationally mastering his world. Man is not helpless against the forces of nature or of his fellow man; God will provide, but only if man does his share. Like Protestantism, Judaism is an intensely individualistic religion and the Jews an intensely individualistic people. While the family was close knit, it was the entire *shtetyl* which was regarded as the inclusive social unit; and in neither case was loyalty to the group considered threatened by physical mobility. The Jews typically have urged their children to leave home if in so doing they faced better opportunities. *Shtetyl* society, from which the vast majority of American Jewry is descended, vigorously stressed the importance of planning and working for the future. A *shtetyl* cultural tradition was that parents save for many years, often at great sacrifice to themselves, in order to improve their son's vocational opportunities or to provide a daughter with a dowry (Zyborowski and Herzog 1952; Rosen 1952; Strodtbeck 1958b).

In some respects, Greek and Jewish cultures were strikingly similar at the turn of the century. The ethos of the town and city permeated the Greek more than most other Mediterranean cultures, although only a small proportion of the population was engaged in trade—with the important exception of the Levantine Greeks, who were largely merchants. The image of the Greek in the Eastern Mediterranean area was that of an individualistic, foresighted, competitive trader. Early observers of the Greek in America were impressed by his activistic, future-oriented behavior. E. A. Ross, a rather unfriendly observer, wrote as early as 1914 that "the saving, commercial Greek climbs. From curb to stand, from stand to store, from little store to big store, and from there to branch stores in other cities—such are the stages in his upward path." (Quoted in Saloutos 1945.)*

Though separated by thousands of miles, French-Canadian and Southern Italian cultures were similar in many respects. Both were primarily peasant cultures, strongly influenced by the Roman Catholic Church. Neither could be described as activistic, individualistic, or future-oriented. In Southern Italian society the closed-class system and grinding poverty fostered a tradition of resignation—a belief that the individual had little control over his life situation and a stress upon the role of fate (*Destino*) in determining success. The living conditions of French-Canadians, although less harsh, were sufficiently severe to sharply limit the individual's sense of mastery over his situation. In neither group was there a strong feeling that the individual could drastically improve his lot; for both groups the future was essentially unpredictable, even capricious. Extended family ties were very strong in both groups: there is the Southern Italian saying, "the family against all others;" the French-Canadian farmer in need of help will travel many miles to hire a kinsman rather than an otherwise convenient neighbor (Miner 1939; see also Williams 1938; Strodtbeck 1958).

* The writer is indebted to J. Gregoropoulos, a native of Athens, for many helpful comments on European and American Greek communities.

Ironically, although Negroes are usually Protestant (however, not ordinarily of the Calvinistic type) and have been exposed to the liberal economic ethic longer than most of the other groups considered here, their culture, it seems, is least likely to accent achievement values. The Negro's history as a slave and depressed farm worker, and the sharp discrepancy between his experiences and the American Creed, would appear to work against the internalization of the achievement values of the dominant white group. Typically, the Negro life-situation does not encourage the belief that one can manipulate his environment or the conviction that one can improve his condition very much by planning and hard work.* Generally, family ties have not been strong among Negroes, although traditionally the mother was an especially important figure and ties between her and her children, particularly sons, may still be very strong (Frazier 1939; Frazier 1957, chapters 13, 24).

Another and more direct way of studying ethnic values is to talk with group members themselves; thus our personal interviews with the mothers. (Their sons in many cases were too young to give meaningful answers.) They were asked whether they agreed or disagreed with the following statements, listed here under the appropriate value orientation categories:

(1) Activistic-Passivistic Orientation.
   Item 1. "All a man should want out of life in the way of a career is a secure, not too difficult job, with enough pay to afford a nice car and eventually a home of his own."
   Item 2. "When a man is born the success he is going to have is already in the cards, so he might just as well accept it and not fight against it."
   Item 3. "The secret of happiness is not expecting too much out of life and being content with what comes your way."

* We recognize that to infer a group's values from its life-situation and then to use these values to explain an aspect of that situation is to reason circularly. However, the temporal sequence between values and mobility has a chicken-egg quality which is difficult to avoid because values and life-situation interact. To some extent, knowledge of ethnic cultures prior to their arrival in the United States helps to establish the priority of values to mobility. In the case of the Negroes, however, relatively little is known about their several cultures before their transportation to this country.

(2) *Individualistic-Collectivistic Orientation.*

Item 4. "Nothing is worth the sacrifice of moving away from one's parents."

Item 5. "The best kind of job to have is one where you are part of an organization all working together even if you don't get individual credit."*

(3) *Present-Future Orientation.*

Item 6. "Planning only makes a person unhappy since your plans hardly ever work out anyway."

Item 7. "Nowadays with world conditions the way they are the wise person lives for today and lets tomorrow take care of itself."

Responses indicating an activistic, future-oriented, individualistic point of view (the answer "disagree" to these items) reflect values, we believe, most likely to facilitate achievement and social mobility. These items were used to form a value index, and a score was derived for each subject by giving a point for each achievement-oriented response. In examining the mothers' scores two assumptions were made: (1) that they tend to transmit their values to their sons, and (2) that the present differences between groups are indicative of at least equal, and perhaps even greater, differences in the past.

The ethnographic and historical materials led us to expect higher value scores for Jews, white Protestants, and Greeks than for Italians, French-Canadians, and Negroes. In large measure, these expectations were confirmed. Table 3 shows that Jews have the highest mean score (5.54), followed closely by Protestants (5.16), Greeks (5.08), and Negroes (surprisingly) (5.03). The Italians' score (4.17) is almost a point lower, and the French-Canadian score (3.68) is the lowest for any group. The scores for Jews, Protestants, and Greeks do not significantly differ when the two-tail test is used (we were not able to predict the direction of the differences), but they are all significantly higher than the scores for Italians and French-Canadians. When Italian and French-Canadian scores are combined to form a "Roman Catholic" score,

---

* Of course, if Whyte (1957) is correct about the growth of the organization man and the importance of the "social ethic," agreement with this statement may indicate an asset rather than a handicap to social mobility.

TABLE 3

MEAN VALUE SCORES BY ETHNICITY AND SOCIAL CLASS

| Ethnicity | Social Class | | | | | |
	I-II	III	IV	V	$\bar{x}$	N
French-Canadian	4.00	4.21	4.60	2.46	3.68	62
Italian	5.86	4.00	3.96	3.40	4.17	74
Greek	6.33	5.52	4.80	3.25	5.08	47
Jew	5.94	5.47	5.41	4.80	5.54	57
Negro	6.00	5.00	4.90	4.67	5.03	65
Protestant	5.86	5.50	4.97	3.54	5.16	122
$\bar{x}$	5.91	5.08	4.78	3.49		

Ethnicity: $F = 11.62$ $P < .001$
Social Class: $F = 33.80$ $P < .001$
Ethnicity X Class: $F = 2.43$ $P < .01$

the latter is significantly lower $(P < .001)$ than the scores for Jews, Protestants, or Greeks.

The prediction for the Negroes proved to be entirely wrong. Their mean score (5.03) is significantly higher $(P < .001)$ than the scores for Italians and French-Canadians. Nor is the Negro score significantly different from those for Protestants and Greeks, although it is significantly lower than the Jewish score $(P < .05)$ when the one-tail test is used. The skeptic may regard the relatively high Negro value score as merely lip-service to the liberal economic ethic, but it may in fact reflect, and to some extent be responsible for, the economic gains of Negroes in recent years.*

Social class also is significantly related to achievement values and accounts for more of the variance than ethnicity: the F ratio for class is 33.80 $(P < .001)$ for ethnicity 11.62 $(P < .001)$. Almost without exception, the mean score for each ethnic group is reduced with each decline in status. *Social class, however, does not wash out the differences between ethnic groups.* A series of "t"

---

* The relatively high value score for Negroes supports our contention that achievement motivation and achievement values are genuinely different components of the achievement syndrome. It will be remembered that the Negroes had the lowest mean motivation score. If achievement motivation and values are conceptually and empirically identical, there should be no difference between the two sets of scores.

tests between cells across each social class reveals that Greek, Jewish, and Protestant scores remain significantly higher than Italian and French-Canadian scores. Negro scores also remain among the highest across each social class. Ethnicity and social class interact and each contributes something to the differences between groups: the individual with high social status who also belongs to an ethnic group which stresses achievement values is far more likely to have a high value score than an individual with low status and membership in a group in which achievement is not emphasized. For example, the Class I-II Greek score is 6.33 as compared with the Class V French-Canadian score of 2.46—the difference between them is significant at the .001 level. On the other hand, the score for Class I-II Italians, an ethnic group in which achievement values are not stressed, is 5.86 as compared with 3.25 for Class V Greeks—the difference between them is significant at the .001 level. Neither variable, then, is sufficient to predict an individual's score; and for some groups social class seems to be the more significant factor, for others ethnicity appears to play the greater role. Thus, for Jews and Negroes the mean scores remain relatively high for each social class; in fact, Class V Jews and Negroes have larger mean scores than many French-Canadians and Italians of higher social status.

ASPIRATION LEVELS

Achievement motivation and values influence social mobility by affecting the individual's need to excel and his willingness to plan and work hard. But they do not determine the areas in which such excellence and effort take place. Achievement motivation and values can be expressed, as they often are, through many kinds of behavior that are not conducive to social mobility in our society, for example, deviant, recreational, or religious behavior. Unless the individual aims for high vocational goals and prepares himself appropriately, his achievement motivation and values will not pull him up the social ladder. Increasingly, lengthy formal education, often including college and post-graduate study, is needed for movement into prestigeful and lucrative jobs. An educational aspiration level which precludes college training may seriously affect the individual's chances for social mobility.

Their cultures, even before the arrival of the ethnic groups in the Northeast, were markedly different in orientation towards education.* The Protestants' stress upon formal education, if only as a means of furthering one's career, is well known. Traditionally, Jews have placed a very high value on educational and intellectual attainment; learning in the *shtetyl* society gave the individual prestige, authority, a chance for a better marriage. Contrariwise, for Southern Italians, school was an upper class institution, not an avenue for social advancement for their children, booklearning was remote from everyday experience, and intellectualism often regarded with distrust. French-Canadians, although not hostile to education and learning, were disinclined to educate their sons beyond the elementary level. Daughters needed more education as preparation for jobs in the event they did not marry, but sons were destined to be farmers or factory workers, in the parents' view, with the exception at times of one son who would be encouraged to become a priest. Greeks—generally no better educated than Italians or French-Canadians—on the whole were much more favorably disposed towards learning, in large part because of their intense nationalistic identification with the cultural glories of ancient Greece.† This identification was strengthened by the relatively hostile reception Greeks met on their arrival in this country, and is in part responsible for the rapid development of private schools supported by the Greek community and devoted to the teaching of Greek culture—an interesting parallel to the Hebrew School among American Jews. Finally, Negroes, who might be expected to share the prevalent American emphasis upon education, face the painfully apparent fact that positions open to educated Negroes are scarce. This fact means that most Negroes, in all likelihood, do not consider high educational aspirations

*For a comparison of ethnic group education and vocational aspirations see Williams (1951, chapter 8); and Woods (1956, chapters 5 and 7).

† Attempts by Mussolini to create a similar bond between his people and ancient Rome, or even the more recent Renaissance, were unsuccessful. French-Canadians for the most part have long refused to be impressed by the "secular" achievement of European anti-clerical French society.

realistic. And the heavy drop-out in high school suggests that the curtailment of educational aspirations begins very early.

To test whether and to what degree these differences between groups persist, the mothers were asked: "How far do you *intend* for your son to go to school?" It was hoped that the term *intend* would structure the question so that the reply would indicate, not merely a mother's pious wish, but also an expression of will to do something about her son's schooling. The data show that 96 percent of the Jewish, 88 percent of the Protestant, 85 percent of the Greek, 83 percent of the Negro (much higher than was anticipated), 64 percent of the Italian, and 56 percent of the French-Canadian mothers said that they expected their sons to go to college. The aspirations of Jews, Protestants, Greeks, and Negroes are not significantly different from one another, but they are significantly higher than the aspirations of Italians and French-Canadians (P < .05).

Social class, once more, is significantly related to educational aspiration. When class is controlled the differences between ethnic groups are diminished—particularly at the Class I–II–III levels—but they are not erased: Jews, Protestants, Greeks, and Negroes tend to have aspirations similar to one another and higher than those of Italians and French-Canadians for each social class. The differences are greatest at the lower class levels: at Class V, 85 percent of the Protestants, 80 percent of the Jews, and 78 percent of the Negroes intend for their sons to go to college as compared with 63 percent of the Greeks, 50 percent of the Italians, and 29 percent of the French-Canadians.

The individual, to be socially mobile, must aspire to the occupations which society esteems and rewards highly. An individual, strongly motivated to excel and willing to plan and work hard, who sets his heart on being the best barber will probably be less vertically mobile than an equally endowed person who aspires to become the best surgeon. Moreover, the individual who aspires to a high status occupation is likely to expend more energy in competitive striving—and in so doing improve his chances for social mobility—than someone whose occupational choice demands relatively little from him.

Since many of the boys in this study were too young to appraise occupations realistically, we sought to obtain a measure of ethnic group vocational aspiration by questioning the mothers about their aspirations for their sons, once again assuming that they would tend to communicate their views of status levels and their expectations for their sons. Ten occupations were chosen which can be ranked by social status; seven of our ten occupations (indicated below with italics) were selected from the N.O.R.C. (National Opinion Research Center 1947) ranking. The occupations, originally presented in alphabetical order, are given here in the order of status: *Lawyer,* Druggist, Jewelry Store Owner, *Machinist,* Bank Teller, *Insurance Agent, Bookkeeper, Mail Carrier, Department Store Salesman,* and *Bus Driver.* * The mothers were asked: "If things worked out so that your son was in the following occupations, would you be satisfied or dissatisfied?" To obtain aspiration scores for each mother, her responses were treated in three ways:

1. The number of times the mother answered "Satisfied" to the ten occupations was summed to give a single score. In effect this meant giving each occupation a weight of one. Since the subject must inevitably select lower status occupations as she increases her number of choices, the higher the summed score, the lower the aspiration level. The basic limitation of this method is that it is impossible to know from the summed score whether the occupations chosen are of low or high status.

2. To correct for this, a second index was derived by assigning weights to the seven occupations taken from the N.O.R.C. study according to their position in the rank order. Thus the highest status position, lawyer, was given a rank weight of 1.0 and the lowest a weight of 6.5 (store salesman and bus driver were tied for last place). Here again, the higher the score, the lower the aspiration level.

3. A third method of weighting the occupations was devised by taking the percentage of the entire sample of mothers who said

* We substituted store salesman for store clerk and bus driver for streetcar motorman. The position of the three occupations which did not appear in the N.O.R.C. survey are ranked according to their similarity to occupations in the survey.

that they would be satisfied with a particular occupation, and using the reciprocal of each percentage as the weight for that occupation. (The reciprocal was first multiplied by one thousand to eliminate decimals.) The mothers ranked the occupations somewhat differently than the N.O.R.C. ranking (assigning a higher status to bookkeeper and insurance agent and lower status to machinist and mail carrier). The assumption here is that the higher the percentage who answered "satisfied," the higher the status of the occupation. A score for each mother was obtained by summing the reciprocal weights for each occupation chosen. With this method, the highest status occupation is lawyer (score of 11.0), the lowest bus driver (48.0). All ten occupations were used in this index. The higher the subject's score, the lower her aspiration level.

Although these indexes differ somewhat, they provide very similar data on ethnic group vocational aspirations. Table 4 shows the same rank ordering of groups for all three indexes, in descending order as follows: Jews, Greeks, Protestants, Italians, French-Canadians, and Negroes. A series of "t" tests of differences between group mean scores revealed differences and similarities much like those found for achievement motivation. Thus the Jews, Greeks, and Protestants show significantly higher mean scores (that is, they tend to be satisfied with fewer occupations and

TABLE 4

MEAN SCORES AND RANK POSITION OF SIX ETHNIC GROUPS
USING THREE INDEXES OF VOCATIONAL ASPIRATION*

| | Index of Vocational Aspiration | | | |
Ethnicity	Number Satisfied	Rank Weight	Reciprocal Weight	N
French-Canadian	6.60 (5)	14.43 (5)	119.90 (5)	62
Italian	5.96 (4)	12.66 (4)	104.55 (4)	74
Greek	4.70 (2)	7.78 (2)	73.51 (2)	47
Jew	3.51 (1)	6.02 (1)	59.48 (1)	57
Negro	6.95 (6)	16.18 (6)	138.74 (6)	65
Protestant	5.28 (3)	10.12 (3)	88.19 (3)'	122

* Rank positions are shown by figures in parentheses.

indicate satisfaction with only the higher status positions) than the Roman Catholic Italians and French-Canadians. (Similar Jewish-Italian differences are reported in Strodtbeck, et al 1957.) The mean score for Jews is significantly higher than the scores for Protestants and Greeks, but there are no significant differences between Greeks and Protestants, or between Italians and French-Canadians. The mean score for Negroes is significantly lower than the scores for all other groups except French-Canadians. In examining the aspirations of Negroes it should be remembered that most of these occupations are considered highly desirable by many Negroes, given their severely limited occupational opportunities, so that their aspiration level may appear low only by "white" standards. There are, however, these problems: are the Negro mothers (83 percent) in earnest in saying that they intend for their sons to go to college? And, if so, how is this to be reconciled with their low vocational aspirations?

Social class, too, is significantly and directly related to vocational aspiration—a familiar finding—*but it is not as significant as ethnicity.* Analysis of variance of data for each of the three indexes reveals that ethnicity accounts for more of the variance than social class. For example, when the number of occupations with which the mother would be satisfied for her son is used as an index of vocational aspiration, the F ratio for ethnicity is 12.41 (P < .001) as compared with a ratio of 9.92 for social class (P < .001). The same pattern holds for data derived from the other two indexes. Although ethnicity and class interact, each contributing to the differences between groups, the effects of class are more apparent at the middle class (Classes I–II–III) than at the working and lower class (Classes IV–V) levels.

As the question was worded in this study, in one sense it is misleading to speak of the "height" of vocational aspirations. For all groups have "high" aspirations in that most mothers are content to have their sons achieve a high status. The basic difference between groups is in the "floor," so to speak, which they place on their aspirations. For example, at least 80 percent of the mothers of each ethnic group said that they would be satisfied to have their sons be lawyers, but only 2 percent of the Greeks and 7 percent of the Jews were content to have their sons become bus drivers, as compared with 26 percent of the French-Canadians and 43 percent of the Negroes. Again, 12 percent of the Jewish, 22 percent of the Protestant, and 29 percent of the Greek mothers said that they would be satisfied to have their sons become department store salesmen, as compared with 48 percent of the Italians, 51 percent of the Negro, and 52 percent of the French-Canadian mothers.

SUMMARY

This paper examines differences in motivation, values, and aspirations of six racial and ethnic groups which may explain in part their dissimilar social mobility rates. Analysis of ethnographic and attitudinal and personality data suggests that these groups differed, and to some extent still differ, in their orientation toward achievement. The data show that the groups place different emphases upon independence and achievement training in the rearing of children. As a consequence, achievement motivation is more characteristic of Greeks, Jews, and white Protestants than of Italians, French-Canadians, and Negroes. The data also indicate that Jews, Greeks, and Protestants are more likely to possess achievement values and higher educational and vocational aspirations than Italians and French-Canadians. The values and educational aspirations of the Negroes are higher than expected, being comparable to those of Jews, Greeks, and white Protestants, and higher than those of the Italians and French-Canadians. Vocational aspirations of Negroes, however, are the lowest of any group in the sample. Social class and ethnicity interact in influencing motivation, values, and aspirations; neither can predict an individual's score. Ethnic differences persist when social class is controlled, but some of the differences between ethnic groups in motivations, values, and aspirations are probably also a function of their class composition.

COMMENTARY on
ALIENATION, RACE, AND EDUCATION

Though the effects of minority group status on self-esteem are uncertain, its effects on alienation are clear. The studies uniformly suggest that, compared to whites, blacks are more likely to be pessimistic, despairing, and cynically distrustful. The evidence for this pattern is the relatively high scores of blacks on several related variables—anomia (Angell 1962; Lefton 1968), estrangement and cynicism (Baughman and Dahlstrom *8*; Harrison and Kass 1967), and alienation, which Middleton examines in the following selection.*

To study a sample of adults who live in a small southern city, Middleton employs a measure of alienation that the author himself developed. He shows that items tapping five different dimensions of alienation all seem to have what he calls an "underlying unity." His major finding is that on each of the five items, blacks are far more likely than whites to give an alienated response.

Despite the agreement of findings of several studies, the work on racial differences in alienation nonetheless illustrates how knowledge in the social sciences is never final but always subject to future refinement and revision. For there are a number of methodological weaknesses in the existing studies. The measure Middleton devised, for example, suffers from a lack of control for agreement response set (Robinson and Shaver 1969, pp. 161–62, 165). In an interview, some respondents tend to agree with attitude items regardless of their content. As all of Middleton's items are worded in one direction, a respondent who agrees with them would score high on alienation. Thus a person could score high on Middleton's items not because he is really alienated but simply because he has a set to voice agreement with statements presented to him. To complicate matters even further, there is some evidence

---

* McCarthy and Yancy (1971, pp. 661–62) question whether blacks are, in fact, more alienated than whites. In my opinion, however, the evidence they present to justify their skepticism is weak and is outweighed by the findings cited here.

that blacks are more prone than whites to agreement response set. Hence racial differences on Middleton's measure of alienation could to some extent be spurious. Despite such methodological problems, the similarity in the findings from several studies suggests that we can be fairly confident that minority group status does engender feelings of alienation.

One component of alienation, as Middleton defines it, is a sense of powerlessness—the feeling that one does not have much control or influence over his environment. Powerlessness, more commonly called "internal versus external control of reinforcements," has itself been the object of much research. Part III of this reader will present several studies suggesting how internal-external control affects the behavior of American blacks (Coleman and others *13*; Gurin and others *14*).

Alienation, Race, and Education

RUSSELL MIDDLETON*

One of the problems empirical studies of alienation must confront is the multiplicity of meanings attached to the concept. Seeman has suggested that there are five major meanings: powerlessness, meaninglessness, normlessness, isolation, and self-estrangement (Seeman 1959). Most studies have dealt with only one of these variants of alienation—or at most two or three, singly or in combination—and there is little evidence regarding the relative frequency of different types of alienation in the population or of their differential association with various causal factors. We shall adopt, with some modifications, Seeman's variants of alienation and examine their incidence in a small southern city.

On the basis of the theoretical formulations of the classic social theorists as well as the fragmentary previous empirical research, we hypothesize that the different types of alienation are highly correlated with one another. Further, we hypothesize that each type of alienation is directly related to those disabling social conditions that limit or block the attainment of culturally valued objectives. We shall test this hypothesis with regard to two of the most important disabling conditions in American society: subordinate racial status and low educational attainment.

* Reprinted from the *American Sociological Review*, vol. 28 (December 1963), pp. 973-77 by permission from the publisher, the American Sociological Association, and by the author.

One possible exception to the general hypotheses is suggested by the vast literature pointing to the alienation of the intellectual from the dominant culture. Awareness of the more subtle ways in which this dominant culture may thwart human potentialities probably requires a relatively high level of education and sophistication. Cultural estrangement may therefore be inversely related to the disabling conditions specified and less highly correlated with the other types of alienation.

METHOD

This study was conducted in a central Florida city of eighteen thousand during the summer of 1962. All residents above the age of twenty were enumerated, and a simple random sample of 256 persons was drawn. Since the number of Negroes in this sample was inadequate for extensive analysis, an additional 50 Negro subjects were randomly drawn. The final sample thus consisted of 107 whites and 99 Negroes. Generalizations about the community as a whole, however, are based on the original sample of 256.

This study constituted a part of a larger cooperative survey of attitudes on a variety of subjects: civil defense, mental illness, political leadership, and the employment of married women. Since exigencies of the larger study permitted us to include only a few items dealing with alienation, a single attitude statement was formulated for each of the variants of alienation. It would have been desirable to construct scales for each type of alienation, but the single items are useful at least for exploratory analysis.*

The types of alienation and the attitude statements associated with each are as follows:

Powerlessness. "There is not much that I can do about most of the important problems that we face today."

* Prior to the study the six items were presented without identification to fourteen graduate students in a seminar in sociological theory who had previously read and discussed the work of Durkheim, Merton, Srole, Nettler, Meier and Bell, Seeman, and Dean on the subjects of anomie and alienation. The students, working independently, showed little hesitation in classifying the items, and they were in unanimous agreement concerning the type of alienation represented by each of the six items.

Meaninglessness. "Things have become so complicated in the world today that I really don't understand just what is going on."

Normlessness. "In order to get ahead in the world today, you are almost forced to do some things which are not right." The concept of normlessness has also been used in several senses (Dean 1961), but here we follow the more restricted usage of Merton (1957) and Seeman (1959) emphasizing the expectation that illegitimate means must be employed to realize culturally prescribed goals.

Cultural estrangement. "I am not much interested in the TV programs, movies, or magazines that most people seem to like." Like many of the questions in Nettler's (1957) scale for alienation,* the present item focuses on the individual's acceptance of popular culture.

Social estrangement. "I often feel lonely." Seeman's point that social isolation cannot readily be separated from differences in associational style—the fact that some men are sociable and some are not—makes clear the desirability of distinguishing social isolation from social estrangement. In his study of the aged, Townsend (1957) makes such a distinction: ". . . to be socially isolated is to have few contacts with family and community; to be lonely is to have an unwelcome *feeling* of lack or loss of companionship. The one is objective, the other subjective and, as we shall see, the two do not coincide." Eric and Mary Josephson (1962) also comment that not all isolates are socially estranged, nor are all nonisolates free from alienation. It is, then, the feeling of loneliness that is crucial to alienation, and the present item is designed to tap this subjective sense of social estrangement.

Estrangement from work "I don't really enjoy most of the work that I do, but I feel that I must do it in order to have other things that I need and want."

In the interviews the six items dealing with alienation were interspersed with a large number of unrelated questions. The

* In addition to questions dealing with political, religious, and familial norms, Nettler asks such questions as the following: "Do you enjoy TV?" "What do you think of the new model American automobiles?" "Do you read *Reader's Digest*?" "Do national spectator sports (football, baseball) interest you?"

respondents were given the following instructions: "Although you may not agree or disagree completely with any of the following statements, please tell me whether you tend more to agree or disagree with each statement." Each agreement was taken as an indication of alienation.

The chi-square test of significance, with the rejection level set at .05, and Yule's coefficient of association (Q) were utilized in the statistical analysis of the data.

FINDINGS

Intercorrelations among the types of alienation are presented in Table 1. With the exception of cultural estrangement, the association between each type of alienation and each other type is moderately strong, with Q's ranging from .46 to .81. As expected, cultural estrangement is not highly correlated with the other variants of alienation; the only statistically significant relation is with normlessness, and even here the Q is a relatively low .31. The type of alienation most highly correlated with the other types is estrangement from work.

If cultural estrangement is excluded, the five remaining items constitute a Guttman scale with a coefficient of reproducibility of .90. Although these five types of alienation may be distinct on a conceptual level, there is apparently an underlying unity. Studies

TABLE 1
INTERCORRELATIONS OF TYPES OF ALIENATION*

	Meaning-lessness	Norm-lessness	Cultural Estrange-ment	Social Estrange-ment	Estrange-ment from work
Powerlessness	.58	.61	.06	.54	.57
Meaninglessness	—	.59	.17	.46	.81
Normlessness	—	—	.31	.48	.67
Cultural estrangement	—	—	—	.08	.20
Social estrangement	—	—	—	—	.71

* The number of cases is 256; the measure of association is Yule's Q. The values of x^2 for all relationships for which Q exceeds .30 are significant at the .05 level.

employing a measure of generalized alienation thus may be feasible, though the nature of the relation of cultural estrangement to the other types of alienation perhaps needs further clarification.

Our present purpose, however, is to determine whether each of the varieties of alienation is associated with conditions of deprivation. The importance of racial status as an alienating condition is immediately apparent from the figures in Table 2. The percentage of Negroes who feel alienated is far higher than the percentage of whites for every type of alienation except cultural estrangement. Approximately two-thirds of the Negro subjects agree with most of the items indicating alienation, whereas a majority of whites disagree with every item. The racial difference is statistically significant in every instance except cultural estrangement.

The difference is largest with respect to estrangement from work. No doubt this reflects the occupational structure of the community, for 72 percent of the employed Negroes are working in semiskilled or unskilled jobs, as compared to only 14 percent of the whites. A marked difference between Negroes and whites also occurs in the case of normlessness. More than half the Negroes but only 16 percent of the whites perceive a conflict between success goals and ethical means. This difference may stem in part from the Negroes' recognition that discrimination leaves few legitimate

TABLE 2

ALIENATION, BY RACE

	Percent Who Feel Alienated		
Type of Alienation	*Negroes**	*Whites*	*Total Community*
Powerlessness	70	40	47
Meaninglessness	71	48	52
Normlessness	55	16	24
Cultural estrangement	35	34	35
Social estrangement	60	27	35
Estrangement from work	66	18	28
Number of cases	(99)	(207)	(256)

* The Negro sample is augmented by an additional 50 cases chosen randomly from the enumeration of Negro adults in the community. Figures for the total community do not include the 50 additional cases.

avenues to success open to them. Observation of the discrepancy between the whites' professed ideals and their actual behavior, particularly in relation to Negroes, may also give Negroes a rather cynical perspective on society.

In Table 3 we may examine the effect of education on aliena-tion within each racial group. Among the Negroes, those who have had twelve or more years of education are in every instance less likely to feel alienated than those with less education, though the differences are statistically significant only for social estrangement and estrangement from work. There is a similar pattern among the whites, with significant differences for powerlessness, meaningless-ness, and estrangement from work.

As one would expect, the inverse relation between education and a sense of meaninglessness is particularly strong, but much more so among the whites than among the Negroes. The per-centage difference between high and low educational groups among the whites is more than twice that for the Negroes. Why is education not a more significant factor in relieving Negroes of the sense that they "really don't understand just what is going on?" We might speculate that the Negroes' greater sense of powerless-ness is responsible. Even educated Negroes may feel little interest

TABLE 3

ALIENATION, BY RACE AND YEARS OF EDUCATION

| | Per Cent Who Feel Alienated | | | |
| | Negroes* | | Whites | |
Type of Alienation	Less Than 12 Years Education	12 or More Years of Education	Less Than 12 Years Education	12 or More Years of Education
Powerlessness	73	60	57	34
Meaninglessness	76	56	80	35
Normlessness	59	40	22	14
Cultural estrangement	39	24	42	31
Social estrangement	67	40	37	24
Estrangement from work	73	44	33	12
Number of cases	(74)	(25)	(60)	(147)

* The Negro sample is augmented by an additional 50 cases chosen randomly from the enumeration of Negro adults in the community.

in attempting to understand things they believe are beyond their control. This interpretation is supported by the fact that education has more effect on powerlessness among whites than it does among Negroes. For each of the other types of alienation, however, the percentage difference between educational groups is greater among the Negroes than among the whites.

Use of the scale for general alienation, which consists of all of the items except cultural estrangement, permits us to gain an overview of the relation between alienation and race and education. If, on the basis of this scale, the sample is divided at the median into groups of high and low alienation, the association between subordinate racial status and alienation is Q=.79. Approximately 6 percent of the Negroes and 28 percent of the whites show no alienation with regard to any of the five types in the scale; 28 percent of the Negroes and only 1 percent of the whites feel alienated in every respect.

The association between education and general alienation is -.67 for the white group and -.56 among the Negroes. Thus, education appears to be of somewhat greater significance among whites than among Negroes. For Negroes in a southern community racial status is far and away the most salient fact; the whites tend to treat Negroes categorically, regardless of education, occupation, or reputation. Yet, education affects most types of alienation, even among the Negroes. On the other hand, there is no significant educational difference among Negroes in the incidence of pessimism. The highly educated Negroes are almost as likely as the poorly educated to agree with the statement, "In spite of what some people say, the lot of the average man is getting worse." Killian and Grigg (1962) report similar findings for Florida Negroes in connection with Srole's anomia scale, of which this item is a part.

CONCLUSION

Among the adults of a small city in central Florida five types of alienation—powerlessness, meaninglessness, normlessness, social

estrangement, and estrangement from work—are highly intercorre-
lated, but a sixth, cultural estrangement, is not closely related to
the others. The hypothesis that social conditions of deprivation
are related to alienation is generally supported. Subordinate racial
status and limited education are strongly associated with all but
one type of alienation. Several other factors, such as occupation of
head of household, family income, sex, marital status, and size of
community of origin, also tend to be related to alienation, but the
coefficients of association are not as high as for race or education.

By far the most striking finding of the study is the pervasiveness
of alienation among the Negro population, a point which is also
dramatically clear in James Baldwin's essay, "Down at the Cross."
In addition to each of the other types of alienation, Baldwin
senses a cultural estrangement among American Negroes so
extreme that "there are some wars . . . that the American Negro
will not support, however many of his people may be coerced. . . ."
(Baldwin 1963). William Worthy, correspondent of the *Baltimore
Afro-American*, has pointed out that the greatest amount of pro-
Castro sentiment in the United States is to be found in Harlem
among lower-class Negroes, and Black Muslim publications have
advocated a policy of "Hands Off Cuba!" This evidence of
estrangement from American culture is not consistent with the
findings of this study, which show that Negroes are no more likely
to be culturally estranged than whites. The discrepancy may be
due to the circumscribed nature of the item used here to determine cultural estrangement, since it deals only with attitudes
toward the popular culture of the mass media. Negroes may feel a
deep estrangement from basic aspects of American culture and yet
turn to the soporific fare of the mass media as a means of escape
from the problems and tensions of life.

COMMENTARY on
WHAT GHETTO MALES ARE LIKE: ANOTHER LOOK

Americans have common notions about which characteristics of behavior and personality are appropriate for males and which for females. Thus males are expected to be aggressive, dominant, independent, and assertive; females to be nurturant, passive, and docile. Such shared expectations constitute the male and female sex roles.

Although there are different theories for the development of sex role characteristics in the child, most students of personality assume that these characteristics are largely learned from the parent of the same sex. It follows from this assumption that in families in which the father is absent or in which he plays a weak, unmasculine role, boys will to some extent fail to acquire appropriate male behavior. In fact, studies have shown that, compared to boys from homes in which the father is present, boys in father-absent homes tend to show less aggression and independence, to behave like girls in their overt behavior and in their fantasies, and to identify more with their mothers. As they grow up, these boys may eventually develop an exaggerated masculinity (e.g., over-toughness) to compensate for the underlying uncertainty they feel about their masculinity (Dager 1964, pp. 759–60; Pettigrew 1964, pp. 18–19).

Because blacks are more likely than whites to be raised in matriarchal homes, many authors maintain that black males are more prone than white males to distorted sex role development (e.g., Pettigrew 1964, pp. 17–24). As with other topics concerning black personality, however, the findings on this topic are problematic. For one thing, the evidence is not consistent. Some findings do, indeed, support the hypothesis that black males are less masculine in their personal makeup than white males (Biller 1968; Lott and Lott 1963; and Hokanson and Calden 1960). But other evidence fails to support this hypothesis (Baughman and Dahlstrom *8*; Biller 1968; Hetherington 1966).*

In addition, the design of two of the most recent studies (Biller 1968; Hetherington 1966) makes it difficult to draw inferences about racial differences in masculinity. The samples for these studies were selected in such a way that the percentage of subjects whose father was absent was the same, or similar, for black and white children. Insofar as black children in the general population are more likely than white children to come from homes without fathers, the samples in these studies were not representative of the population. Hence if blacks are, in fact, more effeminate and this effeminacy is due to the greater incidence of father absence, these studies must understate the extent of racial differences in effeminacy.†

In the selection reprinted here, Hannerz starts with the assumption that, even though they have been reared in matriarchal families, black ghetto males are not really handicapped in acquiring masculine behavior. In defense of his position, he points out that there are ways other than identifying with, or imitating, a father by which a growing boy can learn what it is to be masculine. The boy, for example, can model his behavior on that of other boys and of older males he observes in the streets. Furthermore, Hannerz argues, there need not be a single model of the male sex role. If the middle-class, white, mainstream culture embodies one idea of masculinity, the culture of the ghetto embodies

---

* Biller's paper is listed with both sets of studies because his data are mixed. On the one hand, the two racial groups in this investigation differed on the IT test, a projective measure of sex-role orientation. On the other hand, they did not differ in sex-role preferences or in ratings of masculine behavior.

† Despite this defect in Biller's study, he found that blacks scored comparatively low on masculinity on a projective measure of sex-role orientation. He also found that boys from families without fathers score comparatively low on this measure. Taken together, these two findings suggest that if the black and white samples in his study had been more representative of their respective populations with respect to the incidence of father absence, Biller would have probably found an even more marked difference between the two races.

another.* The models upheld by both cultures, Hannerz maintains, coexist among ghetto residents.

Some authorities would disagree with the position taken by Hannerz. One, for example, claims that studies show that "by the age of three or four boys express clear-cut preferences for masculine activities, toys, and objects" (Mussen 1969, p. 710). Hence essential elements in sex-role learning occur before boys become old enough to be extensively involved in peer groups or to model their behavior on that of men in the streets. Hetherington (1966) found that boys who had lost their fathers at age four or earlier were comparatively feminine both in overt behavior and on a projective measure of sex-role preferences. At the time of the study these boys were nine to twelve years of age, so that they had had opportunity to observe males outside the home. Despite this opportunity, the effects of father absence on their personalities persisted. In addition, Mussen (1969) and Biller (1968) suggest that although the boy can learn certain superficial aspects of masculinity without a father present, other aspects require identification with the father. This is true of an erotic preference for the opposite sex and of general, pervasive interests and attitudes characteristic of the male sex role. If these contentions are correct, the ghetto youngster's chance to observe males other than his father does not compensate for the absence of the father.

Thus the development of masculinity in ghetto males is very much a matter of debate among scholars. Which of the conflicting positions is closer to the truth, is difficult to say at this time.

* The argument that the black ghetto culture has a distinctive model of masculinity is also made by Keil (1966, pp. 20–26).

What Ghetto Males Are Like: Another Look

ULF HANNERZ*

Ever since the beginnings of the study of black people in the Americas investigators have commented on the ways in which black men and women—in particular some men and women—differ in their behavior from their white counterparts.† Most of these comments have focused on the nature of the black family, and especially on female dominance. Herskovits saw the close bond between mother and children, and the peripheral status of the father, as an African vestige, typical of polygynous marriage where every woman with her offspring formed a separate unit. Yet he was aware that this pattern was changed and adapted to New World slavery (Herskovits 1941, p. 181). Frazier is generally regarded as the pioneer among those who have ascribed to American slavery itself the strongest influence in undermining the stability of marital unions (Frazier 1932, 1934, 1939, 1949). But Frazier also saw a strengthening of the marriage institution among rural freedmen in southern states, and another weakening following migration and urbanization. He makes relatively clear that economic insecurity was one characteristic of city life, but this

---

† The term "black" will generally be used here for ethnic identification, in line with the current trend of preference among at least younger and more politically aware Negroes in the U.S.

point is frequently dimmed by his imagery of other urban evils: anonymity, disorganization, lack of social supports and controls. Undoubtedly, he was influenced by his contemporaries in the Chicago school of sociology, who saw the city primarily in such terms. Under those conditions, the lower-class black family allegedly reverted, with matrifocality, to a primitive evolutionary stage (Frazier 1934, p. 298). Obviously, Frazier found practically only weaknesses in the matrifocal family arrangement. His studies contain an abundance of comments on the evils of "broken" families but are quite deficient in social and cultural analysis of a more intensive sort.*

The emphasis on the socio-economic matrix of family life which Frazier's work foreshadowed has emerged as the third major perspective in black American family studies, and this point of view is now probably dominant. It relates the absence or marginality of the husband-father in many black households to the low occupational status, poor income, job insecurity, and unemployment of many black males. Of little importance as a provider and in the articulation of the household with the wider structure of the society, the male is deprived of some of the most important features of the male role as defined in the dominant high-status cultures of New World societies. Consequently, his position in the household is undermined, and the female becomes dominant.

The famous "Moynihan report," although in some ways a curiously ambiguous document, points to the correlation between household form and economic-occupational factors (United States Dept. of Labor 1965, pp. 19–25). In some of the comments on the "Moynihan report," and in other studies which were more or less part of the ensuing debate about the black family, the same point is made more clearly (Gans 1967; Herzog 1967; H. Lewis 1967).

Most of what has been said about the sex roles of New World black people can find its place in one of these three perspectives. However, this means that the studies only marginally involve the discussion of sex roles *per se,* as they are first of all studies of the

---

* For a recent criticism of pejorative elements in the Frazier tradition of family studies see Valentine (1968).

family or household as an institution. This may still provide a reasonably clear view of the female role, since it is clearly enacted to a great extent within the matrifocal household. It is the man's life, then, which tends to occur somehow "out there, somewhere," away from studies of black domestic life, because his major characteristic as far as the household is concerned is absence or marginality.

Under such conditions, what is the male role, and how is it replicated in generation after generation? To what are those boys socialized who again and again grow up to exist on the periphery of households, and how is their role handled in adult life? What we need in order to answer such questions is micro-sociological data concerning cultural management and transmission pertaining to the male role. Such data are seldom offered. Yet it is possible to piece together some kind of a picture of the lower-class black male. In the United States, his popular image was summed up by Norman Mailer in his essay on *The White Negro*: The black male lives in the present, subsists for the kicks of Saturday night, gives up the pleasures of the mind for the pleasures of the body, and gives voice to the character and quality of his existence in his music (Mailer n.d.).

Certainly there is some poetic exaggeration in Mailer's picture, and a great deal of stereotyping in the general public's imagery concerning the people of the black ghetto. But hardly anyone acquainted with life in the ghetto can fail to see that there is also much of reality involved. Rainwater's sketch of the "expressive life style" shows a trained social scientist's picture which is remarkably similar to Mailer's.* Undoubtedly there is a sizeable segment of the male population which is strongly concerned with sex, drinking, sharp clothes, and "trouble," and among these men we find many of those only marginally involved with married life. Of course, a great many men in the ghetto live largely according to the mainstream styles of life, and in stable marriages; there is much heterogeneity in ghetto life styles. But to a considerable

---

* Rainwater's essay offers a social-psychological funtional interpretation of the "expressive life style" which largely complements the perspective of cultural dynamics offered here (1966b, pp. 113ff).

extent, it is to the former that we should turn our attention to see what pattern of maleness goes with matrifocality.

This essay is an attempt to outline the social processes within the ghetto communities of the northern United States whereby the identity of streetcorner males is established and maintained.* Although based on fieldwork in but one North American urban community, the analysis is probably applicable to some extent also to other black communities in the New World where males grow up and exist in similar socio-economic conditions, a similar matrix of interpersonal relationships and, as the quotations above seem to tell us, into a similar complex of cultural values and definitions. As a role analysis, it involves an attempt to consider all significant relationships of the male in which socially induced sex-specific behavior occurs or is commented upon within the black community. In employing such a framework, it tends to differ from the institutional family analysis which has been strong in the social anthropology of New World black life, and stands closer to the kind of network conceptualization which has only recently become generally recognized as an analytical tool in social anthropology (Barnes 1954; Bott 1957; Epstein 1961; Mitchell 1966; Mayer 1966).†

To set the stage and state the issues involved in such an analysis, we may look at the views expressed by two predecessors in the study of the ghetto male role. One of the two is Charles Keil, whose *Urban Blues* (1966) is a study of the bluesman as a "culture hero." According to Keil, the urban blues singer, with his emphasis on sexuality, "trouble," and flashy clothes, gives expression to a cultural model of maleness which is highly valued by the ghetto dwellers and relatively independent of the mainstream cultural tradition. Keil (1966, p. 28) criticizes a number of writings which

---

* The apt term "streetcorner men" is used by Liebow (1967), who may have derived it from Whyte (1954).

† The network, as the term is used here, is an "ego-centric" social structure—that is, one takes as a point of departure one person and traces his relationships. The definitions in the works quoted are somewhat variable, but this seems to be the general use of the concept.

tend to see this conception of the male role as rooted in the individual's anxiety about his maleness, finding them unacceptably ethnocentric:

> Any sound analysis of Negro masculinity should first deal with the statements and responses of Negro women, the conscious motives of the men themselves, and the Negro cultural tradition. Applied in this setting, psychological theory may then be able to provide important new insights in place of basic and unfortunate distortions.

Keil, then, comes out clearly for a cultural interpretation of the male role we are interested in here. But Elliot Liebow, in *Tally's Corner* (1967, p. 223), a study resulting from the author's participation in a research project which definitely considered ghetto life more in terms of social problems than as a culture, reaches conclusions which, in some of their most succinct formulations, quite clearly contradict Keil's:

> Similarities between the lower-class Negro father and son . . . do not result from "cultural transmission" but from the fact that the son goes out and independently experiences the same failures, in the same areas, and for much the same reasons as his father.

Thus father and son are "independently produced look-alikes." With this goes the view that the emphasis on sexual ability, drinking, and the like, is a set of compensatory self-deceptions which can only veil unsuccessfully the streetcorner male's awareness of his failure.

Keil and Liebow, as reviewed here, may be taken as representatives of the differing opinions on why black people in the ghettos, and in particular the males, behave differently from other Americans. One involves a cultural determinism internal to the ghetto, the other an economic determinism involving the links between the ghetto and the wider society.* It is easy to see how

---

* Admittedly, to some extent both Keil and Liebow introduce qualifications. Keil points to the influence of long-lasting poverty and oppression in shaping black culture, but he implies that at the present point of cultural development the ghetto dweller's culture is quite independent of mainstream culture. Liebow (1967, p. 223) writes: "No doubt, each generation does provide role models for each succeeding one." Immediately thereafter, however, he dismisses the point as unimportant.

the two views relate to the perspectives on determinants of domestic structure. As we have said, it seems that the socio-economic determinism (as represented by Liebow) is at present the majority point of view among social scientists engaged in this field of study. Admittedly, the present opportunity structure places serious obstacles in the way of many ghetto dwellers, making a mainstream life style difficult to accomplish. Thus, if research is to influence public policy, it is particularly important to point to the wider structural influences which can be changed in order to give equal opportunity to ghetto dwellers. Yet some of the studies emphasizing such macro-structural determinants involve somewhat crude conceptualizations which are hardly warranted by data and which in the light of anthropological theory quickly appear oversimplified.

First of all, let us dispose of some of the opposition between the two points of view cited above. There is not necessarily any direct conflict between ecological-economic and cultural explanations, and the tendency to create such a conflict in much of the current writings on poverty involves a false dichotomy. Anthropologists assume that culture is transferred from generation to generation, and also that it is influenced by the community's relationship to its environment. (The fact that the environment in this case is social rather than natural does not make a great difference—besides, contemporary ecological anthropology tends to take the social environment into consideration as well.) Economic determinism and cultural determinism can thus go hand in hand in a stable environment. Since the ecological niche of ghetto dwellers has long remained relatively unchanged, there seems to be no reason why their adaptation should not have become in some ways cultural. It is possible, of course, that the first stage in the evolution of the ghetto-specific life style consisted of a multiplicity of identical but largely independent adaptations from the existing cultural background—mainstream or otherwise—to the given opportunity structure, as Liebow suggests, thus creating a statistical norm of behavior which is not truly a cultural norm. But the second stage of adaptation—by the following generations—involves the perception of the first-stage adaptation as a normal condition, a state of affairs which from then on can be expected. What was at first independent adaptation becomes transformed into a ghetto heritage of assumptions about the nature of man and society.

Yet Liebow implies that father and son are independently produced as streetcorner men and that transmission of a ghetto-specific culture has a negligible influence. To those adhering to such a standpoint, strong evidence in its favor is seen in the fact that ghetto dwellers—both men and women—often express mainstream sentiments about sex roles. Most ghetto dwellers would certainly agree, at times at least, that education is a good thing, that gambling and drinking are bad, if not sinful, and that a man and a woman should be true to each other. Finding such opinions, and considering Keil's statement quoted above about deriving the ghetto cultural interpretation from statements and responses of the black people themselves, one may be led to doubt that there is much of a specific ghetto culture. Noting the behavior which contradicts the stated values, then, one arrives at two questions: "Is there any reason to believe that ghetto-specific behavior is cultural?" And, if that should be the case, "What is the nature of the co-existence between mainstream culture and ghetto-specific culture in the black ghetto?"

To answer the first question, one might look again at the communications about behavior related to the male identity in the ghetto. This is where we should trace all significant relationships in the typical streetcorner male network. One set of relationships in which such communications occur frequently is the family; another is the male peer group.

Much has been made of the notion that young boys in the ghetto, growing up in matrifocal households, are somehow deficient in masculinity, or uncertain about masculinity, because their fathers are absent or peripheral in household affairs.* It is said that they lack the role models necessary for learning male behavior, the kind of information about the nature of masculinity which a father would transmit unintentionally merely by going

---

* Matrifocality is defined here in behavioral rather than compositional terms—if the household affairs are female-dominated, it is a matrifocal household even if a marginal husband-father resides in it. Viewed this way, of course, matrifocality becomes a matter of degree.

about his life at home is missing. The boys therefore supposedly experience a great deal of sex role anxiety, as a result of this cultural vacuum. (Writings in this vein include Miller, 1958; Rohrer and Edmonson 1960; Derbyshire, et al. 1963; Pettigrew 1964). It is possible that such a view contains more than a grain of truth in the case of some quite isolated female-headed households. Evidence from studies of such households in other social contexts point in this direction (Burton and Whiting 1961; Pettigrew 1964). In the ghetto situation, however, there may be less to this than meets the eye.* First of all, a female-headed household without an adult male in residence but where young children are growing up—and where it is thus likely that the mother is still rather young—is seldom one where adult males are forever absent. More or less steady boyfriends (sometimes including the separated father, on visits which may or may not result in a marital reunion) pass in and out. Even if these men do not assume a central household role, the boys can obviously use them as source material for identifying male behavior. To be sure, this male role model is not a mainstream role model, but it still shows what males are like.

Furthermore, not only males can teach males about masculinity. Although role-modeling is probably essential, other social processes can contribute to identity formation. Mothers, grandmothers, aunts, and sisters who have observed men at close range have adopted expectations about the typical behavior of men which they express and which influence the boys in the household. The boys will come to share in the imagery of the women

---

* Another aspect of the impact of matrifocality on children in a black community was discussed from an anthropological vantage point by Powdermaker (1939, p. 197), where she also pointed to the difficulties with cross-cultural psychological inferences: "There is little if any indication that the fatherless household among these Negroes tends to result in the kind of psychological complications which clinical workers have come to associate with middle-class white households where there is no father. The economic situation is one guard against this. The Negro mother usually works out during the day, or, if she is home, she is extremely busy doing her own work or the washing she takes in from outside. She lacks time, opportunity and energy to lavish on her children the over-protection which leads to those emotional difficulties characteristic of certain fatherless white families. Equally important is the circumstance that most mothers, even in households which lack a man, do not want for sexual outlet, and therefore are not impelled to seek from their children some substitute for the satisfaction normally derived from a mate."

concerning the men as they are exposed to women's conversations, and often they will find that men who are not regarded as good household partners (that is, in the mainstream male role) are still held to be attractive social companions. Thus the view is easily imparted that the hard men, good talkers, clothes-horses and all, are not altogether unsuccessful as males. The women also act more directly toward the boys in these terms—they have expectations of what men will do, and whether they wish the boys to follow in these steps or not, they instruct them in the model. Boys are advised not to "mess with" girls, which is at the same time emphasized as the natural thing which they will otherwise go out and do—and when the boys start their early adventures with the other sex, the older women may scold them but at the same time point out, not without satisfaction, that "boys will be boys." This kind of maternal (or at least adult female) instruction of young males, also noted by Abrahams (1964, p. 28) and Keil (1966, p. 23), is obviously a kind of altercasting (Weinstein and Deutsch-berger 1963), or more exactly, socialization to an alter role—that is, women cast boys in the role complementary to their own according to their experience of man-woman relationships. One single mother of three boys and two girls put it this way:

> You know, you just got to act a little tougher with boys than with girls, 'cause they just ain't the same. Girls do what you tell them to do and don't get into no trouble, but you just can't be sure about the boys. I mean, you think they're OK and next thing you find out they're playing hookey and drinking wine and maybe stealing things from cars and what not. There's just something bad about boys here, you know. But what can you say when many of them are just like their daddies? That's the man in them coming out. You can't really fight it, you know that's the way it is. They know, too. But you just got to be tougher.*

This is in some ways an antagonistic socialization, but it is built upon an expectation that it would be unnatural for men not to

---

* Portions which are quotations of ghetto dwellers derive from notes made as soon as possible after the statements were made. They are probably quite accurate in terms of content and vocabulary but should not be taken to give any indication of the phonology and the syntax of the actual speech.

turn out to be in some ways bad—that is fighters, drinkers, lady killers, and so forth. There is one thing which is worse than a no-good man—the sissy, who is his opposite. A boy who seems weak is often reprimanded and ridiculed not only by his peers but also by adults, including his mother and older sisters. The combination of role-modeling by peripheral fathers or temporary boy-friends with altercasting by adult women certainly provides for a measure of male role socialization within the family.

However, when I said that the view of the lack of models in the family was too narrow, I did not refer to the lack of insight into social processes in many matrifocal ghetto families so much as to the emphasis on the family as *the* information storage unit of a community's culture.* I believe it is an ethnocentrism on the part of middle-class commentators to take it for granted that if information about sex roles is not transmitted from father to son within the family, it is not transmitted from generation to generation at all. There exists in American sociology, as well as in the popular mind, what Birdwhistell (1966) has termed a "sentimental model" of family life, according to which the family is an inward-turning isolate, meeting most of the needs of its members, and certainly the needs for sociability. The "sentimental model" is hardly ever realistic even as far as mainstream American families are concerned, and it has even less relevance for black ghetto life. Ghetto children live and learn out on the streets just about as much as within the confines of the home. Even if mothers, aunts, and sisters would not have streetcorner men as partners, there is an ample supply of them on the front staircase or down at the corner. Many of them have such a regular attendance record as to become quite familiar to children and are frequently very friendly with them. Thus again, there is no lack of adult men showing what adult men are like. It seems rather unlikely that one can deny all the role-modeling effect of these men on their young neighbors. Some of these men may be missing in the U.S. census records, but they are not missing in the ghetto community.

Much of the information gained about sex roles outside the

* The notion of social groupings as information storage units of culture has been intro-duced and explored by Roberts (1964).

family comes not from adult to child, however, but from persons in the same age bracket or only slightly higher. The idea of culture stored in lower age grades must be taken seriously. Many ghetto children start participating in the peer groups of the neighborhood at an early age, often under the watchful eye of an elder sibling. In this way they are initiated into the culture of the peer group by interacting with children—predominantly of the same sex—who are only a little older than they are. And in the peer group culture of the boys, expressions of the male sex role are a highly salient feature. Some observers have felt that this is a consequence of the alleged sex role anxiety discussed briefly above. This may be true, of course, and it may have had an important part in the development of male peer group life as a dominant element of ghetto social structure. In the present situation, however, there is not necessarily such a simple psycho-social relationship. Most ghetto boys can hardly avoid getting into peer groups, and once they are in them they are efficiently socialized into a high degree of concern with their sex role. Much of the joking, the verbal contests, and more or less obscene singing among small ghetto boys— obligatory forms of interaction among them—serve to alienate them from dependence on mother figures and train them to the exploitative, somewhat antagonistic attitude toward women which is typical of streetcorner men. This is not to say the cultural situation is always very neat and clear-cut, and this is particularly obvious in the case of the kind of insult contest called "playing the dozens," "sounding," or in Washington, D.C., "joning," a form of ritualized interaction which is particularly common among boys in the early teens (Kochman 1970; Dollard 1939; Berdie 1947; and Abrahams 1962). When one boy says something unfavorable about another's mother, the other boy is expected either to answer in kind or fight, in a kind of defense of his honor (on which apparently that of his mother reflects). But the lasting impression is that there is something wrong about mothers—they are not as good as they ought to be ("Anybody can get pussy from your mother"), they take over male items of behavior and by implication too much of the male role ("Your mother smokes a pipe"). If standing up for one's family is the manifest expected consequence of "the dozens," then, it can apparently hardly be avoided that a latent function is a strengthening of the belief that ghetto women are not what they ought to be.* The other point of significance is that the criteria of judgment about what a good woman should be like are apparently mainstream-like. She should not be promiscuous, and she should stick to the mainstream-like female role and not be too dominant. The boys, then, are learning and strengthening a cultural ambivalence involving contradictions between ideal and reality in female behavior. We will return to a discussion of such cultural ambivalence later. But the point remains that even this game involves continuous learning and strengthening of a cultural definition of what women are like which is in some ways complementary to the definition of what men are like. And much of the songs, the talk, and the action—fighting, sneaking away with girls into a park or an alley, or drinking out of half-empty wine bottles stolen from or given away by adult men—are quite clearly preparations for the streetcorner male role. If boys and men show anxiety about their masculinity, one may suspect that this is induced as much by existing cultural standards as by the alleged non-existence of models.†

This socialization within the male peer group is a continuing process; the talk that goes on, continuously or intermittently, in the sociable sessions of adult men at the street corner or on the front steps may deal occasionally with a football game or a human-interest story from the afternoon newspaper, but more often there are tales from personal experience about drinking

---

*The distinction between manifest and latent functions is, of course, that suggested by Merton (1957, pp. 19ff).

† This means that even if peer groups and their culture meet a need for some anxious males, as is generally suggested, they are a part of the ghetto scene which demands adjustment to its standards also by males without such prior anxiety, as a price of a membership which may be difficult to avoid. Whether fathers are present or not, the peer group sets its own model of masculinity for members. Some writers, such as Rohrer and Edmonson (1960), seem to be on the verge of recognizing the peer group as a reality *sui generis* in the socialization of boys, but they are still reluctant to admit that sexual identity anxiety is not necessarily the first-order determinant. In their picture, peer group life seems forever invented anew as an answer to this psychological need. Yet the rituals of this life show that there is a lively cultural tradition.

adventures (often involving the police), about women won and lost, about feminine fickleness and the masculine guile which sometimes triumphs over it, about clothing or there may simply be comments on the women passing down the street: "Hi ugly . . . don't try to swing what you ain't got."

This sociability within the male peer group, then, like much other sociability seems to be a culture-building process (Watson 1958). Shared definitions of reality are created out of the selected experiences of the participants. Women are nagging and hypocritical; you can't expect a union with one of them to last forever. Men are dogs; they have to run after many women. There is something between men and liquor; liquor makes hair grow on your chest. The regularity with which the same topics appear in peer group sociable conversation indicates that they have been established as the expected and appropriate subjects in this situation, to the exclusion of other topics.

> Mack asked me did I screw his daughter, so I asked, "I don't know, what's her name?" And then when I heard that gal was his daughter all right, I says, "Well, Mack, I didn't really have to take it, 'cause it was given to me." I thought Mack sounded like his daughter was some goddam white gal. But Mack says, "Well, I just wanted to hear it from you." Of course, I didn't know that was Mack's gal, 'cause she was married and had a kid, and so she had a different name. But then you know the day after when I was out there a car drove by, and somebody called my name from it, you know, "hi darling," and that was her right there. So the fellow I was with says, "Watch out, Buddy will shoot your ass off." Buddy, that's her husband. So I says, "Yeah, but he got to find me first!"
>
> Let me tell you fellows, I've been arrested for drunkenness more than two hundred times over the last few years, and I've used every name in the book. I remember once I told them I was Jasper Gonzales, and then I forgot what I had told them, you know. So I was sitting there waiting, and they came in and called Jasper Gonzales, and nobody answered. I had forgotten that's what I said, and to tell you the truth, I didn't know how to spell it. So anyway, nobody answered, and there they were calling "Jasper Gonzales! Jasper Gonzales!" So I thought that must be me, so I answered. But they had been calling a lot of times before that. So the judge said, "Mr. Gonzales, you are of Spanish

descent?" And I said, "Yes, your honor, I came to this country thirty-four years ago." And of course I was only thirty-five, but you see I had this beard then, and I looked pretty bad, dirty and everything, you know, so I looked like sixty. And so he said, "We don't have a record on you. This is the first time you have been arrested?" So I said, "Yes, your honor, nothing like this happened to me before. But my wife was sick, and then I lost my job you know, and I felt kind of bad. But it's the first time I ever got drunk." So he said, "Well, Mr. Gonzales, I'll let you go, 'cause you are not like the rest of them here. But let this be a warning to you." So I said, "Yes, your honor." And then I went out, and so I said to myself, "I'll have to celebrate this." So I went across the street from the court, and you know there are four liquor stores there, and I got a pint of wine and next thing I was drunk as a pig.

Were you here that time a couple of weeks ago when these three chicks from North Carolina were up here visiting Miss Gladys? They were really gorgeous, about 30–35. So Charlie says why don't we stop by the house and he and Jimmy and Deekay can go out and buy them a drink. So they say they have to go and see this cousin first, but then they'll be back. But then Brenda [Charlie's wife] comes back before they do, and so these girls walk back and forth in front of the house, and Charlie can't do a thing about it, except hope they won't knock on his door. And then Jimmy and Deekay come and pick them up, and Fats is also there, and the three of them go off with these chicks, and there is Charlie looking through his window, and there is Brenda looking at them too, and asking Charlie does he know who the chicks are.

Peer groups thus give some stability and social sanction to the meanings which streetcorner men attach to their experiences—meanings which may themselves have been learned in the same or preceding peer groups. They, probably more than families, are information storage units for the ghetto-specific male role. At the same time, they are self-perpetuating because they provide the most satisfactory contexts for legitimizing the realities involved. In other words, they suggest a program for maleness, but they also offer a haven of understanding for those who follow that program and are criticized for it or feel doubts about it—and of course, all streetcorner males are more or less constantly exposed to the definitions and values of the mainstream cultural apparatus, so some cultural ambivalence can hardly be avoided. So if a man is a dog for running after women—as he is often said to be, among ghetto dwellers as among Otterbein's Andros Islanders, as quoted above—he wants to talk about it with other dogs who appreciate that this is a fact of life. If it is natural for men to drink, let it happen among other people who understand the nature of masculinity. Thus the group maintains constructions of reality, and life according to this reality maintains the group.*

It is hard to avoid the conclusion, then, that there is a cultural element involved in the sex role of streetcorner males, because expectations about it are manifestly shared and transmitted rather than individually evolved. (If the latter had been the case, of course, it would have been less accurate to speak of these as roles, since roles are by definition cultural.) This turns us to the second question stated above, about the co-existence of mainstream and ghetto-specific cultures. Streetcorner men certainly are aware of the ideal of mainstream male role performance—providing well for one's family, remaining faithful to one's spouse, staying out of trouble, and so on—and now and then everyone of them states it as his own ideal. What we find here, then, may be seen as a bi-cultural situation. Mainstream culture and ghetto-specific culture provide different models for living, models familiar to everyone in the ghetto. Actual behavior may lean more toward one model or more toward the other, or it may be some kind of mixture, at one point or over time. The ghetto-specific culture, including the streetcorner male role, is adapted to the situation and the experience of the ghetto dweller; it tends to involve relatively little idealization but offers shared expectations concerning self, others, and the environment. The mainstream culture, from the ghetto dweller's point of view, often involves idealization, but there is less real expectation that life will actually follow the paths suggested by it. This is not to say that the ghetto-specific culture offers no values at all of its own, or that nothing of mainstream culture ever appears realistic in the ghetto; but in those areas of

---

*A relevant statement on conversation as an instrument for the maintenance of social reality is that by Berger and Luckmann (1966, pp. 140ff).

life where the two cultures exist side by side as alternative guides
to action (for naturally, the ghetto-specific culture, as distinct
from mainstream culture, is not a "complete" culture covering all
areas of life),* the ghetto-specific culture is often taken to forecast
what one can actually expect from life, while the mainstream
norms are held up as perhaps ultimately more valid but less attain-
able under the given situational constraints. "Sure it would be
good to have a good job and a good home and your kids in college
and all that, but you got to be yourself and do what you know."
Of course, this often makes the ghetto-specific cultural expectations into self-fulfilling prophecies, as ghetto dwellers try to attain
what they believe they can attain. (To be sure, self-fulfilling
prophecies and realistic assessments may well coincide.)

On the whole, one may say that both mainstream culture and
ghetto-specific culture are transmitted within many ghetto families. We have noted how socialization into the ghetto-specific male
role within the household is largely an informal process, in which
young boys may pick up bits and pieces of information about
masculinity from the women in the house as well as from males
who may make their entrances and exits in it. On the other hand,
when adult women—usually mothers or grandmothers—really "tell
the boys how to behave," they often try to instill in them mainstream, not to say puritan norms—drinking is bad, sex is dirty, and
so forth. The male peer groups, as we have seen, are the strong-
holds of streetcorner maleness, although there are times when men
cuss each other out for being "no good." Finally, of course, mainstream culture is transmitted in contacts with the outside world,
such as in school or through the mass media. It should be added,
though, that the latter may be used selectively to strengthen some
elements of the streetcorner male role; ghetto men are drawn to

* One may, of course, prefer to speak of the ghetto-specific sub-culture. The amount of
analytical sharpening which the sub-culture concept has brought to sociology and
anthropology has not been impressive, however, so using it consistently here may not
have balanced the clumsiness of expression which it would have added. It should be
clear, however, that ghetto-specific culture consists only of a relatively small number of
cultural items and complexes compared to the amount of general American culture
which ghetto dwellers and others share.

Westerns, war movies, and crime stories both in the movie house and on their TV sets.

As mentioned above, even if the nature of men's allegiance to the two cultures makes it reasonably possible to adhere, after a fashion, to both at the same time, as in the last statement quoted, the bi-cultural situation of streetcorner males involves some ambivalence. The rejection of mainstream culture as a guide to action rather than only a lofty ideal is less than complete. Of course, acting according to one or the other of the two cultures to a great extent involves bowing to the demands of the social context, so that situational selectivity from the point of view of the actor plays a part in guiding his behavior. A man whose concerns in the peer group milieu are drinking and philandering will try to be "good" in the company of his mother or his wife and children, even if a complete switch is hard to bring about. There also are peer groups, of course, which are more mainstream-oriented than others, although even the members of these groups are affected by streetcorner definitions of maleness. To some extent, then, the varying allegiance of different peer groups to the two cultures is largely a difference of degree, as the following statement by a young man implies.

> Those fellows down at the corner there just keep drinking and drinking. You know, I think it's pretty natural for a man to drink, but they don't try to do nothing about it, they just drink every hour of the day, every day of the week. My crowd, we drink during the weekend, but we can be on our jobs again when Monday comes.

Contextual culture change on the part of a man can then also be brought about by a change of peers—and there are men who move from one group to another with concomitant changes of behavior.

However, although situational selectivity brings some order into the picture of this bi-cultural situation, it is still one of less than perfect stability. The drift between contexts is itself not something to which men are committed by demands somehow inherent in the social structure. Ghetto men may spend more time with the family, or more time with the peer group, and the extent to which they choose one or the other, and make a concomitant cultural selection, still appears to depend considerably on personal attachment to roles, and to changes in it.* The social alignments of a few men may illustrate this. One man, Norman Hawkins, a construction laborer, spends practically all his leisure time at home with his family, only occasionally joining in the streetcorner conversations and behavior of the peer group to which his neighbor, Harry Jones, belongs. Harry Jones, also a construction worker, is also married and has a family but stays on the periphery of household life, although he lives with his wife and children. Some of the other men in the group are unmarried or separated and so seldom play the "family man" role which Harry Jones takes on now and then. Harry's younger brother, Carl, also with a family, used to participate intensively in peer group life until his drinking led to a serious ailment, and after he recuperated from this he started spending much less time with his male friends and more with his family. Bee Jay, a middle-aged bachelor who was raised by his grandmother, had a job at the post office and had little to do with street life until she died. Since then, he has become intensively involved with a tough, hard-drinking group and now suffers from chronic health problems connected with his alcoholism. Thus we can see how the life careers of some ghetto men take them through many and partly unpredictable shifts and drifts between mainstream and ghetto-specific cultures, while others remain quite stable in one allegiance or other.

The sociocultural situation in the black ghetto is clearly complicated. The community shows a great heterogeneity of life styles; individuals become committed to some degree to different ways of being by the impersonally enforced structural arrangements to which they are subjected, but unpredictable contingencies have an influence, and their personal attachments to life styles also vary. The socio-economic conditions impose limits on the kinds of life ghetto dwellers may have, but these kinds of life are culturally transmitted and shared as many individuals in the

---

*In adherence to Goffman's definitions (1961, pp. 88-89), *commitment* to a role refers here to impersonal structural arrangements which force an individual to certain lines of action, while *attachment* refers to a person's being "affectively and cognitively enamored, desiring and expecting to see himself in terms of the enactment of the role and the self-identification emerging from this enactment."

present, and many in the past, live or have lived under the same premises. When the latter is the case, it is hardly possible to invent new adaptations again and again, as men are always observing one another and interacting with one another. The implication of some of Frazier's writings, that ghetto dwellers create their way of life in a cultural limbo—an idea which has had more modern expressions—appears as unacceptable in this case as in any other situation where people live together, and in particular where generations live together. The behavior of the streetcorner male is easily experienced as a natural pattern of masculinity with which ghetto dwellers grow up and which to some extent they grow into. To see it only as a complex of unsuccessful attempts at hiding failures by self-deception seems, for many of the men involved, to be too much psychologizing and too little sociology. But this does not mean that the attachment to the ghetto-specific culture is very strong among its bearers. Rodman's concept of a lower class value stretch is a realistic statement of many ghetto dwellers' cultural involvement:*

> Lower-class persons in close interaction with each other and faced with similar problems do not long remain in a state of mutual ignorance. They do not maintain a strong commitment to middle-class values that they cannot attain, and they do not continue to respond to others in a rewarding or punishing way simply on the basis of whether these others are living up to the middle-class values. A change takes place. They come to tolerate and eventually to evaluate favorably certain deviations from the middle-class values. In this way, they need not be continually frustrated by their failure to live up to unattainable values. The resultant is a stretched value system with a low degree of commitment to all the values within the range, including the dominant, middle-class values" (Rodman 1963, p. 209).

The question of whether streetcorner males have mainstream culture or a specific-ghetto culture, then, is best answered by saying that they have both, in different ways. There can be little

---

*Rodman's (1963) "commitment" seems to equal Goffman's (1961) "attachment."

doubt that this is the understanding most in line with that contemporary trend in anthropological thought which emphasizes the sharing of cultural imagery, of expectations and definitions of reality, as the medium whereby individuals in a community interact. It is noteworthy that many of the commentators who have been most skeptical of the idea of a ghetto-specific culture, or more generally a "culture of poverty," have been those who have taken a more narrow view of culture as a set of values about which an older generation consciously instructs the younger ones in the community. Thus Valentine (1968, p. 113) hypothesizes that

> lower-class life does not actually constitute a distinct subculture in the sense often used by poverty analysts, because it does not embody any design for living to which people give sufficient allegiance or emotional involvement to pass it on to their children.

Roach and Gursslin (1967, pp. 387–88) too, in their critique of the "culture of poverty" concept, imply that cultural transmission invariably involves a strong normative system. Obviously, the answer to whether there is a ghetto-specific culture or not will depend to some extent on what we shall mean by culture. Perhaps this is too important a question to be affected by a mere terminological quibble, and perhaps social policy, in some areas, may well proceed unaffected by the question raised by a ghetto-specific culture. On the other hand, in an anthropological study of community life, the wider view of cultural sharing and transmission which has been used here will have to play a part in our picture of the ghetto, including that of what ghetto males are like.

COMMENTARY on
RACIAL DIFFERENCES ON THE MMPI

At least twelve studies have compared blacks and whites on the Minnesota Multiphasic Personality Inventory (MMPI).* This inventory consists of thirteen scales, each denoted by a number (e.g., "scale 1") or an abbreviation (e.g., the "Hs scale"). These scales were originally devised for the clinical assessment of the mentally ill. Each scale, however, has been found to measure personality tendencies in "normal" (i.e., non-psychiatric) samples as well.

Often the samples in the studies making racial comparisons on the MMPI have been from the groups such as prison inmates or medical patients and have therefore not been representative of the general population. Despite these sampling biases, racial differences have consistently been found on certain scales.†

Most of the studies have found that blacks tend to score higher on scale 1 (Hs) than whites. Extremely elevated scores indicate that a person is defeatist, complaining, and cynical. Moderately high scores suggest lack of ambition, stubbornness, lethargy, and egocentrism.

Blacks make comparatively low scores on scale 3 (Hy). Thus they are less likely to need affection and support, and they are less likely to be idealistic and naive. They are more likely to be socially isolated and misanthropic.

Blacks score relatively high on scale 8 (Sc). High scores on this scale indicate tendencies toward withdrawal, feelings of alienation and of being misunderstood, and doubts about self-worth.

Compared to whites, blacks make high scores on scale 9 (Ma). Such scores characterize energetic, tense, hyperactive, warm—even uninhibited—persons. They have pleasant, outgoing temperaments.

---

* Nine of these studies are summarized by Harrison and Kass (1967), whose paper reports the tenth study. The eleventh study is reported by Miller (1968). The twelfth is the research by Baughman and Dahlstrom reported in the following selection.

† The following interpretation of each scale is based on Carson (1969) and Kleinmuntz (1967, chapter 8).

The following selection by Baughman and Dahlstrom is from one of the most recent studies of blacks and whites using the MMPI. The primary virtue of this selection is that the sample studied—consisting, as it does, of eighth graders—is more representative of the general population than many other samples investigated with the MMPI. Since few students drop out by the eighth grade, various segments of the population have been adequately covered.

Although the findings reported in the following selection agree with most of the previously mentioned findings, there is one important difference: Baughman and Dahlstrom fail to find racial differences on scale 3 (Hy), the scale that measures qualities such as idealism, sociability, and need for affection.

In addition to making racial comparisons on specific scales, Baughman and Dahlstrom also compute the percentage of respondents in each group that have a "primed code." A primed code is a profile having an extremely high score on one or more of the scales—a score that is higher than all but a few individuals in the general population would exhibit and that therefore indicates psychiatric pathology. The authors report that blacks are somewhat more likely than whites to have primed codes.

Finally the selection compares the races on special scales developed by Harrison and Kass (1967). In finding that blacks score higher on measures of estrangement and cynicism, the selection confirms the conclusion of Middleton's study (selection 6)—namely, that blacks are more likely to feel alienated than whites.*

The MMPI has several disadvantages. The main one is that the scales of the inventory are not unidimensional: a given scale does not correspond to a single characteristic, say, impulsiveness. Hence one cannot say that a high score indicates that a person is impulsive, and a low score that he is controlled. Indeed, any scale of the

---

* Nonetheless, the findings based on these special scales are problematic. In devising these scales, Harrison and Kass began by examining the statistical relation between race and each item in the MMPI. They then conducted a factor analysis—but this was based only on those items that strongly differentiated between blacks and whites. Their special scales were derived from this factor analysis. Thus racial differences in the average scores on these special scales were built into the scales. Would these scales have shown as strong a relation to race as they did if these measurement biases had not been present? Probably not.

MMPI may connote several different qualities, and one cannot be sure which of these a given score represents. Does a high score on scale 8 (Sc) signify that a person has a low sense of self-esteem or that he is socially isolated or that he feels estranged from others? It could signify any or all of these. The multi-dimensional nature of each scale also gives rise to seemingly contradictory findings. Thus the high scores of blacks on scale 9 suggest sociability while their high scores on scale 8 suggest social isolation.

In addition, moderately elevated scores on a scale may connote one set of personality tendencies while highly elevated scores connote a different set. Carson (1969) writes that a moderately elevated score on scale 9 (Ma) suggests a pleasant outgoing temperament. An extremely elevated score, on the other hand, is indicative of maladaptive hyperactivity, irritability, and lack of inhibitions. This makes for a problem. A relatively high mean score for blacks on scale 9 could be due to the moderately elevated scores of many individuals or to the highly elevated scores of a few. Thus a given mean score is difficult to interpret.

Despite these problems, Baughman and Dahlstrom's selection is a worthwhile piece. For the MMPI, as these investigators use it, permits us to obtain a comprehensive picture of the differences in modal personality between blacks and whites.

Racial Differences on the Minnesota Multiphasic Personality Inventory

E. EARL BAUGHMAN and W. GRANT DAHLSTROM*

This project was initiated to learn more about a neglected group of American children, those residing in the rural South. Most of our data describe white and Negro boys and girls who live in a rural area of central North Carolina [Millfield] under a racially segregated pattern of social and educational organization. Although the Negro population outnumbers the white, the majority group does not control the power structure.

Although poverty is not unknown to many of the white families, it is experienced much more frequently by the Negro families. On the other hand, we must make it clear that the typical families in Millfield are neither destitute nor in abject poverty. They often have very low cash incomes, but, living on the land and raising produce, they are considerably better nourished, for example, than equally large families would be if they were completely dependent upon so small a cash income. While some families live in houses that are dilapidated, primitive, and repellent, many landowners keep even their rental houses in fair repair.

With respect to racial matters, Millfield resists change, although not violently. No legal constraints stand today to maintain racial separation in the schools, and some Negro students have recently entered all-white schools. Yet it is also true that this breakdown of

* Excerpted from *Negro and White Children: A Psychological Study in the Rural South,* by E. Earl Baughman and W. Grant Dahlstrom (1968), pp. 451–53, 232–57, and 467–70, by permission of the publisher, Academic Press, and of the senior author.

complete segregation in the schools has been very slow. Changes in racial relationships have been even less evident in organizations like PTAs, churches, or political parties. The basic pattern of parallel activities rather than interactive relationships between members of the two racial groups continues to exist very much as it has for many decades.

THE MMPI

To obtain objective and quantitative data on certain personality characteristics of the children in Millfield, the Minnesota Multiphasic Personality Inventory (MMPI) was included in our assessment battery.... The content and form of the MMPI limited its use to the eighth-grade level, precluding age comparisons in personality development.

CONSTRUCTION OF THE INVENTORY

There are five hundred fifty separate statements (sixteen of them are used twice) in the MMPI to which each subject is asked to answer true or false as they apply to him. The content of these items ranges widely over views of one's self and others, over personal feelings and social attitudes, over physical and mental symptoms, over beliefs, habits, and past experiences. The pool of items was collected with the hope that the major personality dimensions would be covered.

For general use of the MMPI, ten personality scales and three validity scales are scored and plotted in a profile. The original scales were constructed empirically by contrasting the item replies of highly selected groups of psychiatric patients to the way a large group of normal adults answered these items. Only those items that actually separated each criterion group from the normals were retained to make up these scales. In addition, some items were eliminated from these component scales to reduce the biases of age, marital status, and socioeconomic status. Sex differences could not be eliminated from most of the scales, however, and separate norms are used in the profiles for each sex.

Although the original scales were derived from patients showing extreme forms of personality deviation, early research studies indicated that useful and meaningful separations within normal ranges of personality variation were possible. These normative groups were primarily made up of adults and included subjects only as young as the age of sixteen. More recent work, however, has indicated that the test is appropriate and valid for literate subjects as young as thirteen or fourteen years of age.

VALIDITY SCALES

The MMPI includes some important safeguards against several pervasive difficulties in the use of verbal statements to survey personality status. These safeguards are called validity scales, since they provide information about the acceptability of a particular set of answers from a test subject. The validity scales are scored as a separate group from the clinical, or personality, scales and are evaluated before the rest of the test profile is interpreted.

One common source of difficulty in using these tests is that the subject may not want to cooperate with the examiner or reveal how these various statements may apply to himself. He may prefer to answer them the way he thinks he should to look good, for example, or he may answer the way he thinks the examiner wants him to fill out the answers. The general tendency to distort one's answers in a strongly favorable way is evaluated by the score on the L scale. A score that is high on this scale casts doubt on the dependability of the scores on the rest of the inventory.

In a similar way, the F score reflects the extent to which a subject has marked answers that are very infrequently given to these items either by normal subjects or even by patients of various kinds. Rare answers can reflect valid personality deviations or such kinds of invalidity as unwillingness to cooperate with the test instructions, serious reading difficulties, inattention, confusion, or even a deliberate intention to appear poorly adjusted on the test.

The third validity index, the K score, is a more subtle measure of a subject's tendency to distort his answers to the test in either an unfavorable (low scores) or a favorable direction (high scores). Research has indicated that the influence of these test-taking sets upon the basic personality scales can be offset to a considerable extent by adding parts of the K score to the raw scores of some clinical scales.*

A fourth index of test validity, the number of statements that the subject omits, or fails to answer either true or false, is also plotted on the test profile. No subject is forced to answer all the items, of course, since some subjects are bound to find occasional items that do not apply to them among such a heterogeneous collection. All the answer sheets of the subjects in Millfield were checked for omissions; few of the subjects left any of the items unanswered.†

Together, these validity indices serve as partial checks on the suitability of the MMPI for the subjects in this study. No scores from any subject who had excessively high values on these scales were included in the analyses of the clinical scales. Perhaps as a result of the variations introduced in the test administration described below, very few invalid protocols were found.‡

PERSONALITY SCALES

These scales (also called clinical scales, since they were derived from various clinical groups formed in psychiatric practice and often have provided useful diagnostic information in clinical work) are usually referred to by the number of their position in the regular MMPI profile.** The meaning of each scale has been demonstrated to be greater than the specific, and often extreme, features that were true of the patients used as criterion groups. This psychological breadth of interpretive significance dictated

---

* Five clinical scales (1, 4, 7, 8, and 9) have been corrected by the customary K-scale weights in the results reported below.

† It should be noted, however, that in the 1964 testing program, the white children were not administered the final one hundred items of the test because of time limitations.

‡ Out of two hundred sixty-five tests, six records were eliminated for excessive F scores and one for a high L scale value.

** The specific diagnostic groups used to construct the standard MMPI scales were: scale 1 (hypochondriacs); scale 2 (depressives); scale 3 (hysterical conversions); scale 4 (psychopathic personalities); scale 5 (male inverts); scale 6 (paranoids); scale 7 (obsessive-compulsives); scale 8 (schizophrenics); scale 9 (hypomaniacs); and scale 0 (social introverts).

abandoning the original diagnostic labels and substituting the numerical system. The personality correlates of the component scales have been collated in several reference works on the MMPI, including Welsh and Dahlstrom (1956), Dahlstrom and Welsh (1960), Marks and Seeman (1963), and Gilberstadt and Duker (1965).

ADMINISTRATION AND SCORING

In the usual form in which the MMPI is now administered, the statements are printed in a booklet and the subject marks his responses to them on a separate answer sheet. This version permits testing large groups of subjects in a single session, if they can read and follow the general test instructions. The validity scale values of each subject (see above) provide checks on the appropriateness of this form of administration for each member of the group tested.

TAPE-RECORDED VERSION

Most of the MMPI statements do not demand more than a fifth-grade reading level to understand them, although occasional items require somewhat higher levels of reading comprehension. However, some of the eighth-grade students in Millfield were not able to demonstrate even fifth-grade reading mastery. Accordingly, a tape-recorded form of the MMPI was prepared in an attempt to circumvent their serious limitation in reading comprehension.

The tape was specially prepared for this project.* After a brief introduction, the tape presents each MMPI statement in the same order as it appears in the standard test booklet. Initially, a pause of ten seconds is made after each item to allow the subject to think over the item and mark his answer to it. After the first ten

---

* We are indebted to James N. Butcher for the preparation and reading of the tape-recorded version of the MMPI used in this study. His West Virginian accent appeared to provide an excellent compromise between the clarity of enunciation needed for full communicative efficiency and the familiarity of accent and emphasis for use with Southern rural subjects. He also carried out the equivalence studies which demonstrated satisfactory stability of the MMPI component scores between examinations by tape and by test booklet on college level subjects (see Butcher and Dahlstrom 1965).

test items, the pacing of the items is speeded up and five-second intervals are used for the rest of the test.*

This tape version of the MMPI was given to each eighth-grade class in their own classroom at the end of the school year in 1963 by our regular field research staff workers. In 1964, however, the white eighth-graders were attending a separate junior high school and had to be examined by a special testing staff in the music room of that school. The subjects, grouped by homerooms, were examined by two women who were not part of our field research staff.† The eighth-grade students in the Negro schools were available for testing as usual by the regular research staff in the spring of 1964, as they were in 1963.

The classroom teachers were not present during this examination, but the project staff members were by now quite well-known to these students. The subjects were each given a Hankes answer sheet for the MMPI and told the purpose and nature of the test. The tape recorder was started, and the first MMPI item was played to the group. The research staff made certain that the children understood the instructions and procedures and then resumed the tape. Circumspect proctoring was carried out during the session; the proctors tried to make sure that the subjects continued to be attentive and that they were able to keep up with the tape delivery, but they also tried to avoid any appearance of prying into the specific answers given by any of the test subjects. Routinely, the tape was stopped every half-hour in order to allow the subjects a chance to stand, stretch, and relax before proceeding with the examination. The examiners were successful in maintaining a serious and business-like testing

* Preliminary research indicated that subjects soon accommodate to the task and do not need more than five or six seconds between items to keep up with the tape recording. We are indebted to the Recording Laboratories of the Department of Radio, Television, and Motion Pictures at the University of North Carolina, which provided the equipment and technicians for editing this tape.

† The testing was fitted into the regularly scheduled periods of these students, and consequently the last one hundred items on the tape could not be given. This curtailment of the test did not affect any of the regular MMPI scales, but some of the special scales had to be prorated to make them comparable to scores from subjects given the full test.

atmosphere. The children's reactions to the items were generally accepting; questions were postponed until completion of the test. The examiners then went back over any items that the children wished to have repeated or failed to understand. Usually there were no more than ten or fifteen such queries, mostly items that some subject wanted to complete after previously skipping them. Some requests for definitions were made, but the examiners provided only occasional synonyms and asked the subjects to make up their own minds about the general meaning of the statements. The comments of the children indicated that they had found the test session long, but interesting.

SCORING METHODS

The scoring of the MMPI is completely objective and highly reliable. Once the subject has completed his marking of spaces on the answer sheet, the tallying of scores is a simple clerical task: a scoring template for each component scale is placed over the answer sheet, and the number of items showing through the spaces constitutes the score for that scale. Each test protocol was scored twice to assure clerical accuracy; the scores were entered on a standard MMPI profile form appropriate to the sex of the subject. In addition, some research scales were scored for each answer sheet by means of special scoring templates.*

PERSONALITY SCALE FINDINGS

Data obtained from a multivariate instrument like the MMPI can be analyzed in a number of meaningful ways. Each component score can be treated independently and analyzed by the usual statistical methods to describe each subgroup—for example, where the group falls on the scale, and how widely it is distributed over the scale range. This scale-by-scale approach was carried out on both the validity and the personality scales of the MMPI, and the results are reported [below]. These analyses were based on the raw scores obtained from scoring each subject's test record. The

* We are indebted to Stephen Flanagan for scoring and tabulating many of these MMPI data.

means and standard deviations found for each subgroup on the component scales are summarized in Table 1 in raw score form.

TABLE 1

RAW SCORE MEANS AND STANDARD DEVIATIONS
ON THE BASIC MMPI SCALES FOR EIGHTH–GRADE CHILDREN
(1963 and 1964)

MMPI scales	White boys (N = 52)		White girls (N = 66)		Negro boys (N = 59)		Negro girls (N = 81)	
	Mean	S.D.	Mean	S.D.	Mean	S.D.	Mean	S.D.
Validity scales								
L	3.3	2.1	3.6	2.0	3.9	3.0	4.0	2.1
F	10.1	6.7	7.8	5.2	12.5	7.2	10.0	5.7
K	10.2	4.3	11.3	4.2	10.0	4.6	10.7	4.3
Personality scales								
1	6.9	5.3	7.0	4.8	8.1	4.1	8.4	4.7
2	17.9	4.5	19.4	4.4	20.3	5.0	21.9	4.2
3	17.9	4.5	19.1	5.3	16.8	4.8	17.9	4.9
4	19.9	4.8	18.6	4.8	21.3	5.1	20.1	4.5
5	20.3	4.6	32.7	4.4	22.4	3.6	31.6	3.7
6	11.1	3.5	9.9	3.7	12.3	3.5	11.8	4.8
7	18.8	7.0	17.4	7.6	20.4	6.8	20.7	6.6
8	21.8	8.7	19.8	10.1	26.4	9.2	26.1	10.2
9	21.8	5.0	19.2	5.3	23.2	4.2	21.0	3.7
0	28.7	6.9	29.2	6.8	30.9	6.0	30.6	5.5

Since each scale has a different number of items and a different range of variation, it is difficult to compare relative levels on different scales for any one group. In addition, as noted above, there are important sex differences on some of the personality scales which further complicate cross-sex comparisons based on raw score values. Therefore, in addition to the raw score means described above, group mean profiles were prepared based upon standard T-score scales.* These profiles for each subgroup are presented in Figure 1.

---

* On each MMPI scale, a standard reference scale is used, called a T-score scale, to facilitate direct comparisons of a subject's standing on each of the various personality dimensions being evaluated. Arbitrarily, the value of the mean earned by a reference

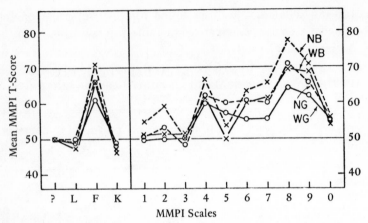

Fig. 1: Mean MMPI profiles of eighth-grade white boys (WB), white girls (WG), Negro boys (NB), and Negro girls (NG), from Millfield (1963 and 1964).

The personality implications of the mean values earned by the various subgroups under study here are given below. Higher values on these different scales usually mean a greater likelihood of some form of emotional maladjustment.

Scale 1. Extreme values on this scale reflect both a narrow self-centeredness and an over-concern with various bodily symptoms. In its lower ranges, this scale often reflects degrees of lethargy, inactivity, and fatigue. Both white subgroups and the Negro girls seem quite free of any of these features (see Figure 1). Only the Negro boys scored high enough to suggest that some of these characteristics may be attributed to them. Generally, these youngsters do not appear to have serious physical preoccupations or overinvolvement with their health and physical well-being.

Scale 2. Both ends of this scale appear to have important

group of Minnesota normal adult men or women is set at the fifty mark for each separate scale. The amount of deviation above or below the mean is scaled by setting the standard deviation of the norm group equal to ten T-score points. Thus, a score of sixty-five signifies that a subject has scored above the Minnesota group of that sex by one and a half standard deviations, in the direction of the psychiatric criterion group used to develop that scale. A score of forty-seven indicates that he has scored below the mean by 0.3 of a standard deviation.

personality implications: high values measure unhappiness, poor morale, self-dissatisfaction, and a sober and serious outlook on life (consistent with the depressed individuals used to construct the scale). Low scores are related to buoyancy, self-confidence, and naturalness; cheerfulness, energy, and good spirits can also be inferred from these low scores. Youngsters this age often score below the Minnesota adult norms on this scale, but no subgroup in this study scored below average. In fact, both Negro groups fell significantly above the mean. Negro boys are particularly likely to show evidence of poor morale and a pessimistic outlook on the world.

Scale 3. This scale was constructed to identify individuals who are likely to get ill under stress, as a partial solution to their emotional problems. High scores are related to this tendency to form conversion reactions, and to the basic personality traits associated with that form of hysteria: naiveté, religious idealism, social dependency, and childishness. None of the groups in Millfield showed an appreciable elevation on scale 3. This is particularly noteworthy in the light of claims in the clinical psychiatric literature that there is a high incidence of this personality pattern among people residing in the South.

Scale 4. Individuals high on this scale are generally rebellious, socially aggressive, and selfish, and show a cynical disregard for rules and authority. The scale was constructed to identify people who continually get into one kind of trouble or another because they lack basic character and integrity. All four subgroups earned scale 4 mean scores in the range of moderate elevation, Negro boys earning the highest value. Scores in this middle range are more likely to reflect impulsivity and interpersonal insensitivity than direct expression of hostility, resentment, or defiance of authority, which are implied by the more extreme values. Judging by their scores on scale 4, these youngsters as a group are not yet ready for adult demands and responsibilities.

Scale 5. This scale measures the extent to which a person expresses an interest pattern characteristic of the opposite sex. Thus among boys, higher scores reflect interests in cultural, scholarly, or academic pursuits, gentlemanly behavior, and, at the higher levels, feminine attitudes and values. Neither white nor Negro boys scored appreciably above the mean for men in general on this scale. This finding thus fails to support some contentions in the current literature that Negro males as a group have in some fashion been feminized by their upbringing and experiences in (supposedly) matriarchal families.

The scores of the two groups of girls, however, are elevated moderately on scale 5. They score more like men on this scale than do most adolescent groups or than women in general do, suggesting some systematic rejection of feminine roles and patterns. High-scoring girls on this scale are characterized as rather coarse, striving, and ambitious. Other evidence in this study indicates that the girls, particularly Negro girls, are dissatisfied in many ways with both their present lot and future prospects in this community. Perhaps, from the scores they earned on scale 5, it could be added that their future roles as women here may include levels of dominance and self-assertiveness that are not in keeping with the usual concept of femininity.

Scale 6. High scores on this scale reflect such personality features as oversensitivity, stubbornness, irritability, and proneness to misinterpret the actions and intentions of other people. These traits are consistent with the paranoid disorders that made up the group on which this scale was constructed. Moderate elevations on this scale, however, show only the basic emphasis upon rationality, self-dedication, and devotion to others, without the sense of self-importance so characteristic of extreme forms of this personality pattern. If anything, people with only moderately elevated scores on scale 6 are likely to appear more as martyrs than as vain and overbearing egotists. All four subgroups scored within moderate limits on scale 6, the Negro youngsters slightly higher than the white eighth-graders. These children can best be described as sensitive, rather self-effacing and self-conscious, with significant degrees of suspiciousness and guardedness in their relations with others.

Scale 7. Increasing elevations on this scale measure agitation, insecurity, perplexity, and feelings of inferiority. High scorers have many apprehensions, self-doubts, and anxieties. All four subgroups scored at a moderate level on scale 7, in the range that reflects lack of self-confidence, unsureness about personal worth, and worries about social acceptance and popularity. The boys (especially the Negro boys) showed more of these various concerns than the girls did; the white girls were most self-confident and comfortable.

Scale 8. Very high scores on this scale indicate severe personality disorganization or a break with reality. Moderate scores reflect underlying self-doubts, alienation from others, convictions of being inferior or different, and inability to experience the feelings and reactions that normal people do. All the subgroups in this sample had their highest elevations on this scale; the Negro boys and girls were most elevated, exceeding both of the white subgroups. Their scores are consistent with deep crises in personal identity, isolation from others, important doubts about their own capabilities, and lack of a sense of personal worth.

High scores on scale 8 are often accompanied by elevation on the F scale in the validity set. Both scales provide the subject with opportunities to report unusual and atypical experiences, beliefs, attitudes, or feelings. These four groups are ranked in a similar way by both the F scale and scale 8. It is quite likely that these subjects are demonstrating similar personality trends in their answers to both scales, trends which will be explored further by means of the special factor scales from Harrison and Kass (1967). These elevations on scale 8 indicate that the youngsters may be going through important crises in personality organization. Such inferences, however, are at variance with both the reports of their teachers and the findings from personal interviews with them. These discrepancies are large; they require considerable additional research to provide adequate explanations for them.

Scale 9. Very high scores on this scale reveal driving energy, overoptimism, ambitiousness, and inability to see one's own limitations or liabilities. The subgroups from Millfield scored in the moderate ranges where nonconformity, excessive energy, lack of control, and poor judgment can more appropriately be inferred. The boys are higher than the girls on this scale, but all four groups are likely to show the impulsiveness, lack of sustained interest, and many short-lived enthusiasms that these scores imply and that are typical of this age range.

Scale 0. This scale was not originally part of the MMPI scale development work at Minnesota. It was devised later to measure differences in social introversion, or the tendency to stay by one-self and avoid wide-ranging social ties and relationships (indicated by high scores). Low scores on scale 0 mean that the person is likely to engage in many different activities, usually seeking out the company of others and actively participating in clubs, socials, and groups. Neither extreme in sociability characterizes the eighth-grade subgroups from Millfield. They are very similar to one another and, as a total group, show only a slight trend toward avoidance of social activities. This level can be best interpreted as lack of assertiveness and social initiative. Once social activities are underway, initiated perhaps by others, Millfield youngsters as a group should be fully participating.

PROFILE PATTERNS

The profile elevation is important in forming the appropriate inferences of personality characteristics from the component MMPI scales or from the patterns of scores in the profile. Therefore, a tabulation was made of the number of subjects in each group having one or more scores in their profile exceeding a T-score of seventy and thus obtaining a primed code. (This cutting score lies two standard deviations above the mean of normal adults of that sex and indicates, in general, the level at which a person's scores approach the score elevations of various clinical reference groups.) The results of these tabulations of the frequencies of primed codes in each of the subgroups are reported in Table 2.

Both Negro subgroups had significantly more highly elevated, or primed, profiles than their white counterparts, and the boys had more primed profiles than the girls did. These data serve to document further the appropriateness of the mean profiles shown in Figure 1 to summarize the MMPI performances of the sub-groups. That is, the mean profiles showed the same relationships among these subgroups in relative deviation from the profile norms as these tabulations of individual records reveal. It is note-worthy that only the white girls, among these subgroups, have

TABLE 2

FREQUENCIES OF MMPI PROFILES WITH PRIMED CODES
(HIGH ELEVATIONS) AND NONPRIMED CODES AMONG THE
EIGHTH–GRADE SAMPLES (1963 and 1964)

	White boys			White girls		
Year	Nonprimed	Primed	Total	Nonprimed	Primed	Total
1963	13	18	31	21	13	34
1964	8	13	21	14	18	32
TOTALS*	21	31	52	35	31	66

	Negro boys			Negro girls		
	Nonprimed	Primed	Total	Nonprimed	Primed	Total
1963	9	25	34	17	25	42
1964	8	17	25	11	28	39
TOTALS*	17	42	59	28	53	81

* Two profiles from the white children and five profiles from the Negro children were
excluded on the basis of excessively high validity scale values.

more profiles that are nonprimed than are primed. The majority of
children in each of the other groups have one or more scale elevations that deviate from the test norms by at least two standard
deviations. Two-thirds to three-fourths of the profiles from the
Negro children had some score (and often several scores) falling
beyond a T-score of seventy. The personality characterizations
offered above, therefore, would be applicable to a great many of
the children in these subgroups, not just to a few, highly deviant
youngsters.

FACTOR SCALE FINDINGS

One additional method of data analysis was carried out. Five
special scales were scored on these MMPI records. These scales
come from some recent research of Harrison and Kass (1967)
based upon their studies of young white and Negro women in
Boston, Massachusetts, who were tested when they came to an
obstetrical clinic for care during pregnancy. Valid records were
available on three hundred eighty-nine white and three hundred

eighty-three Negro mothers-to-be, a large enough sample of each group to permit detailed item analyses in addition to statistical analyses of the standard MMPI scales. Although two hundred thirteen of the five hundred fifty MMPI items showed stable differences in endorsement patterns between the two groups, only the one hundred fifty most discriminating items were chosen for more elaborate analyses. Using factor analytic procedures on a high-speed electronic computer, these workers were able to find twenty stable groupings among these selected items which they used to form special factor scales. Some of these special scales proved to be quite short and unreliable, but a few seem to be useful in characterizing the differences between these white and Negro women in their self-descriptions on the MMPI. Five of these scales were selected for use in this study; they represent the first five factors to emerge from their analyses and serve to summarize many of the differences that were found. Naming such scales has to be quite arbitrary until further research clarifies the significance each may have for personality interpretations, but the tentative titles suggested by Harrison and Kass appear to be reasonable summaries of the content of the items making up each scale. In the present study they provide us with additional means of examining some of the ways these youngsters are viewing and presenting themselves at this stage of their development.

Factor I is a twenty-six-item scale called, tentatively, Estrangement. It is made up of such items as: The future seems hopeless to me (True); No one seems to understand me (True); I am sure I get a raw deal from life (True); I have a daydream life about which I do not tell other people (True); and These days I find it hard not to give up hope of amounting to something (True). This scale showed higher scores for Negro subjects in Harrison and Kass' study.

Factor II has twenty-one items and has been labeled Intellectual and Cultural Interests. Some of the items include: I like poetry (True); I like to read about history (True); I like dramatics (True); I read in the Bible several times a week (True); and I think I would like the work of a librarian (True). The Negro subjects in Harrison and Kass' study earned higher scores on this scale, too.

Factor III, called Denial of Deviant Behavior, contains only ten items, among which are: I have never had a fit or convulsion (True); I have never seen a vision (True); and It wouldn't make me nervous if any members of my family got into trouble with the law (False). This scale showed higher scores for the white subjects in the derivational study.

Factor IV is a somewhat longer scale, made up of twenty-six items, and is labeled Cynicism. Some representative items include: It takes a lot of argument to convince most people of the truth (True); I think most people would lie to get ahead (True); Most people make friends because friends are likely to be useful to them (True); Most people will use somewhat unfair means to gain profit or an advantage rather than lose it (True); and People generally demand more respect for their own rights than they are willing to allow for others (True). On this scale the Negro women earned higher scores than the white women did.

Factor V, Admission of Minor Faults, is a nine-item scale on which the white women earned the higher scores. It contains such items as: I played hookey from school quite often as a youngster (True); I can remember "playing sick" to get out of something (True); At times I feel like swearing (True); and I enjoy gambling for small stakes (True).

By restricting their factor analyses to the items that showed the largest and most dependable differences between their samples of white and Negro women, Harrison and Kass concentrated primarily upon those personality features and behavioral characteristics that most strikingly separate these two groups. This method serves to minimize the many important personality features that people from these different ethnic backgrounds have in common. It must be kept in mind, therefore, in the results that follow that the purpose is to try to characterize the nature of the differences rather than to put into a balanced perspective a complete set of personality descriptions. In addition, only one set of the variables from the Harrison and Kass study were selected for an application to the Millfield protocols.* Their other scales could have been

* We gratefully acknowledge the kindness of Robert D. Harrison in allowing us to make use of these findings prior to their publication.

included, although these additional measures probably would not have been so dependable as the ones that were used.*

The means and standard deviations, in raw score form, are reported on each factor scale for the four subgroups in Table 3. Even though these scales were devised to represent different and important sources of variance among the MMPI differences found in their samples, the authors were not able to keep these scales independent. They reported one large correlation in this set (.83 between scale I and scale IV) and several moderate values among some of the other scales. Scale III correlated positively with scale V (the two scales that showed higher values for white women than Negro women) but negatively with the other three scores reported here.

TABLE 3

RAW SCORE MEANS AND STANDARD DEVIATIONS
ON HARRISON AND KASS' MMPI FACTOR SCALES
ON EIGHTH–GRADE CHILDREN (1963 and 1964)

Factor scales	White boys (N = 52)		White girls (N = 66)		Negro boys (N = 59)		Negro girls (N = 81)	
	Mean	S.D.	Mean	S.D.	Mean	S.D.	Mean	S.D.
I. Estrangement	11.9	4.2	10.7	4.1	14.2	3.9	13.3	4.5
II. Intellectual and Cultural Interests	8.5	3.0	10.2	4.5	12.9	3.1	14.3	3.1
III. Denial of Deviant Behavior	6.6	1.9	7.2	1.9	7.2	1.4	7.4	1.6
IV. Cynicism	16.9	4.1	14.6	4.2	19.9	3.1	18.9	3.9
V. Admission of Minor Faults	3.6	1.4	2.8	1.5	2.6	1.5	2.5	1.5

In the present study, scales II [Intellectual and Cultural Interests] and IV [Cynicism] showed the most dependable differences both between white and Negro subgroups and between the sexes within the racial groupings. All comparisons were highly significant in the statistical evaluations made of these means. On scale I [Estrangement], the contrasts involving the racial subgroups were

* The MMPI protocols from the white children in 1964 did not include answers to the last hundred items of the test. Three of these scales had to be prorated to allow for the fact that the last few items had been omitted and were unavailable.

stable, but the other differences were not. On scale V [Admission of Minor Faults], the white boys were differentiated from the other groups (significantly higher), but no other differences were stable. The same finding was obtained for scale III [Denial of Deviant Behavior], in the opposite direction and at a lower level of significance; the white boys were significantly lower than the other groups on this scale.

Comparing the direction and the magnitude of differences obtained on the original derivational samples and on the Millfield subgroups for these scales, an impressive degree of consistency was found. On four of the five scales the differences between the white and Negro children were in the same direction as those reported by Harrison and Kass; on one (scale III), there was a slight reversal. These separations were obtained in spite of differences in age, geographic locale, marital status, and, for some comparisons, differences in sex as well between the Massachusetts and North Carolina samples.

Equally striking in these findings is the absolute level of the mean scores on these scales earned by the Millfield groups. For example, there are only twenty-six items on scale IV, but the means for these groups ranged between fifteen and twenty items endorsed in the significant direction. The elevations on scales I and II, although less dramatic, also indicate that the Millfield children agreed with the original groups on a majority of the items scored on these scales.

These findings mean that by the time these children have reached the eighth grade, at the age of thirteen or fourteen, many of the attitudes, beliefs, and self-perceptions that differentiate white and Negro adults have already appeared in the self-reports of these Southern rural children. The Negro children describe themselves, and the world as they know it, in terms of estrangement and cynicism. Yet the data from these scales, and from the regular MMPI scales as well, indicate that they are not just reflecting strong and pervasive negative feelings about themselves. On scales III and V, in describing various personal faults and peccadillos, they are likely to place themselves in a moderately favorable light. On scale II, these same youngsters describe themselves as

possesing interests and values in general cultural pursuits that are
strongly endorsed by middle-class and upper-class adults. In the
area of emotional ties and interpersonal relationships, however,
these children show pervasive mistrust of themselves and others,
extreme pessimism about receiving fair treatment or justice, and
expectations that people will be self-seeking, dishonest, and
double-dealing. Many of these cynical attitudes extend to social
institutions and agencies as well.

Within the data summarized in Table 3 it can also be seen
that the patterns separating white and Negro children are different
from the patterns separating boys and girls within each racial
group. It is important to determine in future research whether
these same differences appear in other groups of white and Negro
subjects examined under a variety of other circumstances.

ARE THE MMPI DATA CONSISTENT
WITH THE OTHER PERSONALITY DATA?

In some respects, the answer to this question is yes; in other
respects, the answer is unquestionably no. Certainly the personality picture that emerges from the analysis of the MMPI data is
less sanguine than that reflected in some of the other assessment
data. Indeed, there are clear indications that large numbers of the
Millfield children might manifest severe behavior problems, if they
were to move to more complex and stressful settings (see below).

When the four groups are compared, there is an essential consistency between the MMPI data and much of the other data that
we have presented in this volume. Thus, the Negro boys, according
to this test, appear to be in the deepest psychological "trouble."[*]
The white girls, in contrast, show the fewest deviations in a
psychopathological direction.[†] The mean test profiles for the
Negro girls and white boys, interestingly enough, are almost identical, except for their scores on the masculinity-femininity scale.

---

[*] On eight out of the ten clinical scales, the mean score for the Negro boys deviated
more from the normal position than the scores for the other three groups (see Figure 1).

[†] On seven out of the ten clinical scales, the score for the white girls showed the smallest
deviation from the normal position (see Figure 1).

In regard to this scale, it is noteworthy that girls, both Negro and white, show a stronger tendency to reject the feminine position than the boys, either Negro or white, show with regard to rejection of the masculine position. It is also true that the Negro boys show more of a feminine orientation than the white boys, while the Negro girls show more of a masculine orientation than the white girls.

The scales designed primarily to identify neurotic components of personality structure reveal that such tendencies are not very salient among these children. (Negro boys, however, show a meaningful departure from the remaining three groups in such tendencies.) Instead, these children tend to score high on scales that suggest the likelihood of impulsive acting-out, an inadequate sense of self, alienation from self and society, a deficiency in sustained interests and commitments, and an overall disorganization within the personality. Such trends are most pronounced among the Negro boys, and least so among the white girls. Although to some extent this personality pattern can be regarded as "typically adolescent," the deviations are too pronounced (except among the white girls) to be explained as simply an adolescent phenomenon. In other words, the particular characteristics of life in Millfield appear to be creating additional stresses within the personality structures of the Negro boys, the Negro girls, and the white boys.

These personality problems revealed by the MMPI are, in our judgment, more severe than would be suggested by the information elicited either from the eighth-grade children in interviews or from their teachers. We believe this to be true even though there were, from time to time, indications throughout our study of certain psychological realities that are consistent with the inferences drawn from the MMPI data. Thus, the consistently poor intellective work of the Negro boys along with their poor peer standing would suggest that this group is in serious psychological trouble. Also, the relatively high dissatisfaction of the Negro girls, along with a strong tendency to reject the prospect of marriage (and with it the mother role) for themselves and their great difficulty in identifying even one positive attribute of their fathers, suggests at least a highly uncomfortable psychological condition for many of them. Among the white boys, their relatively weak commitment to pursuing further education in today's world along with the poor quality of their academic work, is probably a strong indication that their inner resources are not as effectively organized as one would like them to be. On the other hand, and still consistent with the MMPI findings, is the fact that the white girls are working effectively in school, they are embracing the idea of marriage for themselves, and in a variety of other ways they are manifesting well-integrated behavior.

The point is still valid, however, that the frequency of severe personality problems, as identified by the MMPI, is greater than that suggested by the other investigative techniques and greater than can be written off as "typically adolescent." It is also apparent from the teachers' evaluations that these personality problems are not manifested in the day-to-day behavior of many of the children. Nor did the problems always show themselves clearly in face-to-face interviews with the children. How can we explain these seeming contradictions?

With regard to the interview data, two factors are probably of critical importance. First, the structure and content of the interview questions simply did not probe deeply into many of the behavioral domains that are comprehensively scrutinized by the large pool of MMPI items. And, clearly, the MMPI items often refer to feelings and overt behaviors that the child cannot or will not bring up on his own volition; he is not accustomed to talking about many of these with anyone, least of all an adult authority figure. Second, even if the interview items had been more comparable to the MMPI statements, the face-to-face situation with a prestigious adult might very well have resulted in a significantly different pattern of responses.* In such interpersonal contexts, most respondents tend to present themselves in a favorable light, whereas the MMPI format seems to the respondent to be more

---

* The reader should recall here that, on the validity scales (L and K), the children's scores were such as to indicate that they were being very nondefensive in their responses. It would be interesting to administer the MMPI orally in a two-person context to a comparable group of children to see if the interpretation that we have suggested is reflected in less deviant profiles.

private or anonymous. That is, many individuals may be able to acknowledge problems or tensions on the MMPI answer sheet that they would have great difficulty attributing to themselves in an interpersonal situation.

The seeming discrepancy between the teachers' ratings and the MMPI findings may also in part be attributable to the fact that there were many differences between the behavioral domains covered by the ratings and by the MMPI items. We do not believe, however, that this is a full explanation for the discrepancy, nor do we believe that the teachers were biasing their ratings so as to provide us with more favorable descriptions than the actual behavior of the children warranted. Rather, we believe that the structure of life in Millfield is such that many of the internal psychological problems that it is helping to create are not readily externalized in the children's overt behavior. Thus, the MMPI data are pointing to what, for many (but not all) children, is a latent condition, an inadequacy in personality structure and process that often may go unrecognized (both by the child himself and by others)—as long as the demands made upon him are relatively simple, or as long as he can avoid more taxing confrontations than he is accustomed to meeting in the day-to-day affairs of Millfield.*

What we are suggesting is that if many of these children were moved to more complex environments (such as urban locales), or if the demands and confrontations pressed upon them in Millfield were intensified significantly, overt behavior pathology among them would become much more prevalent than it currently is. Such a formulation recognizes that visible behavior is a function not only of the personality processes existent within a person but of the context within which he exists. We believe, therefore, that the teachers are providing reasonably accurate reports of the children's behavior as it is manifested in Millfield, but that their

---

* Let the reader recall, for example, that most children tended to view Millfield in very simple terms, as a place where everyone was about like everyone else. And in their classrooms (especially those in the Negro schools) many children are protected from the realities of their poor performance by being given better grades than their performance merits, by being passed instead of failed in the grade, and so on. In these and other ways, many children are shielded from many of the realities of their existence, even including the fact that they are poor and that they are not being adequately prepared to reach the goals which they are being taught to embrace.

reports would be altered sharply if they observed the children confronting very different situational pressures. The MMPI, on the other hand, is identifying an internal structure which would have quite different implications if the children were functioning in a more complex environment than Millfield.

Having reached the above formulation, we were especially interested in the observation offered by a Negro principal in Millfield during the spring of 1967.* In talking with him, he commented on the fact that his school's enrollment had increased appreciably during the on-going academic year, even though the overall trend in enrollment for the past several years had been downward. We asked him why his enrollment had increased, and he pointed to several factors. Among these was the fact that a number of families living in a not-too-distant urban area had sent their children to live with relatives in his school district. The reason for this was the fact that these children had gotten into trouble in their home community. Spontaneously, then, the principal went on to point out that these children were no problem at all in Millfield and that if he had not known of their histories he would have no way of separating them from the other children in his school. To this observation we would add the prediction that if these children, as well as many of Millfield's own, were moved to the street corners of a city's ghetto, problem behavior would not be too difficult to identify.

* This was an experienced school administrator, but it was his first year in Millfield. We had not had an opportunity to communicate our observations or interpretations to him.

Part III: Personality Influences on Behavior

COMMENTARY on
THE PSYCHOLOGICAL CONTEXT OF MILITANCY

We saw in Part II of this reader that discrimination and minority group status foster certain personality characteristics in black Americans. In the following selection, Marx suggests that it is some of these very characteristics that dampen militancy in the struggle for civil rights.

Blacks, for example, tend to be more alienated than whites (Middleton 6). And alienation—which Marx calls "low morale"—is associated with lack of militancy (also see Orbell 1967). Discrimination also discourages identification with one's racial group (Morland 3) and blunts an awareness of how its plight is due to the social environment (Gurin et al. 14). Marx's data suggest that a lack of identification—a lack of a "favorable self-image"—and a lack of awareness of social factors also impede the development of militancy (also see Johnson 1966; Maliver 1965; Noel 1964; Gurin et al. 14; Lao 1970). There is some evidence that blacks are more authoritarian in their personal makeup than whites (Prothro and Smith 1957).* And Marx's data indicate that authoritarianism undermines militancy (also see Grossack 1957). Thus discrimination perpetuates itself in part by engendering in its victims those personality characteristics that undermine the will to resist and that foster resignation to minority group status.

This insight, however, should not be a cause for pessimism. For it suggests that if American society will lower the barriers of discrimination, it will be enhancing the insistence of blacks on having their rights. This last assertion received some support from Marx's data. Marx finds that personality characteristics such as those

---

* Whether the racial difference in average level of authoritarianism found in this study characterizes the population as a whole is, however, problematic. The sample consisted of college students, and college students are not representative of the general population. Black students, for example, probably have higher IQs, have greater achievement motivation, and come from higher status homes than most blacks. It is conceivable, therefore, that a more representative sample would yield different levels of authoritarianism than the sample used by Prothro and Smith.

discussed earlier (e.g., alienation and attitudes towards one's racial group) intervene between militancy and what he calls social involvement. Since social involvement largely reflects income and education, one can surmise that as the income and education of blacks go up, their personalities will change in a way that will make them more militant. If so, the enlarging of the civil rights of blacks is an accumulative, snow-balling process. Insofar as the society moves toward equality of opportunity, it reinforces the refusal of the black population to be resigned to discrimination. Thus measures to abolish discrimination and to increase equality of opportunity create the psychological impetus to more such measures.

Marx did his field work in 1964, when militants were trying to lower the barriers of discrimination and achieve integration in American society. Since then the mood of the black community has changed. Many who are considered militant no longer stress desegregation. The emphasis, rather, is on cultural nationalism, black pride, and community control. Would the personality characteristics that Marx found to be correlated with militancy of the early 1960s variety be correlated with the more nationalistic type of militancy so conspicuous today? We really don't know the answer. And the absence of an answer is an illustration of how social change can occur so quickly that the social scientist sometimes finds it difficult to keep his research "relevant."

The Psychological Context of Militancy

GARY T. MARX*

INTRODUCTION

The more perceptive and realistic social analysts have realized that conflict goes hand in hand with the eradication of the color line. Still, there remains the open and highly significant question of the extent to which an aroused Negro community, demanding its Constitutional rights, and being to some extent aware of the crippling consequences of its participation in what Malcolm X has called "the American Nightmare" (others have called it "The American Dream"), need become caught up in the blind hatred and categorical negative thinking that tends to characterize the dominant group. The violent protests of those sympathetic to the KKK and White Citizens Councils against efforts at desegregation clearly involve the most virulent hatred of Negroes. To what extent is the protest of Negroes against enforced segregation and inferior status related to antiwhite attitudes? This study was conceived in the hope that the Negro American community can become ever more militant and yet remain relatively tolerant.

The interviews on which this study is based were conducted in October, 1964, at a time when civil rights interest seemed to have reached a peak. Congress had just passed the most comprehensive

* Abridged from pp. 80-93 (excluding introductory quotations by Henley, Bunton, and King), pp. xvi-xvii (Introduction) and pp. 40–43 of *Protest and Prejudice* (Torchbook edition, 1969) by Gary T. Marx. Copyright 1967 by Anti-Defamation League of B'Nai B'rith by permission of Harper and Row, Publishers, Inc., and of the author.

civil rights act in a hundred years; Negro rioting in Northern cities and the brutal murder of three young civil rights workers in Mississippi were constantly in the news.

In all, 1,119 interviews were conducted with Negro adults. These were obtained from several different samples. The first, the metropolitan sample, consists of 492 persons and is representative of Negroes living in metropolitan areas of the nation outside the South. To obtain the sample, metropolitan areas outside the South were randomly sampled. From these sampled areas, Negro respondents were selected through modified probability procedures.

In addition to the metropolitan sample, four urban centers were chosen for special study and a representative sample of Negroes selected from each. These cities were Chicago, New York, Atlanta, and Birmingham. These four were chosen because they are among the most important urban centers of Negro population and because they differ in region, history, and present Negro-white relations. It was hoped that differences in the climate of Negro opinion among these four urban centers, and between them and the general metropolitan sample, might yield insights.

At many points in the analysis, respondents from the metropolitan sample and from the four cities are combined to provide more cases for analysis. This procedure is warranted on empirical grounds since in most cases relations found in the combined sample hold in each of the subsamples.

Interviewing and sampling were done by the National Opinion Research Center at the University of Chicago. NORC has conducted national surveys for several decades and its methods are widely respected.

The actual interviews lasted from an hour to an hour and a half. The original research design called for all interviews to be conducted by Negro interviewers. This was possible for almost nine out of ten respondents. For the non-Southern metropolitan area sample Negro interviewers sometimes were unavailable (for example, in Waterbury, Connecticut, and Hamilton, Ohio) and experienced white poll takers were used instead. This did not bias the results to any significant degree. Where analysis suggested that the race of the interviewer had a biasing effect on expressed attitudes toward whites, those interviewed by whites were excluded from consideration.*

AN INDEX OF MILITANCY

The dictionary defines militancy as a "fighting spirit, attitude, or policy." To be sure, there are many styles of fighting racial injustice and types of militancy. Thus far the most significant in bringing about social change has been that of the organized civil rights movement.

One of the aims of this study was to assess Negro response to the civil rights struggle. To this end we are here concerned with support for the kind of militancy manifested by the conventional civil rights groups in 1964.

The concept of militancy used here is that of *conventional militancy*. At the time of the interviews, the outlook of the conventional civil rights groups and spokesmen had a great deal in common. Each of these groups was urgently aware of the extensiveness of discrimination faced by the American black man. All called for an end to discrimination and segregation and demanded the admission of the Negro to the economic and political mainstream of American life. And they wanted these changes quickly— "Freedom Now." In pursuit of this end, participation in peaceful non-violent demonstrations was encouraged. For the purposes of this study, we judge militancy by commonly held standards of

* Using Negro interviewers does not eliminate all sources of bias. One of the ways of making out as a working-class Negro in America is to be suspicious of outsiders, even if they are black, and hence some respondents may have been hesitant to give their true feelings.

In addition, the interviewer, whether Negro or white, was usually higher in social position than the respondent. In some cases this may have inhibited expressions of militancy.

A further problem lies in obtaining a sample which is representative of certain segments of the Negro community, in particular unattached younger males. Even the U.S. Census seems to undersample this group. Given the unique experience and perspective of many in this group it is possible that they are somewhat more militant and anti-white than our sample indicates.

civil rights activists at the time the interviews were conducted.*

The following eight items were used as the test of Negro militancy in 1964; the response scored as militant is indicated for each.

In your opinion, is the government in Washington pushing integration too slow, too fast, or about right? (Too slow.)

Negroes who want to work hard can get ahead just as easily as anyone else. (Disagree.)

Negroes should spend more time praying and less time demonstrating. (Disagree.)

To tell the truth I would be afraid to take part in civil rights demonstrations. (Disagree.)

Would you like to see more demonstrations or less demonstrations? (More.)

A restaurant owner should not have to serve Negroes if he doesn't want to. (Disagree.)

Before Negroes are given equal rights, they have to show that they deserve them. (Disagree.)

An owner of property should not have to sell to Negroes if he doesn't want to. (Disagree.)

These eight items were combined into an Index of Conventional Militancy. Respondents received one point for responding to each question in a militant way. Those who said they had no opinion,

---

* There were, of course, important differences in the tactics, short-run goals, and sources of support among the NAACP, the Urban League, SCLC, CORE, and SNCC. The differences between the last two groups and the others became even more pronounced in the summer of 1966 with the raising of the issue of black power and the questioning of nonviolence and the role of whites in the civil rights struggle. But even in 1966 there is some similarity beneath the divergent rhetorics, particularly if one contrasts these involved and concerned Negroes with those uninvolved and relatively unconcerned.

It should be clearly understood that by militancy here we are not referring to black nationalist or extremist attitudes, although our measure of militancy does not preclude the holding of such attitudes. As will be noted later, the relative lack of support for black nationalism prevented a more elaborate analysis.

or who responded in an unmilitant way, received no score on the item. Scores on the index could range from zero (not a single militant response) to eight (militancy shown on all eight questions).

Scores were combined to produce three categories of respondents: militants, moderates, and conservatives. *Militants* were all those who scored six or higher on the index. Persons who scored three, four, of five were classified as *moderates*. Those with scores of two or less were classified as *conservatives*. The average score on the index was 3.7 in the South, slightly above four in both Chicago and the national sample, and nearly five in New York. Since the average respondent in all samples is a moderate, conservative respondents fall below the norm everywhere, while militants exceed it. Before proceeding, it is important to clarify just what it means in terms of responses to concrete questions for an individual to be classified in each of these three categories.

The militant Negro is one who actively opposes discrimination and segregation. He feels barriers now exist which keep Negroes from getting ahead, and is impatient with the speed of social change. He demands his rights *now* and is likely to agree with Martin Luther King that "the oft-repeated clichés, 'the time is not ripe,' 'Negroes are not culturally ready,' are a 'stench in the nostrils of God' (King 1964, p. 168). The militant Negro encourages civil rights demonstrations and his concern with the here and now leads him to think that Negroes should spend more time in the secular activity of demonstrating than in the otherworldly one of praying. He also would, or already has, taken part in such demonstrations and is likely to agree with St. Augustine that "those that sit at rest while others take pains [to act] are tender turtles and buy their quiet with disgrace."

On the other hand the conservative seems happy in his place or, rather, the place relegated to him by racism; he is not opposed to discrimination, thinks that Negroes who want to work hard can get ahead as well as anyone else, is content with the speed of social change (or even thinks it is moving too fast), feels that Negroes must show they deserve equal rights before they are given them, desires fewer civil rights demonstrations and would not participate in such demonstrations, and thinks that Negroes should spend more time praying and less time demonstrating. Those scored as moderates fall somewhere in between these two types: they protest some inequities, but accept others.*

Combining single items into a composite index has many advantages in measuring social and psychological phenomena. Responses to single questions are never entirely reliable; they can be based on such idiosyncratic factors as misunderstanding the question or interviewer error. By its very nature, an index measures *consistency* of response. On the Index of Militancy, an individual is classified as militant or conservative only if he is consistently so.

Aside from considerations of accurate and reliable measurement, an index of militancy has important descriptive functions. A summary assessment of Negro militancy cannot be arrived at if only single questions are considered; depending on the question asked, militancy varies widely. However, after constructing an index of militancy, one can decide on a single standard of militancy, in this case, at least six militant responses out of eight. It then becomes possible to say that, using this standard, such and such a percentage of Negroes are militant, moderate, or conservative in their civil rights orientation.

It should be emphasized that employing an index can never overcome the relative nature of social and psychological measurement. The concept of militancy used in this study is relative in at least two senses. It is relative to the questions included in the index; furthermore, those termed "militant" are militant not in an absolute sense but only relative to respondents with lower scores. Nevertheless, only an index of militancy allows us to judge, in a rough way, the extent of militancy in the Negro community as militancy is defined in this study.

---

* This measure is of necessity abstract and general. In particular local situations Negro militancy is not an easily defined homogeneous entity. The concrete demands of "militant" middle-class Negroes may be very different from, and even conflict with, the demands of "militant" working-class Negroes. Related to class differences in the substantive content of "militancy" are the differences in ideology and approach of groups such as the NAACP and SNCC. In addition, *within* these same organizations there is often bitter factionalism between the "moderates" and "radicals." In spite of this diversity of approach and the difficulty in narrowly defining militancy, at a more general level there is likely to be some basic agreement (such as over the items included in the index).

INTELLECTUAL SOPHISTICATION

It has been suggested that social class and social participation influence militancy because they result in intellectual sophistication, high morale, and a positive self-image. These factors are positively related to militancy and do in fact partly explain why social privilege and social participation lead to militancy. The intellectually sophisticated, as a result of their greater cognitive powers, their greater knowledge about the world, and to some extent the possession of a unique set of values, are likely to view the world differently from the unsophisticated. In this section four separate indicators of intellectual sophistication will be related to militancy.

THE *F* SCALE OR BREADTH OF PERSPECTIVE

An excellent indication of general sophistication is the well-known *F*-scale items (Adorno, et al. 1950). Although the scale was originally designed to measure a personality characteristic—authoritarianism—ever since the publication of *The Authoritarian Personality* a lively controversy has existed among social scientists over the meaning of the items included in the *F*-scale (e.g., Christie and Jahoda 1954). Much persuasive evidence argues for the view that the items in the *F*-scale measure intellectual sophistication or the breadth of a person's perspective, rather than deep-seated personality traits. Following this view, items from the *F*-scale were combined into a measure of breadth of perspective. The following items were used:

—Sex crimes, such as rape and attacks on children, deserve more than mere imprisonment; such criminals ought to be publicly whipped, or worse.
—No weakness or difficulty can hold us back if we have enough will power.
—Reading the stars can tell us a great deal about the future.
—People can be divided into two distinct classes—the weak and the strong.
—Much of our lives are controlled by plots hatched in secret places.

For each item an individual agreed to, or indicated he had no opinion on, a score of one was given.

Table 1 shows that this index has a powerful inverse relation to militancy. Among those with a narrow view of the world and the most restricted perspective (agreeing to all five F-scale items), only twelve percent were militant. This percentage increases to forty-one and seventy-two for those with the broadest perspective (accepting one or less of the F-scale items). Intellectual sophistication, as measured by these items, seems a crucial factor in determining militancy.

The broader and more liberated his outlook, the more likely a Negro is to be militant.

TABLE 1

MILITANCY BY SCORE ON F SCALE

| | Narrow Perspective | | | Broad Perspective | | |
	5	4	3	2	1	0
Militant	12%	21%	21%	33%	41%	''2%
Number	(101)	(267)	(315)	(261)	(117)	(25)

AWARENESS OF THE ROLE OF SOCIAL FACTORS

The F-scale items indicate a general kind of sophistication. But a more specific kind of sophistication is sensitivity to the way social factors shape human behavior: To what extent do persons recognize the degree to which their behavior is conditioned by their sociocultural environment? This requires an ability to detect the complexity of the world.

The questionnaire included several items designed to measure whether individuals were aware of the importance of environment in affecting social outcomes.* Militancy would seem almost to require recognition of the role of social forces in determining the present low status of Negroes. To think otherwise shifts the blame away from an unjust social order onto the failure of individual

---

* In a recent paper Glock (1964) has suggested that people's attitudes on a wide variety of public issues are influenced by their conception of man's nature, especially the weight they give to the role of the social environment.

Negroes. The following questions were asked and combined into an index of awareness of how social factors shape behavior:

—Poor people have no one to blame but themselves.
—Most people on welfare could take care of themselves if they really wanted to.
—If you try hard enough you can usually get what you want. *

A score of one was given for each instance of disagreement.

This measure is strongly related to militancy. Among those least aware of the effect of the social environment, only about one in ten was militant. This proportion increases steadily up to five out of ten among those who indicated maximum awareness of the effect of the social environment (Table 2). Thus, almost a necessary condition for militancy seems to be at least a mild awareness of how social factors affect behavior and, related to this, the perception that problems of Negroes are common to them as a group rather than as random individuals. Danzig has recently stressed the latter in noting that the concept of collective struggle rather than individual achievement is now dominant in the civil rights movement. He notes: "What is now perceived as the 'revolt of the Negro' amounts to this: the solitary Negro seeking admission into the white world through unusual achievement has been

---

* Kenneth Clark (1965, pp. 75 and 55), has recently noted that an important white rationalization for maintaining the *status quo* is the belief "that the poor are to blame for the squalor and despair of the slums; that the victims of social injustice are somehow subhuman persons who cause and perpetuate ther own difficulties."

Clark further suggests that "in response to white society's criticisms of Negro family instability and the patterns of poverty, many *middle-class* [italics added] Negroes have tended to accept the judgment of many whites that they [Negroes in general] are responsible for their own troubles, that economic dependency is related directly to immorality." It would be appropriate to add that such beliefs are held to an even greater extent by many working-class Negroes. In response to the statement "Poor people have no one to blame but themselves," 30 percent of those low in social class and 15 percent of those high in social class indicated agreement.

In a somewhat similar vein Le Roi Jones (1963, p. 134) has written of the "smell of the dry rot of the middle-class Negro mind: the idea that, somehow, Negroes must *deserve* equality." In this regard it is interesting to note that in response to the statement, "Before Negroes are given equal rights, they have to show that they deserve them," 55 percent of those low in social class indicated agreement, while for those high in social class this figure dropped to 27 percent.

replaced by the organized Negro insisting upon a legitimate share for his group of the goods of American society" (Danzig 1964, p. 43). Recognition that the problems of Negroes are group problems, and that the rights and privileges of an individual depend in large measure upon the status of the group to which he belongs, is an important defining characteristic of the current civil rights movement, and those who have this perspective are much more likely to be militant than those who do not.

TABLE 2

MILITANCY BY AWARENESS
OF HOW SOCIAL FACTORS SHAPE BEHAVIOR

	Score on Index of Awareness of Social Factors			
	Low			*High*
	0	*1*	*2*	*3*
Militant	11%	22%	36%	50%
Number	(219)	(457)	(312)	(92)

KNOWLEDGE OF NEGRO CULTURE FIGURES

Factual knowledge about the world is a general indicator of sophistication and breadth of perspective, regardless of race. For Negroes, having greater knowledge of Negro history and of important Negro cultural and political leaders is a type of sophistication that should be strongly related to civil rights interest, a more positive self-image, and militancy. While the questionnaire did not ask about knowledge of Negro history, it did ask respondents to identify a number of prominent Negro figures. Inferences can be made from knowledge of these figures to general level of information. It can be seen in Table 3 that having knowledge of Negro civil rights leaders and writers is strongly related to militancy. Among those unable to identify any of the civil rights leaders (Martin Luther King, James Farmer, Medgar Evers, and Roy Wilkins) only about three percent were militant, and this figure consistently increases up to a high of forty-two percent for those able to identify all four. Similarly, in identifying three writers concerned with protest themes (Richard Wright, Ralph Ellison, and Langston Hughes) sixteen percent among those unable to identify any were militant, whereas for those correctly identifying all three, fifty-seven percent scored as militant. When these two measures are combined into an index of knowledge of Negro culture figures, the percentage militant goes from three for those with least knowledge to sixty for those with the most (Table 4). It is the informed Negro who is militant; the uninformed are more likely to be sunk in apathy.

TABLE 3

MILITANCY BY KNOWLEDGE OF NEGRO CULTURE FIGURES

	Number of Civil Rights Leaders Correctly Identified				
	0	1	2	3	4
Militant	3%	9%	19%	20%	42%
Number	(32)	(193)	(151)	(268)	(448)

	Number of Negro Writers Correctly Identified			
	0	1	2	3
Militant	16%	29%	41%	57%
Number	(555)	(242)	(220)	(61)

TABLE 4

MILITANCY BY INDEX OF KNOWLEDGE
OF NEGRO CULTURE FIGURES

	Score on Index							
	Low 0	1	2	3	4	5	6	High 7
Militant	3%	9%	15%	19%	22%	35%	46%	60%
Number	(29)	(159)	(131)	(178)	(204)	(162)	(157)	(55)

INTELLECTUAL VALUES

The possession of intellectual values is also an important indication of a sophisticated world view. Respondents were asked to agree or disagree with the following three statements:

—I don't like to hear a lot of arguments I disagree with.
—A little practical experience is worth all the books put together.
—I like to hear all sides of an argument before I make up my mind.

These items were combined into an index of acceptance of intellectual values. (A score of one was given for disagreeing with the first two items and agreeing with the third.) This index shows a powerful relationship to militancy: Only two percent of the "nonintellectually oriented" were militant, and this figure increases steadily to fifty percent for those considered the most "intellectually oriented" (Table 5).

TABLE 5

MILITANCY BY ACCEPTANCE OF INTELLECTUAL VALUES

| | Nonintellectually Oriented | | Intellectually Oriented | |
	0	1	2	3
Militant	2%	17%	31%	50%
Number	(41)	(511)	(373)	(165)

A COMBINED MEASURE

The indexes of Acceptance of Intellectual Values, Knowledge of Negro Culture Figures, and Awareness of Social Factors, as well as the F scale, are each powerfully related to militancy. They are also strongly interrelated and may be viewed as components of a general intellectual sophistication. When they are combined into a single index, the impact of general sophistication on militancy is shown to be great. The proportion militant steadily increases as intellectual sophistication increases, from a low of only *five percent* among those least sophisticated to *eighty-five* among the most sophisticated (Table 6). When this index is collapsed into categories of very unsophisticated, low on sophistication, and sophisticated, the percentages are nine, twenty-five, and fifty-two, respectively.

MORALE

Movements for radical social change are unlikely to originate with "children of despair." They require a certain hope that a

TABLE 6

MILITANCY BY INDEX OF INTELLECTUAL SOPHISTICATION

Score on Index of Intellectual Sophistication[a]

	Very Unsophisticated 0	1	2	3	4	5
Militant Number	5% (20)	6% (88)	7% (102)	13% (143)	22% (175)	23% (141)

	6	7	8	9	10	Very Sophisticated 11,12
	31% (118)	40% (107)	56% (72)	49% (41)	67% (27)	85% (20)

Collapsed Scores

	Very Unsophisticated (0-3)	Low on Sophistication (4-6)	Sophisticated (7-12)
Militant Number	9% (353)	25% (434)	52% (264)

[a]Composed of *F*-scale score (5 scored 0; 3,4 scored 1; 2 scored 2; 0,1 scored 3); Awareness of How Social Factors Shape Behavior (0,1 scored 0; 2 scored 1; 3 scored 2); Acceptance of Intellectual Values (0,1 scored 0; 2 scored 1; 3 scored 2); and Knowledge of Negro Culture figures (0,1 scored 0; 2 scored 1; 3 scored 2; 4 scored 3; 5 scored 4; 6 scored 5).

better future, if not just around the corner, is at least a possibility, and the will or desire to do something to help bring about change. Demoralized people are unlikely to believe that an improved future is possible, and their sense of futility is likely to lead to apathy, not action, and to despair rather than demonstrations.

Our questionnaire included the following three questions, which have been combined into an index of morale:

—You sometimes can't help wondering whether anything is worthwhile anymore.

—Nowadays a person has to live pretty much for today and let tomorrow take care of itself.

—I often feel quite lonely.*

For each item disagreed with a score of one was given. This index is strongly related to militancy (Table 7). Of those with low morale (agreeing to all three questions) only fifteen percent were militant. This figure increases steadily up to forty-two percent for those with high morale (rejecting all three of the items).

TABLE 7

MILITANCY BY MORALE

	Low Morale 0	1	2	High Morale 3
Militant	15%	22%	31%	42%
Number	(270)	(356)	(259)	(203)

That low morale is related to lack of militancy may also be seen by using a different indicator: subjective evaluation of one's health. Other factors being equal, people who consider themselves in poor health should be more likely to be demoralized and concerned with their own bodies than with the body politic. Respondents were asked to evaluate their own health with respect to the categories of excellent, good, fair, or poor. It can be seen that having a low evaluation of one's health serves to reduce militancy. Only seven percent of those who described themselves as in poor health evidenced concern over the civil rights struggle. The figures are twenty-four, twenty-nine, and thirty-one percent, respectively, among those who said they were in fair, good, or excellent health

* These items were all strongly interrelated. They are similar to those used in the past by Srole (1956) to indicate anomie. The concept of anomie emphasizes weakening of an individual's attachment to society and his sense of isolation from others. However, they are used here simply as indicators of the somewhat less abstract concept of morale.

The criticism might be made that the middle question, rather than measuring morale, is simply a measure of acceptance of certain lower-class values involving the rejection of deferred gratification. But even the value itself no doubt arose from certain functional exigencies involving lack of opportunity, and hence can be seen as related to demoralization.

Two studies using somewhat similar items report findings comparable to those in Table 7. See Orbell (1967) and Gore and Rotter (1963).

(Table 8). This pattern was maintained even when the effect of age was controlled for.

TABLE 8
MILITANCY BY STATE OF HEALTH

	Excellent	Good	Fair	Poor
Militant	31%	29%	24%	7%
Number	(302)	(432)	(261)	(98)

A sense of life's utter futility and concern only with day-to-day existence have been found by novelists and social scientists to characterize a large proportion of Negroes in ghetto areas. Rainwater, in studying Negro life in the slums, notes: "In the white and particularly in the Negro slum worlds little in the experience that individuals have as they grow up sustains a belief in a rewarding world." He contrasts the "strategies of living" of the middle class to the "strategies for survival" of the slum Negro. One of the most prominent of the latter is the "depressive strategy." "As members of the Negro slum culture grow older, there is the depressive strategy in which goals are increasingly constricted to the bare necessities for survival (not as a social being but simply as an organism). This is the strategy of I don't bother anybody and I hope nobody's gonna bother me: I'm simply going through the motions to keep body (but not soul) together" (Rainwater 2).* Although our data imperfectly measure this strategy for survival, they do suggest that the "deadness of the depressed style" is a factor retarding the development of a militant orientation.

NOTHING BUT A MAN

Although slum children are still bitten by rats and their unemployed or underemployed parents face various types of subtle and blatant discrimination, for many the most biting

* He notes that the "strategies for living" of the middle class "are predicated on the assumption that the world is inherently rewarding if one behaves properly and does his part. The rewards of the world may come easily or only at the cost of great effort, but at least they are there."

and poignant aspect of the race situation in America lies at
the symbolic rather than the material level.* It involves the denial
of dignity to blacks and the acceptance among the subjugated of
many negative attitudes about their own group.

A low self-image among Negroes was consciously created by
many slave owners. According to those who wrote discourses
on how best to manage slaves, a crucial factor was developing
in them a sense of personal inferiority. "They had 'to know
and keep their places,' to 'feel the difference between master
and slave,' to understand that bondage was their natural status.
They had to feel that African ancestry tainted them, that their
color was a badge of degradation" (Stampp 1956, p. 145).

What was at one time consciously created became a natural
product of the organization of race relations in America. No better
example of the self-fulfilling prophecy can be found. The literature on race relations abounds with studies of "self-hate," "group
disparagement," and "negative group identification" among
Negroes and minority groups in general. Past research has clearly
documented that the negative stereotypes held by whites about
Negroes are often held by Negroes too.

One factor often thought to be associated with the upsurge of
racial protest in America is a change in self-image on the part of
American black men. The head of an important civil rights organization in the South states: "For years whites have decreed that
Negroes must think of themselves as whites thought of them.
Negroes are now insisting that the white majority revise its opinion
of them in accord with their own newly fashioned self-conception" (Dunbar 1964, p. 11).

Since the present study collected data at just one point in time,
it cannot document this presumed change in self-image. It also can
tell us little about the deep-seated processes of identity through
which this change is occurring. However, on the basis of two very
general questions, respondents can be separated into those who

---

* King (1958, p. 29) clearly notes this when he states: "Their minds and souls were so
conditioned to the system of segregation that they submissively adjusted themselves to
things as they were. This is the ultimate tragedy of segregation. It not only harms one
physically but injures one spiritually. It sears the soul and degrades the personality."

seem to have a positive image of their group and those with a negative image.

Only seventeen percent of the sample agreed to the traditional stereotype "Generally speaking, Negroes are lazy and don't like to work hard." But fifty-four percent agreed that "Negroes blame too many of their problems on whites."* These two questions have been combined into an index of self-image.† For each item disagreed with a score of one was given.

To protest the *status quo* would seem to entail the belief that the disadvantages of Negroes as a group are traceable to the systems of status degradation imposed on Negroes by the white majority. It would also seem to entail rejection of the belief that Negroes are lazy and do not like to work hard, since to believe otherwise would shift concern away from changing the social world to changing the individual. The data show that, among those considered to have an unfavorable self-image, only ten percent score as militant, while militancy increases to thirty-nine percent for those having a favorable self-image (Table 9). People who have more doubts about their group's behavior will no doubt find it more difficult to argue convincingly with others on its behalf.

TABLE 9

MILITANCY BY SELF–IMAGE

	Unfavorable Self-Image (0)	*Neutral* (1)	*Favorable Self-Image* (2)
Militant	10%	23%	39%
Number	(156)	(563)	(370)

* Another question included in the study which might have been relevant in the past was: "In general, do you think that Negroes are as intelligent as white people—that is, can they learn things just as well if they are given the same education and training?" Ninety-nine percent now say "yes." That Negroes have a higher estimation of their group's potentialities than whites is brought out by a recent nationwide survey of whites which found that among Southerners 57 percent said "yes"; among Northerners, 80 percent. The figures of 57 and 80 percent represent a steady increase over a twenty-year period (Sheatsley 1966, p. 223).

† It should be noted that in the strictest sense this measures group image rather than personal image.

It is difficult to say that having a positive self-image is a direct cause of militancy, since it is hard to establish which comes first. Most probably, the two go hand in hand and are themselves the result of other factors. However, table 9 suggests an important fact about militancy. While it is obvious that militant attitudes are a precondition of efforts to change the external world, they are also apt to produce changes in individual self-conception as well. Thus the development of a positive concern over civil rights can be seen as combating the unfortunate consequences of America's racial system at two levels.*

PSYCHOLOGICAL FACTORS AS LINKS
BETWEEN THE SOCIAL STRUCTURE AND MILITANCY

We earlier noted that higher social position and greater social participation result in militancy.† The suggestion was made that people with these characteristics are more likely to be intellectually sophisticated, to have a more positive self-image, and to have a higher morale. It was hypothesized that these were important subjective mechanisms through which sociocultural factors produce increased militancy.‡ We can now proceed to test the above hypotheses.

We have seen that these subjective factors are powerfully related

---

* This is brought out more clearly when we observe self-image among our three styles of response to the civil rights struggle. It may be recalled that those receiving scores of zero, one, and two on the Index of Conventional Militancy were called conservative; those with scores of three, four, and five, moderates; and those with scores of six, seven, and eight, militants (the group which the analysis has been concerned with thus far). Among conservatives about one in four had an unfavorable self-image. For militants this figure was only one in twenty.

In considering the development of protest in historical perspective, Rose (1948) sees protest and the development of a positive self-image as intricately linked.

† By "social position" (or social class), the author means level of education, of occupational prestige, and of income. The measure of social participation has two components: (1) actual participation—the number of organizations belonged to, the frequency of visits with friends, and voting in 1960, and (2) symbolic participation—the extent to which the respondent reads magazines and newspapers, both Negro and general.—Ed.

‡ These hypotheses were developed on the basis of participation in CORE and from the literature before the analysis of the data began.

to militancy. Furthermore, though each was positively related to the other, each had an independent effect on militancy. They are now combined into an index of subjective predisposition to militancy. On this measure, among those scored as low on subjective predisposition, only six percent support militant attitudes. This figure increases to fifty-six percent for those high in subjective predisposition to militancy (Table 10).

TABLE 10

MILITANCY BY INDEX OF SUBJECTIVE PREDISPOSITION

	Score on Index of Subjective Predisposition to Militancy *			
	Low (0,1)	*Medium* (2,3)	*Medium High* (4)	*High* (5,6)
Militant	6%	22%	43%	56%
Number	(247)	(478)	(176)	(138)

* Composed of indexes of Intellectual Sophistication (0–3 scored 0; 4–6 scored 1; 7–12 scored 2); Morale (0,1 scored 0; 2 scored 1; 3 scored 2); and Self-Image (0 scored 0; 1 scored 1; 2 scored 2).

Since it is hypothesized that both social participation and social class relate to militancy for similar reasons, and since these measures are strongly related to each other, they have been combined into an index of social involvement. As Table 11 indicates, the number militant runs from eight percent among those low in social involvement to fifty percent for those high.*

We are now ready to consider the joint effect of social and psychological factors on militancy. We have suggested that the sociological variables summarized in the Index of Social Involve-

* It should be clearly noted that the figures in this index and the one just above are based on categories collapsed in such a way as to provide adequate cases for more refined analysis. When these two measures are observed uncollapsed, for the social involvement measure militancy goes from a low of 0 percent to a high of 75 percent and for the subjective orientation index from 0 to 70 percent. However, the concern in this section is not with showing the separate predictive power of these measures but rather with seeing how much of the effect of social involvement can be understood in terms of subjective orientations when they are brought together.

The two measures are strongly related to each other. Among those lowest in social involvement, 44 percent are low in subjective predisposition. This figure is only 3 percent among those highest in involvement.

TABLE 11
MILITANCY BY INDEX OF SOCIAL INVOLVEMENT
Score on Index of Social Involvement*

	Low 0	1	2	3	High 4
Militant	8%	16%	27%	39%	50%
Number	(188)	(243)	(290)	(247)	(118)

*Based on Social Class and Social Participation indexes. Scores of 0, 1, and 2 were given for those in lower, middle, and upper social position and for those low, medium, and high in social participation.

ment are related to militancy primarily through the intervening mechanism of the psychological variables summarized in the Index of Subjective Predisposition. That is, the social variables result in the psychological, which in turn result in militancy. If this is the case, then when the Index of Subjective Predisposition is controlled, the relation between social involvement and militancy ought to disappear. To the extent that this relation disappears we can say that we have located the psychological consequences of social involvement that in turn are translated into militancy.

Table 12 considers the joint effects of social and psychological variables on militancy. The outcome confirms our expectations.

TABLE 12
RELATION BETWEEN SOCIAL INVOLVEMENT AND MILITANCY
WITH SUBJECTIVE PREDISPOSITION HELD CONSTANT
(Percent militant; number of respondents shown in parentheses)

Social Involvement	Subjective Predisposition to Militancy			
	High	Medium High	Medium	Low
Very isolated 0	*	31% (21)	7% (81)	4% (78)
1	40% (15)	34 (32)	13 (102)	8 (78)
2	62 (37)	40 (35)	21 (138)	5 (62)
3	49 (41)	50 (64)	33 (106)	12 (25)
Very involved 4	60 (40)	48 (27)	54 (48)	†

*Of the two respondents, one scored as militant.

†Of the four respondents, none scored as militant.

While the range of the original relation between social involvement and militancy was forty-two percentage points, it tends to disappear into meaningless fluctuations within two of the four categories of the Index of Subjective Predisposition and is greatly reduced in a third category. Only among those classified as medium on the subjective index do the original effects of social involvement remain strong. Within the other three categories (reading down the table), relatively no important relation remains between social involvement and militancy. With the exception of this one category, then, we see evidence that the social factors help produce militancy through the mechanisms of high morale, intellectual sophistication, and positive self-image.

Because this is an important but somewhat complex point, it should be elaborated. What we find is that, with the exception noted, social participation does not have much *direct* affect on militancy. Rather, social participation produces certain psychic states, such as high morale, and it is these which facilitate the development of a militant outlook. This is not to reject social factors as "causes" of militancy. Rather, it is to specify the way in which social factors seem to operate in producing militancy.

The failure of the relation to be reduced in the medium category of the Subjective Index may result from the fact that these persons are strongly predisposed neither toward nor away from militancy. They are likely to be neither very sophisticated nor very ignorant, to have neither a very high morale nor a defeatist morale, neither a positive self-image nor one that is consistently negative. Lacking a subjective view of the world that would prompt them either to militancy or to apathy, such people are more directly influenced by their social involvements. Among persons who lack a consistent subjective orientation (those scored medium) to inform their response to the civil rights struggle, external social considerations remain relevant. They may be primarily conforming to what those around them are doing (being militant if they are high in social involvement or apathetic if low), and their reactions are more likely to be fairly unstable and ambivalent. Where a consistent subjective orientation has developed, which either predisposes persons toward militancy or toward apathy, then the effects of social involvement are wiped out.

To an important extent, we have seen that the psychological factors examined in this chapter provide the mechanism by which social factors act upon militancy. The main reason why the most privileged and least socially isolated Negroes are the most militant is because they have the necessary psychological outlook to support and encourage militancy: morale, sophistication, and pride in self.* However, where such an outlook is found among the less privileged and more isolated, militancy is also found. When the privileged fail to hold such views, they also fail to be militant.

* While it is argued here that these factors tend to result from a high degree of social participation and higher social position, two qualifications should be noted. First, there is a margin of indeterminancy between the variables of social structure and subjective orientations, shown by the fact that some (but not many) of those low in social involvement were nevertheless high in subjective predisposition to militancy and some (but again not many) of those high in social involvement were low in subjective predisposition to militancy. Secondly, being subjectively predisposed to militancy may sometimes lead to social involvement. High morale and positive self-image are often no doubt relevant factors in determining an individual's eventual social position.

COMMENTARY on
THE SIGNIFICANCE OF "SOUL"

Since blacks are subject to discriminatory, and often degrading, treatment and since they have low prestige in the American system of ethnic stratification, it has been commonly assumed that they have relatively low levels of self-esteem (Rosenberg 4). Even though the findings bearing on this assumption are mixed—some supporting it, some not—this supposed lack of self-esteem has been used by social analysts in explaining a variety of behavior among blacks.

In his discussion of ghetto streetcorner men, for example, Liebow (1967, pp. 208–31) argues that a key expectation for men in our culture is that they earn enough to support a family. Lacking the education, training, and skills necessary for holding a good job, the ghetto male is unable to meet this expectation. Hence his sense of self-worth is very fragile. Motivated, Liebow maintains, by a desire to escape the nagging doubts about the self, the ghetto male indulges his appetites for whiskey and women and spends much time ingratiating himself with other streetcorner men—behavior designed to hide his failures and to prove himself.

Arguing in a similar vein, Clark (1965, pp. 63–67) writes about the fantasy life led by ghetto adolescents, who doubt their own worth. According to him, these teenagers often pretend to know about crime or to be doing something ghetto residents think important (e.g., going to college). By eliciting the admiration and respect of acquaintances, such fantasy behavior bolsters the pretender's flagging self-esteem.

Employing the concept of self-esteem in an analogous way, Hannerz (*10*) describes what blacks mean by "soul" and analyzes why the soul rhetoric has emerged. He argues that as the chances for social mobility start to open up, ghetto blacks find it difficult to continue blaming discrimination for economic failure. Many come to blame themselves. As a result, a latent sense of self-doubt develops. One way those who fail to "make it" have of protecting their self-esteem is to reject the success ethic of American culture and emphasize an alternative system of values and ideals. The alternative system commonly selected by ghetto blacks is "soul." Since an individual's self-esteem depends on living up to certain standards and soul provides standards that ghetto residents can live up to, the soul rhetoric enhances the ghetto black's self-respect.

Hannerz has entered a very controversial area of discussion. With the increasing emphasis on black pride and black consciousness in recent years, some scholars have argued that the black ghetto does have a culture distinct from the American mainstream (Keil 1966; Blauner 1970). They mean that there are distinctive norms and values shared by, and transmitted among, ghetto residents and that these norms and values govern their behavior. A social scientist holding this position might argue, for example, that marital infidelity is frequent in the ghetto because men there are commonly *expected* to be unfaithful. Other authors, however, doubt the existence of this distinctive culture. They believe that the behavior of ghetto residents can better be understood as an adaptation to their conditions of degradation and discrimination (Berger 1967; Liebow 1967, pp. 208–31). A proponent of this view might argue, as Liebow does, that running around with other women is a psychologically defensive maneuver to shore up a precarious sense of self-worth.

Hannerz does not seem to accept either point of view completely. On the one hand, he agrees that the black ghetto contains distinctive cultural items, such as soul food and soul music. On the other, he interprets the emphasis in the ghetto on these items as an adaptation to current situational strains. Implicit in this interpretation is the hypothesis that if equality of opportunity were to become a genuine and widespread reality in our society, blacks would progressively have little need for soul and would become assimilated into the mainstream culture.

The Significance of "Soul"

ULF HANNERZ*

In the black ghettos of the large cities of the northern United States, the last few years have witnessed the emergence of the concept of "soul." For instance, in every riot from Watts to Washington, hastily printed signs were rushed to doors and windows of Negro-owned businesses, all carrying the same message: Soul Brother. These businesses were usually spared. Perhaps this is why the term cropped up in a cartoon during the Washington riots—the cartoon showed a "Soul Brother" sign on the iron fence surrounding the White House.

Recently, while doing field work in a lower-class Negro area in Washington, D.C., I considered soul from the standpoint of its typical meanings in Negro slums in Northern American cities. The neighborhood's inhabitants share the characteristics of America's lower-class urban poor: a high rate of unemployment; a considerable amount of crime (including juvenile delinquency); and households headed, more often than not, by adult women, while the men are either absent or only temporarily attached to the family.

Of the people at the field site, a minority were born in Washington, D.C. The majority are emigrants from the South, particularly from Virginia, North Carolina, and South Carolina. Apart from conducting field work in this area by means of traditional participant observation, I also paid attention to those impersonal media

* Reprinted from "The Rhetoric of Soul," pp. 57–61 of Transaction, vol. 5 (July-August 1968) by permission from Transaction and the Institute of Race Relations, and of the author.

that are specifically intended for a lower-class Negro audience: radio stations (three in Washington were clearly aimed at Negroes); the recording industry; and stage shows featuring Negro rock and roll artists and comedians. (The phrase "rhythm and blues" used by whites to denote Negro rock and roll is now widely used by the Negroes themselves.) These media have played a prominent part in promoting the vocabulary of soul. On the other hand, both the local Negro press, such as the Washington *Afro-American,* and the national Negro publications, like the monthly *Ebony,* are largely middle-class-oriented and thus of limited value for understanding life in the ghetto.

THE NATURE OF SOUL

What, then, is soul? As the concept has come to be used in urban ghettos, it stands for "the essence of Negroness." And, it should be added, this "Negroness" refers to the kind of Negro with which the urban slum-dweller is most familiar—people like himself. The question whether a middle-class, white-collar, suburban Negro also has soul is often met with consternation. In fact, soul seems to be a folk conception of the lower-class urban Negro's own "national character." Modes of action, personal attributes, and certain artifacts are given the soul label. In conversations one typically hears statements such as "Man, he got a lot of soul." This appreciative opinion may be given concerning anybody in the ghetto, but more often by younger adults or adolescents about their peers. Soul talk is particularly common among younger men. This sex differentiation in the use of soul may be quite important in understanding the basis of the soul concept.

The choice of the term "soul" for this "Negroness" is in itself noteworthy. First of all, it shows the influence of religion on lower-class Negroes, even those who are not themselves active church members. Expressions of religious derivation—such as "God, have mercy!"—are frequent in everyday speech among all lower-class Negroes, in all contexts. A very great number of people, of course, have been regular churchgoers at some point, at least at the time they attended Sunday school, and many are involved in church activities—perhaps in one of the large Baptist churches, but more often in small spiritualist storefront churches. Although the people who use the soul vocabulary are seldom regular churchgoers themselves, they have certainly been fully (although sometimes indirectly) exposed to the religious idiom of "soul-stirring" revival meetings.

Further, the choice of soul (a term that in church usage means "the essentially human") to refer to "the essentially Negro," as the new concept of soul does, certainly has strong implications of race pride. If soul is Negro, the non-Negro is non-soul, and, in a unique turnabout, somewhat less human. Although I have never heard such a point of view spelled out, it seems to be implicitly accepted as part of soul ideology. What is soul is not only different from what is not soul (particularly what is mainstream, middle-class American); it is also superior. The term "soul" appraises as well as describes. If one asks a young man what a soul brother is, the answer is usually something like "Someone who's hip, someone who knows what he's doing." It may be added here that although both soul brother and soul sister are used for soul personified, the former is more common. Like soul, soul brother and soul sister are terms used particularly by younger men.

SOUL MUSIC—SOUL FOOD

Let us now note a few fields that are particularly soulful. One is music (where the concept may have originated), especially progressive jazz and rock and roll. James Brown, a leading rock and roll singer, is often referred to as "Soul Brother Number One"; two of the largest record stores in Washington, with almost exclusively Negro customers, are the "Soul Shack" and the "Soul City." Recently a new magazine named *Soul* appeared; its main outlet seems to be these de facto segregated record stores. It contains stories on rock and roll artists, disc jockeys, and so on. Excellence in musical expression is indeed a part of the lower-class Negro's self-conception, and white rock and roll is often viewed with scorn as a poor imitation of the Negro genius. Resentment is often aimed at the Beatles, who stand as typical of white intrusion into a Negro field. (Occasionally a Beatles melody has become a hit in the Negro ghetto as well, but only when performed in a local version by a Negro group, such as the recording of "Day Tripper" by the Vontastics. In such a case, there is little or no mention of the melody's Beatles origin.)

The commercial side of Negro entertainment is, of course, directly tied to soul music. The Howard Theater in Washington, with counterparts in other large Negro ghettos in the United States, stages shows of touring rock and roll groups and individual performers. Each show usually runs a week, with four or five performances every day. Larger shows also make one-night appearances at the Washington Coliseum. Occasionally, a comedian takes part; Moms Mabley, Pigmeat Markham, and Red Foxx are among those who draw large, predominantly Negro audiences.

The emcees of these shows are often celebrities in their own right. Some, such as "King" Coleman and "Georgeous" George, tour regularly with the shows, and others are local disc jockeys from the white-owned Negro radio stations. In Washington, such disc jockeys as "The Nighthawk," Bob Terry of the WOL "Soul Brothers," and "Soulfinger," Fred Correy of the WOOK "Soul Men," make highly appreciated appearances at the Howard. It is clear that the commercial establishments with a vested interest in a separate Negro audience have latched onto the soul vocabulary, using it to further their own interests as well as to support its use among the audience. Thus there is also, for instance, a WWRL "soul brother radio" in New York. But the soul vocabulary is not just a commercial creation. It existed before it was commercialized, and the fact that it seems so profitable for commercial establishments to fly the banner of soul indicates that, whatever part these establishments have had in promoting soul, it has fallen into already fertile ground.

A second area of widespread soul symbolism is food. The dishes that Negroes now call soul food they once called "Southern cooking" and still do to some extent; but in the Northern ghettos these foods increasingly come to stand for race rather than region. In the center of the Washington Negro area, for instance, the Little Harlem Restaurant advertises "soul food." There are a number of such foods: chitlins, hog maw, black-eyed peas, collard greens, corn bread, and grits. Typically, they were the poor man's food in the rural South. In the urban North, they may still be so to some degree, but in the face of the diversity of the urban environment they also come to stand as signs of ethnicity. References to soul food occur frequently in soul music—two of the hits of the winter 1966–67 were "Grits and Cornbread" by the Soul Runners and the Joe Cuba Sextet's "Bang! Bang!," with the refrain "corn bread, hog maw, and chitlin." Sometimes the names of soul foods may themselves be used as more or less synonymous with soul— Negro entertainers on stage, talking of their experiences while journeying between ghetto shows around the country, sometimes refer to it as "the chitlin circuit," and this figure of speech usually draws much favorable audience reaction.

THE NEGRO WAY OF LIFE

What, then, is "soul" about soul music and soul food? It may be wise to be cautious here, since there is little intellectualizing and analyzing on the part of the ghetto's inhabitants on this subject. I believe that this comparative absence of defining may itself be significant, and I will return to this later. Here, I will only point to a few basic characteristics of soul that I feel make it "essentially Negro"—referring again, of course, to urban lower-class Negroes.

There is, of course, the Southern origin. The "Down Home" connotations are particularly attached to soul food; but while Negro music has changed more, and commercial rock and roll is an urban phenomenon, this music is certainly seen as the latest stage of an unfolding heritage. Thus the things that are soul, while taking on new significance in the urban environment, provide some common historical tradition for ghetto inhabitants. One might also speculate that the early and, from then on, constant and intimate exposure to these foods and to this music— radios and record players seem to belong to practically every ghetto home—may make them appear particularly basic to a "Negro way of life."

When it comes to soul music, there are a couple of themes in style and content that I would suggest are pervasive in ghetto life, and are probably very close to the everyday experience of ghetto inhabitants.

One of these is lack of control over the environment. There is a very frequent attitude among soul brothers that one's environment is somewhat like a jungle, where tough, smart people may survive and where a lot happens to make it worthwhile and enjoyable just to "watch the scene"—if one does not have too high hopes of controlling it. Many of the reactions to listening to progressive jazz seem connected with this view: "Oooh, man, there just ain't nothing you can do about it but sit there and feel it goin' all the way into you." Without being able to do much about proving it, I feel that experiences—desirable or undesirable—in which one can only passively percieve what is happening are an essential fact of ghetto life, for better or for worse; thus it is soul.

Related to this theme are unstable personal relationships, in particular between the sexes. It is well known that among lower-class urban Negroes there are many "broken" families (households without a husband and father), many temporary common-law unions, and in general relatively little consensus on sex roles. It is not much of an exaggeration, then, to speak of a constant battle of the sexes. Indeed, success with the opposite sex is a focal concern in lower-class Negro life. From this area come most of the lyrics of contemporary rock and roll music. (It may be objected that this is true of white rock and roll as well; but this is very much to the point. For white rock and roll is predominantly adolescent music, and reaches people who also have unstable personal relationships. In the case of lower-class urban Negroes, such relationships are characteristic of a much wider age-range, and music on this theme also reaches this wider range.) Some titles of recent rock and roll hits may show this theme: "I'm Losing You" (Temptations), "Are You Lonely" (Freddy Scott), "Yours

Until Tomorrow" (Dee Dee Warwick), "Keep Me Hangin' On" (Supremes). Thus soul may also stand for a bitter-sweet experience that arises from contacts with the other sex (although there are certainly other sources). This bitter-sweetness, of course, was already typical of the blues.

Turning to style, a common element in everyday social inter-action—as well as among storefront-church preachers, Negro comedians, and rock and roll singers—is an alternation between aggressive, somewhat boastful behavior and plaintive behavior from an implicit underdog position. This style occurs in many situations and may itself be related to the unstable personal relationships mentioned above. In any case, it seems that this style is seen as having soul; without describing its elements, soul brothers tend to describe its occurrences in varying contexts as "soulful."

I have hesitated to try to analyze and define soul, because what seems to be important in the emergence of the present soul con-cept is the fact that there is *something* that is felt to be soul; *what* that something is isn't so important. There is, of course, some logic to this. If soul is what is "essentially Negro," it should not be nec-essary for soul brothers to spend much time analyzing it. Asking about soul, one often receives answers such as, "You know, we don't talk much about it, but we've all been through it, so we know what it is anyway." Probably this is to some extent true. What the lack of a clear definition points to is that soul vocabulary is predominantly for the in-crowd. It is a symbol of solidarity among the people of the ghetto—but not in more than a weak and implicit sense of solidarity *against* anybody else. Soul is turned inward; and so everybody who is touched by it is supposed to know what it means.

The few interpreters of soul to the outside world are, in fact, outsiders. LeRoi Jones, the author, is a convert to ghetto life who, like so many converts, seems to have become more militantly partisan than the authentic ghetto inhabitants. Originally he rather impartially noted the ethnocentric bias of soul:

> . . . The soul brother means to recast the social order in his own image.
> White is then not "right," as the old blues had it, but a liability, since
> the culture of white precludes the possession of the Negro "soul."

Now he preaches the complete destruction of American society,
an activist program that I am sure is far out of step with the
immediate concerns of the average soul brother. Lerone Bennett,
an editor of the middle-class *Ebony* magazine, is not particularly
interested in what he calls "the folk myth of soul," yet he explains
what he feels soul really is:

> . . . the American counterpart of the African concept of Negritude, a
> distinct quality of Negroness growing out of the Negro's experience and
> not his genes. . . . Soul is the Negro's antithesis to America's thesis
> (white), a confrontation of spirits that could and should lead to a
> higher synthesis of the two.

I am not convinced that Bennett's conception is entirely correct; it
is certainly not expressed in the idiom of the ghetto. Charles Keil,
an ethnomusicologist, probably comes closer to the folk conception than anyone else—by giving what amounts to a catalogue
of those ghetto values and experiences that the inhabitants recognize as their own:

> "The breath of life"; "It don't mean a thing if you ain't got that
> swing"; "Grits and greens"; and so on.

In doing so, of course, one does not get a short and comprehensive
definition of soul that is acceptable to all and in every situation—
one merely lists the fields in which a vocabulary of soul is particularly likely to be expressed.

The vocabulary of soul, then, is a relatively recent phenomenon,
and it is used among younger Negro ghetto dwellers, particularly
young men, to designate in a highly approving manner the experiences and characteristics that are "essentially Negro." As such, it is
employed within the group, although it is clear that by discussing
what is "typically Negro" one makes an implicit reference to
non-Negro society. Now, why has such a vocabulary emerged in
this group at just this point of Negro history?

For a long time, the social boundaries that barred Negro Americans from educational and economic achievements have been highly impermeable. Although lower-class Negroes largely accepted the values of mainstream American culture, the obvious impermeability of social boundaries has probably prevented a more complete commitment on their part to the achievement of those goals that have been out of reach. Instead, there has been an adjustment to the lower-class situation, in which goals and values more appropriate to the ascribed social position of the group have been added to, and to some extent substituted for, the mainstream norms. The style of life of the lower class, in this case the Negro lower class, is different from that of the upper classes, and the impermeability of group boundaries and the unequal distribution of resources have long kept the behavioral characteristics of the groups relatively stable and distinct from each other. However, to a great extent, one of the groups—the lower-class Negroes—would have preferred the style of life of the other group—the middle-class whites—had it been available to them.

Lower-class Negroes have only been able to do the best they could with what they have had. They have had two cultures—the mainstream culture they are relatively familiar with, which is in many ways apparently superior and preferable and which has been closed to them, and the ghetto culture, which is a second choice and is based on the circumstances of the ascribed social position.

This, of course, sounds to some extent like the position of what has often been described as that of "the marginal man." Such a position may cause psychological problems. But when the position is very clearly defined and where the same situation is shared by many, it is perhaps reasonably acceptable. There is a perfectly understandable reason for one's failure to reach one's goal. Nobody of one's own kind is allowed to reach that goal, and the basis of the condition is a social rule rather than a personal failure. There are indications that marginality is more severely felt if the barrier is not absolute—if crossing a boundary, although uncertain, is possible. According to Alan C. Kerckhoff and Thomas C. McCormick:

. . . an absolute barrier between the two groups is less conducive to
personality problems than "grudging, uncertain, and unpredictable
acceptance." The impact of the rejection on an individual's personality
organization will depend to some extent upon the usual treatment
accorded members of his group by the dominant group. If his group as
a whole faces a rather permeable barrier and he meets with more serious
rejection, the effect on him is likely to be more severe than the same
treatment received by a more thoroughly rejected group (one facing an
impermeable barrier).

Recent changes in race relations in the United States have
indeed made the social barriers to achievement seem less impermeable to the ghetto population. One often hears people in the
ghetto expressing opinions such as, "Yeah, there are so many programs, job-training and things going on, man, so if you got
anything on the ball you can make it." On the other hand, there
are also assertions about the impossibility of getting anywhere.
Obviously, a clearcut exclusion from mainstream American culture
is gradually being replaced by ambivalence about one's actual
chances. This ambivalence, of course, seems to represent an
accurate estimate of the situation: The lower-class Negro continues to be disadvantaged, but his chances of moving up and out
of the ghetto are probably improving. People do indeed trickle out
of the ghetto.

It is in this situation that the vocabulary of soul has emerged. It
is a response, I feel, to the uncertainty of the ghetto dweller's
situation. This uncertainty is particularly strong for the younger
male, the soul brother. While women have always been able to live
closer to mainstream culture norms, as homemakers and possibly
with a job keeping them in touch with the middle-class world, men
have had less chance to practice and become competent in mainstream culture. Older men tend to feel that current social changes
come too late for them, but they have higher expectations for the
following generation. Therefore, the present generation of young
men in the Negro ghettos of the United States is placed in a new
situation, to which they are making new responses, and much of
the unrest in the ghettos today is perhaps the result of these
emerging pressures.

This new situation must be taken into account if we are to understand the emergence of the soul vocabulary. The increasing ambivalence about one's opportunities· in the changing social structure may be accompanied by doubts about one's own worth. Earlier, the gap between mainstream culture norms and the lower-class Negro's achievements could be explained easily, by referring to social barriers. Today, the suspicion arises that under-achievement is due to one's own failure, and self-doubt may result.

THE RHETORIC OF ESTEEM

Such self-doubt can be reduced in different ways. Some young men, of course, are able to live up to mainstream norms of achievement, thereby reducing the strain on themselves (but at the same time increasing the strain on the others). Higher self-esteem can also be obtained by affirming that the boundaries are still impermeable. A third possibility is to set new standards for achievement, proclaiming one's own achievements to be the ideals. It is not necessary, of course, that the same way of reducing self-doubt always be applied. In the case of soul, the method is that of idealizing one's own achievements, proclaiming one's own way of life to be superior. Yet the same soul brother may argue at other times that he is what he is because he is not allowed to become anything else.

In any case, soul is by native public definition superior, and the motive of the soul vocabulary, I believe, is above all to reduce self-doubt by persuading soul brothers that they are successful. Being a soul brother is belonging to a select group instead of to a residual category of people who have not succeeded. Thus, the soul vocabulary is a device of rhetoric. By talking about people who have soul food, the soul brother attempts to establish himself in the role of an expert and connoisseur; by talking to others of his group in these terms, he identifies with them and confers the same role on them. Using soul rhetoric is a way of convincing others of one's own worth and of their worth. As Kenneth Burke expresses it:

A man can be his own audience, insofar as he, even in his secret thoughts, cultivates certain ideas or images for the effect he hopes they may have upon him; he is here what Mead would call "an 'I' addressing its 'me' "; and in this respect he is being rhetorical quite as though he were using pleasant imagery to influence an outside audience rather than one within.

The soul vocabulary has thus emerged from the social basis of a number of individuals, in effective interaction with one another, with similar problems of adjustment to a new situation. The use of soul rhetoric is a way of meeting their needs as long as it occurs in situations where they can mutually support each other. Here, of course, is a clue to the confinement of the rhetoric to in-group situations. If soul talk were directed toward outsiders, they might not accept the claims of its excellence—it is not *their* "folk myth." Viewing soul as such a device of rhetoric, it is also easier to understand why the soul brothers do not want it made the topic of too much intellectualizing. As Clifford Geertz has made clear, by analyzing and defining an activity one achieves maximum intellectual clarity at the expense of emotional commitment. It is doubtful that soul rhetoric would thrive on too much intellectual clarity; rather, by expressing soul ideals in a circumspect manner— in terms of emotionally charged symbols such as soul food and soul music—one can avoid the rather sordid realities underlying these emotions. As I pointed out already, the shared lower-class Negro experiences that seem to be the bases of soul are hardly such as to bring out a surge of ethnic pride. That is the psychological reason for keeping the soul concept diffuse.

There is also, I believe, a sociological basis for the diffuseness. The more exactly a soul brother would define soul, the fewer others would probably agree upon the "essential Negroness" of his definition; and, as we have seen, a basic idea of the rhetoric of soul is to cast others into roles that satisfy them and at the same time support one's own position. If people are cast into a role of soul brother and then find that there has been a definition established for that role that they cannot accept, the result may be overt disagreement and denial of solidarity, rather than mutual deference.

As it is, soul can be an umbrella concept for a rather wide variety of definitions of one's situation, and the soul brothers who are most in need of the race-centered conception can occasionally get at least fleeting allegiance to soul from others with whom, in reality, they share relatively little—for instance, individuals who are clearly upwardly mobile. Once I listened to a long conversation about soul music in a rather heterogeneous group of young Negro men, who all agreed on the soulfulness of the singers whose records they were playing. Afterwards I asked one of the men, who was clearly upwardly mobile, about his conception of soul. He answered that soul is earthy, that "There is nothing specifically Negro about it." Yet the very individuals with whom he had just agreed on matters of soul had earlier given me the opposite answer—only Negroes have soul. Thus, by avoiding definitions, they had found together an area of agreement and satisfaction in soul by merely assuming that there was a shared basis of opinion.

THE FUTURE OF SOUL

To sum up: Soul has arisen at this point because of the Negro's increasingly ambivalent conceptions about the opportunity structure. Earlier, lack of achievement according to American mainstream ideals could easily be explained in terms of impermeable social barriers. Now the impression is gaining ground that there are ways out of the situation. The young men who come under particularly great strain if such a belief is accepted must either achieve (which many of them are obviously still unable to do); explain that achievement is impossible (which is probably no longer true); or explain that achievement according to mainstream ideals is not necessarily achievement according to their *own* ideals. The emergence of soul goes some way toward meeting the need of stating alternative ideals, and also provides solidarity among those with such a need. And it is advantageous to maintain a diffuse conception of soul, for if an intellectually clear definition were established, soul would probably be both less convincing and less uniting.

The view of soul taken here is, in short, one of a piecemeal rhetorical attempt to establish a satisfactory self-image. I am sure that, for the great majority of soul brothers, this is the major basis of soul. It may be added that LeRoi Jones and Charles Keil take a more social-activist view of soul, although Keil tends to make it a prophecy rather than an interpretation. At present, I think that there is little basis for their connecting the majority of soul brothers with militant black nationalism. But organized black nationalism may be able to recruit followers by using some kind of transformed soul vocabulary, and I think there are obviously political attempts now under way to make more of soul. Thus, if at present it is not possible to speak of more than a "rhetoric of soul," it may well be that in the future we will have a "soul movement."

COMMENTARY on
THE STUDY OF URBAN VIOLENCE

The classic studies of black modal personality stress that discrimination and caste status constantly frustrate blacks. Whether it is being treated with disrespect or being insulted or seeing one's aspirations thwarted or not having enough money to buy necessities or being physically abused with impunity—such experiences incessantly irritate the black man's psyche. In line with the frustration-aggression hypothesis, it has been assumed that such frustrations naturally arouse anger and aggression in blacks (Dollard 1957, chapters 12–14; Kardiner and Oversey 1951, chapter 9).

A corollary of this assumption is that, compared to whites, blacks harbor a relatively high level of anger and hostile feelings. The evidence of this, however, is problematic. Some studies reinforce the proposition (Hammer 1953; Karon 1958). Others partially support and partially contradict it (Mussen 1953; Grossack 1957). And still others flatly contradict it (Touchstone 1957; Brazziel 1964; Baughman and Dahlstrom 1968, chapter 13). Despite the variety of findings, we should perhaps not reject the proposition out of hand. The measures of anger and hostility used in these studies are mostly projective and are often of dubious validity. Therefore many authors hold to the assumption that blacks have a high level of anger.

One of the main concerns in the literature has been how blacks handle their resentment. Writing in a period during which blacks were less militant than they are today, Dollard (1957, chapter 12) and Kardiner and Ovesey (1951, chapter 9) pointed out that since direct aggression against the natural target of their frustrations (whites) would be hazardous, blacks learn to inhibit it. This argument receives support from several experimental studies (Katz and others 1964; Winslow and Brainerd 1950). If blacks cannot vent their anger on whites, what do they do with it?

One mechanism that has been postulated (Kardiner and Ovesey 1951, chapter 9) involves replacing aggression with "acceptable"

behavior, such as ingratiation and passivity. Such behavior characterized blacks during earlier periods of American history, especially in the South. Another possible mechanism is indirect,
disguised aggression—such as malicious gossip about whites—or
furtive, hard-to-detect aggression—such as killing a white person
from ambush (Dollard 1957, chapter 14). A third mechanism is to
displace aggression onto other blacks. One of the themes in Rainwater's selection (2), for example, is that the anger arising from
their daily frustrations is directed by blacks against members of
their own families in the form of arguments, verbal abuse, and
physical fighting. The displacement of aggression onto other
blacks would also explain, in part, the high rate of violent crimes
that blacks commit against each other (Solomon, et al. *12*).

Inhibitions that once prevented blacks from venting their anger
directly on whites have progressively lost their force over the last
few decades. This decline can be accounted for by several factors.
For one thing, there has been a large-scale shift of the black
population from the rural and small-town South—where open
dissatisfaction by a black was usually punished—to the urban
north—where whites have been more permissive toward black hostility (Sears and McConahay 1970). Second, with the advances in
civil rights and in his overall status, the black American no longer
has as much fear of the white man as he once did. Third, ideological currents have emerged justifying the Negro's use of violence
in the pursuit of his rights. The resultant weakening of the inhibitions on aggression against whites has contributed to the rash of
civil disorders in the black ghettoes that the United States has
experienced since the mid-sixties.

Perhaps even more important in the eruption of ghetto riots,
however, is the increasing frustration experienced by the blacks.
"Increase" may sound strange. After all, the civil rights and the
socioeconomic condition of blacks have significantly improved
over the years. Here, however, the concept of relative deprivation
is illuminating.

Frustration, as Berkowitz points out in the following selection,
is not simply a function of the absolute level of deprivation. It is

always relative to an individual's aspirations and standards. While the condition of blacks has improved since the end of World War II, the gains have not kept pace with the rise in their aspirations. Although the living standards of blacks have increased, for example, there is still a huge gap between the average income of whites and that of blacks, and this gap has started closing only within recent years (U.S. Bureau of Labor Statistics and U.S. Bureau of the Census 1971, p. 25). Thus blacks have not participated to the same extent as whites in the growing affluence of American society.

As the discrepancy between the situation of the blacks as it is and their situation as they would like it to be has grown, their frustration has mounted (Pettigrew 1971, chapter 7; Grinstaff 1968). Empirical research corroborates the role that frustration has played in producing the ghetto riots of recent years (e.g., National Advisory Commission on Civil Disorders 1968, chapters 2 and 4; Ransford 1968; Sears and McConahay 1970). This link between frustration and violence is a major theme in Berkowitz's paper.

The Study of Urban Violence

SOME IMPLICATIONS OF LABORATORY STUDIES OF FRUSTRATION AND AGGRESSION

LEONARD BERKOWITZ*

The frustration-aggression hypothesis is the easiest and by far the most popular explanation of social violence—whether political turmoil, the hot summers of riot and disorder, or robberies and juvenile delinquency. We are all familiar with this formulation, and there is no need to spell out once again the great number of economic, social, and psychological frustrations that have been indicted as the source of aggression and domestic instability. Espoused in the social world primarily by political and economic liberals, this notion contends that the cause of civil tranquility is best served by eliminating barriers to the satisfaction of human needs and wants. Indeed, in the version that has attracted the greatest attention, the one spelled out by Dollard and his colleagues at Yale in 1939, it is argued that "aggression is always the result of frustration" (Dollard, et al 1939).

The widespread acceptance of the frustration-aggression hypothesis, however, has not kept the formula safe from criticism. Since we are here concerned with the roots of violence, it is important to look closely at the relationship between frustration and aggression and consider the objections that have been raised. These criticisms have different, sometimes radically divergent, implications for social policy decisions. Before beginning this discussion,

* Reprinted from *The American Behavioral Scientist*, vol. 11, number 4 (March-April 1968), pp. 14–17, by permission of the Publisher, Sage Publications, Inc., and the author.

two points should be made clear. One, I believe in the essential validity of the frustration-aggression hypothesis, although I would modify it somewhat and severely restrict its scope. Two, with the Yale psychologists I prefer to define a "frustration" as the blocking of ongoing, goal-directed activity, rather than as the emotional reaction to this blocking.

One type of criticism is today most clearly associated with the ideas and writings of the eminent ethnologist Konrad Lorenz. Throughout much of his long and productive professional career Lorenz has emphasized that the behavior of organisms—humans as well as lower animals, fish, and birds—is largely endogenously motivated; the mainsprings of action presumably arise from within. Behavior, he says, results from the spontaneous accumulation of some excitation or substance in neural centers. The external stimulus that seems to produce the action theoretically only "unlocks" inhibitory processes, thereby "releasing" the response. The behavior is essentially not a reaction to this external stimulus, but is supposedly actually impelled by the internal force, drive, or something, and is only let loose by the stimulus. If a sufficient amount of the internal excitation or substance accumulates before the organism can encounter a releasing stimulus, the response will go off by itself. In his latest book, *On Aggression*, Lorenz (1966, p. 50) interprets aggressive behavior in just this manner. "It is the spontaneity of the [aggressive] instinct," he maintains, "that makes it so dangerous." The behavior "can 'explode' without demonstrable external stimulation" merely because the internal accumulating *something* had not been discharged through earlier aggression. He strongly believes that "present-day civilized man suffers from insufficient discharge of his aggressive drive . . ." (p. 243). Lorenz's position, then, is that frustrations are, at best, an unimportant source of aggression.

We will not here go into a detailed discussion of the logical and empirical status of the Lorenzian account of behavior. I should note, however, that a number of biologists and comparative psychologists have severely criticized his analysis of animal behavior. Among other things, they object to his vague and imprecise concepts, and his excessive tendency to reason by crude analogies. Moreover, since Lorenz's ideas have attracted considerable popular attention, both in his own writings and in *The Territorial Imperative* by Robert Ardrey, we should look at the evidence he presents for his interpretation of human behavior. Thus, as one example, he says his views are supported by the failures of "an American method of education" to produce less aggressive children, even though the youngsters have been supposedly "spared all disappointments and indulged in every way" (Lorenz 1966, p. 50). Since excessively indulged children probably expect to be gratified most of the time, so that the inevitable occasional frustrations they encounter are actually relatively strong thwartings for them, Lorenz's observation must leave the frustration-aggression hypothesis unscathed. His anthropological documentation is equally crude. A psychiatrist is quoted who supposedly "proved" that the Ute Indians have an unusually high neurosis rate because they are not permitted to discharge the strong aggressive drive bred in them during their warlike past (p. 244). Nothing is said about their current economic and social frustrations. Again, we are told of a psychoanalyst who "showed" that the survival of some Bornean tribes is in jeopardy because they can no longer engage in head-hunting (p. 261). In this regard, the anthropologist Edmund Leach has commented that Lorenz's anthropology is "way off," and reports that these Bornean tribes are actually having a rapid growth in population.

Another citation also illustrates one of Lorenz's major cures for aggressive behavior. He tells us (p. 55) that quarrels and fights often tear apart polar expeditions or other isolated groups of men. These people, Lorenz explains, had experienced an unfortunate damming up of aggression because their isolation had kept them from discharging their aggressive drive in attacks on "strangers or people outside their own circle of friends" (p. 55). In such circumstances, according to Lorenz, "the man of perception finds an outlet by creeping out of the barracks (tent, igloo) and smashing a not too expensive object with as resounding a crash as the occasion merits" (p. 56). According to this formulation, then, one of the best ways to prevent people from fighting is to provide them with "safe" or innocuous ways of venting their aggressive urge. Efforts to minimize their frustrations would presumably be wasted or at least relatively ineffective.

I must strongly disagree with Lorenz's proposed remedy for conflict. Informal observations as well as carefully controlled laboratory experiments indicate that attacks upon supposedly safe targets do not lessen, and can even increase, the likelihood of later aggression. We know, for example, that some persons have a strong inclination to be prejudiced against almost everyone who is different from them. For these prejudiced personalities, the expression of hostility against some groups of outsiders does not make them any friendlier toward other persons. Angry people may perhaps feel better when they can attack some scapegoat, but this does not necessarily mean their aggressive tendencies have been lessened. The pogroms incited by the Czar's secret police were no more successful in preventing the Russian Revolution than were the Russo-Japanese and Russo-Germanic wars. Attacks on minority groups and foreigners did not drain away the hostility toward the frustrating central government. Aggression can stimulate further aggression, at least until physical exhaustion, fear, or guilt inhibits further violence. Rather than providing a calming effect, the destruction, burning, and looting that take place during the initial stages of a riot seem to provoke still more violence. Further, several recent laboratory studies have demonstrated that giving children an opportunity to play aggressive games does not decrease the attacks they later will make upon some peer, and has a good chance of heightening the strength of these subsequent attacks (e.g., Mallick and McCandless 1966).

These misgivings, it should be clear, are not based on objections to the notion of innate determinants of aggression. Some criticisms of the frustration-aggression hypothesis have argued against the assumption of a "built-in" relationship between frustration and aggression, but there is today a much greater recognition of the role of constitutional determinants in human behavior. However, we probably should not think of these innate factors as constantly active instinctive drives. Contemporary biological research suggests these innate determinants could be likened to a "built-in wiring diagram" instead of a goading force. The "wiring" or neural connections makes it easy for certain actions to occur, but only in response to particular stimuli (Berkowitz 1965). The innate factors are linkages between stimuli and responses—and an appropriate stimulus must be present if the behavior is to be elicited. Frustrations, in other words, may inherently increase the likelihood of aggressive reactions. Man might well have a constitutional predisposition to become aggressive after being thwarted. Clearly, however, other factors—such as fear of punishment or learning to respond in non-aggressive ways to frustrations—could prevent this potential from being realized.

It is somewhat easier to accept this interpretation of the frustration-aggression hypothesis, if we do not look at frustration as an emotionally neutral event. Indeed, an increasing body of animal and human research suggests that the consequences of a severe thwarting can be decidedly similar to those produced by punishment and pain. In the language of the experimental psychologists, the frustration is an aversive stimulus, and aversive stimuli are very reliable sources of aggressive behavior. But setting aside the specific emotional quality of the frustration, more and more animal and human experimentation has provided us with valuable insights into the frustration-aggression relationship.

This relationship, first of all, is very widespread among the various forms of life; pigeons have been found to become aggressive following a thwarting much as human children and adults do. In a recent experiment by Azrin, Hutchinson, and Hake (1966), for example, pigeons were taught to peck at a key by providing them with food every time they carried out such an action. Then after the key-pressing response was well established, the investigators suddenly stopped giving the bird food for his behavior. If there was no other animal present in the experimental chamber at the time, the pigeon exhibited only a flurry of action. When another pigeon was nearby, however, this burst of responding did not take place and the thwarted bird instead attacked the other pigeon. The frustration led to aggression, but only when a suitable target was present. This last qualification dealing with the nature of the available target is very important.

Before getting to this matter of the stimulus qualities of the target, another aspect of frustrations should be made explicit. Some opponents of the frustration-aggression hypothesis have assumed a person is frustrated whenever he has been deprived of the ordinary goals of social life for a long period of time. This assumption is not compatible with the definition of "frustration" I put forth at the beginning of this paper or with the results of recent experimentation. Contrary to traditional motivational thinking and the motivational concepts of Freud and Lorenz, many psychologists now insist that deprivations alone are inadequate to account for most motivated behavior. According to this newer theorizing, much greater weight must be given to anticipations of the goal than merely to the duration or magnitude of deprivation per se. The stimulation arising from these anticipations—from anticipatory goal responses—is now held to be a major determinant of the vigor and persistence of goal-seeking activity. As one psychologist (Mowrer) put it, we cannot fully account for goal-striving unless we give some attention to "hope." Whether a person's goal is food, a sexual object, or a color TV set, his goal-seeking is most intense when he is thinking of the goal and anticipating the satisfactions the food, sexual object, or TV set will bring. But similarly, his frustration is most severe when the anticipated satisfactions are not achieved (Berkowitz 1965 and 1968).

The politico-social counterpart of this theoretical formulation is obvious; the phrase "revolution of rising expectations" refers to just this conception of frustration. Poverty-stricken groups who had never dreamed of having automobiles, washing machines, or new homes are not frustrated merely because they had been deprived of these things; they are frustrated only after they had begun to hope. If they had dared to think they might get these objects and had anticipated their satisfactions, the inability to fulfill their anticipations is a frustration. Privations in themselves are much less likely to breed violence than is the dashing of hopes.

James Davies (1962) has employed this type of reasoning in his theory of revolutions. The American, French, and Russian Revolutions did not arise because these people were subjected to prolonged, severe hardships, Davies suggests. In each of these revolutions, and others as well, the established order was overthrown when a sudden, sharp socio-economic *decline* abruptly thwarted the hopes and expectations that had begun to develop in the course of gradually improving conditions. Some data recently reported by Feierabend and Feierabend (1966) can also be understood in these terms. They applied the frustration-aggression hypothesis to the study of political instability in a very impressive cross-national investigation. Among other things, they observed that rapid change in modernization within a society (as indicated by changes in such measures as the percentage of people having a primary education and the per capita consumption of calories) was associated with a relatively great increase in political instability (p. 265). It could be that the rapid socio-economic improvements produce more hopes and expectations than can be fulfilled. Hope outstrips reality, even though conditions are rapidly improving for the society as a whole, and many of the people in the society are frustrated. Some such process, of course, may be occurring in the case of our present Negro revolution.

Let me now return to the problem of the stimulus qualities of the target of aggression. Recall that in the experiment with the frustrated pigeons the thwarted birds did not display their characteristic aggressive behavior unless another pigeon was nearby. The presence of an appropriate stimulus object was evidently necessary to evoke aggression from the aroused animals. Essentially similar findings have been obtained in experiments in which painful electric shocks were administered to rats (Ulrich and Azrin 1962). Here too the aroused animals only attacked certain targets; the shocked rats did not attack a doll placed in the experimental chamber, whether the doll was moving or stationary. Nor did they attack a recently deceased rat lying motionless in the cage. If the dead animal was moved, however, attacks were made. Comparable results have been obtained when electrical stimulation was applied to the hypothalamus of cats (Levison and Flynn 1965). Objects having certain sizes or shapes were attacked, while other kinds of objects were left alone.

This tendency for aroused animals to attack only particular targets can perhaps be explained by means of Lorenz's concept of the releasing stimulus. The particular live and/or moving target "releases" the animal's aggressive response. But note that the action is not the product of some gradually accumulating excitation or instinctive aggressive drive. The pigeon, rat, or cat, we might say, was first emotionally aroused (by the frustration, pain, or hypothalamic stimulation) and the appropriate stimulus object then released or evoked the action.

Similar processes operate at the human level. A good many (but not all) aggressive acts are impulsive in nature. Strong emotional arousal creates a predisposition to aggression, and the impulsive violent behavior occurs when an appropriate aggressive stimulus is encountered. Several experiments carried out in our Wisconsin laboratory have tried to demonstrate just this. Simply put, our basic hypothesis is that external stimuli associated with aggression will elicit relatively strong attacks from people who, for one reason or another, are ready to act aggressively. A prime example of such an aggressive stimulus, of course, is a weapon. One of our experiments has shown that angered college students who were given an opportunity to attack their tormentor exhibited much more intense aggression (in the form of electric shocks to their frustrator) when a rifle and pistol were nearby than when a neutral object was present or when there were no irrelevant objects near them (Berkowitz and LePage 1967). The sight of the weapons evidently drew stronger attacks from the subjects than otherwise would have occurred in the absence of these aggressive objects. Several other experiments, including studies of children playing with aggressive toys, have yielded findings consistent with this analysis (e.g., Mallick and McCandless 1966). In these investigations, the aggressive objects (guns) acquired their aggressive stimulus properties through the use to which they were put. These stimulus properties can also come about by having the object associated with aggression. Thus, in several of our experiments, people whose name associated them with violent films shown to our subjects later were attacked more strongly by the subjects than were other target-persons who did not have this name-mediated connection with the observed aggression. (See Berkowitz 1965 for a summary of some of this research.)

These findings are obviously relevant to contemporary America. They of course argue for gun-control legislation, but also have implications for the riots that have torn through our cities this past summer. Some of our political leaders seem to be looking for single causes, whether this is a firebrand extremist such as Stokely Carmichael or a history of severe social and economic frustrations. Each of these factors might well have contributed to this summer's rioting; the American Negroes' frustrations undoubtedly were very important. Nevertheless, a complete understanding of the violence, and especially the contagious spread from one city to another, requires consideration of a multiplicity of causes, all operating together. Some of these causes are motivational; rebellious Negroes may have sought revenge, or they may have wanted to assert their masculinity. Much more simply, a good deal of activity during these riots involved the looting of desirable goods and appliances. Not all of the violence was this purposive, however. Some of it arose through the automatic operation of aggressive stimuli in a highly emotional atmosphere.

This impulsive mob violence was clearly not part of a calculated war against the whites. Where a deliberate anti-white campaign would have dictated attacks upon whites in all-white bastions, it was often Negro property that was destroyed. Moreover, aggressive stimuli had an important role. A lifetime of cruel frustrations built up a readiness for aggression, but this readiness had to be activated and inhibitions had to be lowered in order to produce the impulsive behavior. Different types of aggressive stimuli contributed to the aggressive actions. Some of these stimuli originated in the news reports, photographs, and films from other cities; research in a number of laboratories throughout this country and Canada indicates that observed aggression can stimulate aggressive behavior. This media-stimulated aggression may not always be immediately apparent. Some aggressive responses may operate only internally, in the form of clenched fists and violent ideas, but they can increase the probability and strength of later open aggression. The news stories probably also lower restraints against this open violence. A person who is in doubt as to whether destruction and looting are safe and/or proper behavior might have his doubts resolved; if other people do this sort of thing, maybe it isn't so bad. Maybe it is a good way to act and not so dangerous after all. And again the likelihood of aggression is heightened.

Then a precipitating event occurs in the Negro ghetto. The instigating stimulus could be an attack by whites against Negroes—a report of police brutality against some Negro—or it might be the sight of aggressive objects such as weapons, or even police. Police probably can function as stimuli automatically eliciting aggression from angry Negroes. They are the "head thumpers," the all-too-often hostile enforcers of laws arbitrarily imposed upon Negroes by an alien world. Mayor Cavanagh of Detroit has testified to this aggression-evoking effect. Answering criticisms of the delay in sending in police reinforcements at the first sign of rioting, he said experience in various cities around the country indicates the presence of police can inflame angry mobs and actually increase violence (Meet the Press, July 30, 1967). Of course the events in Milwaukee the week after Mayor Cavanagh spoke suggest that an army of police and National Guardsmen swiftly applied can restrain and then weaken mob violence fairly effectively. This rapid, all-blanketing police action obviously produces strong inhibitions, allowing time for the emotions inflamed by the precipitating event to cool down. Emptying the streets also removes aggression-eliciting stimuli; there is no one around to see other people looting and burning. But unless this extremely expensive complete inhibition can be achieved quickly, city officials might be advised to employ other law-enforcement techniques. Too weak a display of police force might be worse than none at all. One possibility is to have Negroes from outside the regular police department attempt to disperse the highly charged crowds. There are disadvantages, of course. The use of such an extra-police organization might be interpreted as a weakening of the community authority or a sign of the breakdown of the duly constituted forces of law and order. But there is also at least one very real advantage. The amateur law enforcers do not have a strong association with aggression and arbitrary frustration, and thus are less likely to draw out aggressive reactions from the emotionally charged people.

There are no easy solutions to the violence in our cities' streets. The causes are complex and poorly understood, and the possible remedies challenge our intelligence, cherished beliefs, and pocketbooks. I am convinced, however, that the roots of this violence are not to be found in any instinctive aggressive drive, and that there is no easy cure in the provision of so-called "safe" aggressive outlets. The answers can only be found in careful, systematic research free of the shopworn, oversimplified analogies of the past.

COMMENTARY on
*CIVIL RIGHTS ACTIVITY
AND REDUCTION IN CRIME AMONG NEGROES*

Psychologists distinguish two ways of handling aggression. A frustrated person may direct it "outward" or "inward." "Outward" means blaming others or physically or verbally abusing others —in general, seeking to hurt others. On the other hand, "inward" means blaming himself, feeling guilty, or feeling depressed.

Although historically the black person has tended, as we saw earlier (commentary on Berkowitz *11*), to inhibit his aggressiveness against whites, this does not mean that he has directed his aggression inward on himself. On the contrary, it is commonly presupposed that blacks usually handle aggression by directing it outward (Breen 1968; Figelman 1968; Gold 1958).* Several different explanations have been offered for this outward form. One is that blacks have a system of values that condones physical aggression, so that fighting, for example, is a socially acceptable way of resolving quarrels (Wolfgang 1968). A different explanation focuses on child-rearing procedures. Gold (1958) presents empirical evidence showing that black parents are more likely than white parents to use physical punishment as a disciplinary measure. For a number of reasons, this kind of discipline fosters the predisposition to outward aggression. These two explanations, of course, are not mutually exclusive.

The outward expression of aggression markedly influences the forms of deviance found among blacks. The paranoid, for example, attributes malicious intent to others, so he can be said to

---

* Several studies have compared blacks and whites on the Rosenzweig Picture Frustration Study—an instrument specifically designed to measure individual differences in methods of handling aggression (McCary 1950, 1956; Portnoy and Stacey 1954; Winslow and Brainerd 1950). At first glance, these studies appear to test the assumption that blacks are inclined to outward aggression. Closer inspection, however, reveals that Rosenzweig's instrument does not really permit such a test. The problem is that the scoring system is based on an extremely broad definition of aggression—one that equates aggression with whatever reactions a person may have to frustration. For example, looking to someone else for a solution to a frustrating situation is regarded as aggression. For us, on the other hand, such behavior does not indicate aggression at all since a reaction is aggressive only if it involves the intent to injure a person or thing.

direct aggression outward. When a black becomes mentally ill, he is more likely than a mentally ill white person to exhibit paranoid features (Breen 1968; Figelman 1968). He is less likely, on the other hand, to be depressed or show other signs of inward aggression (Prange and Vitols 1962; Lane 1968). Since suicide, moreover, is commonly thought to involve inward aggression, it is not surprising that black rates of suicide are much lower than white rates (Lalli and Turner 1968; Gibbs 1966; Gold 1958).

Outward aggression is an important element in crime among blacks. The proportion of apprehended criminals who are black greatly exceeds the proportion of blacks in the general population. This disproportion is especially pronounced for crimes of violence (Wolfgang 1968; Lalli and Turner 1968; Pettigrew 1964, chapter 6). Thus in 1969 blacks comprised only 11 percent of the United States population, but they accounted for 62 percent of the arrests for murder and nonnegligent manslaughter and 49 percent of the arrests for aggravated assault (Federal Bureau of Investigation 1970, p. 118). The overrepresentation of blacks on various indices of crime is, in part, spurious, reflecting discrimination by law-enforcement and judicial agencies. The authorities, for example, have generally been more likely to arrest, convict, and incarcerate blacks than whites for the same offense (Pettigrew 1964, pp. 136–40). The effect has been artificially to inflate the extent of crime among blacks reported in official statistics.

Nonetheless, the high rate of violent crimes committed by blacks is not entirely spurious. For example, cause-of-death data, which are more reliable than crime statistics, suggest that homicides are far more common among blacks than among whites (Pettigrew 1964, p. 142). The victims of violent crimes committed by blacks are ordinarily black themselves (Wolfgang 1968). The elevated incidence of such crimes seems due to several factors. Among the more important of these is the high level of outward aggression that blacks vent on each other—an aggression that is a response to the frustrations produced by discrimination, poverty, and relative deprivation (Gold 1968; Pettigrew 1964, chapter 6).

In the following selection, Solomon and his associates present data suggesting that during periods of mass civil rights activity, there is a sharp reduction in violent crimes among blacks. To explain this reduction, one has to consider three possible ways mass protest may affect the aggression of the participants. First, mass action may displace aggression. That aggression ordinarily channeled into violent crimes against other blacks may instead be channeled into protests against discriminatory conditions. Second, civil rights activity may give a participant hope and a sense of power, the feeling that he can do something about his situation. By reducing the sense of powerlessness, mass civil rights activity may diminish frustration and, with it, the aggression that ordinarily finds an outlet in crime. Third, direct action may promote unity and cohesiveness among blacks. One consequence is that social control would be more effective. Since violence against one's fellows would endanger unity, blacks could employ this enhanced social control to discourage it.

Whichever of these interpretations is correct—and more than one may be—the effect of protest activity is not only to change the social order but also to alter, if perhaps only temporarily, the psychology of the participants.

Civil Rights Activity and Reduction in Crime Among Negroes

FREDRIC SOLOMON, WALTER L. WALKER,
GARRETT J. O'CONNOR, and JACOB R. FISHMAN *

INTRODUCTION

In this preliminary report, data are presented on a possible reduction in crime among Negroes in certain cities during periods of organized community action for civil rights in those cities. The existence of such a phenomenon has been remarked upon by leaders of "direct action" civil rights groups in several communities. Yet, to date there has been no documentation of this phenomenon except for newspaper accounts of the one-day "March on Washington for Jobs and Freedom" of August 28, 1963.

According to the *Washington Evening Star*, there were only seven "major crimes" recorded by the District of Columbia police in the twenty-four-hour period ending at 8:00 AM on August 29, 1963. The *Star* noted that during the same time period in the previous week, there had been nineteen such crimes. Thus, reported major crime in Washington apparently dropped sixty-three percent for the day of and the night after The March.

Somewhat more surprising is an article which appeared in the *New York Times*. A reporter spent most of August 28th in Harlem

---

*Reprinted from the *Archives of General Psychiatry*, vol. 12 (1965), pp. 227-36, by permission of the publisher and by Frederic Solomon. Copyright 1965, American Medical Association.

and then wrote a story about the serious but happy mood that seemed to pervade Harlem on that day (Talese 1963). The story in the *Times* concluded with the following:

> Police cars patrolled Harlem's streets all day, thinking it would be a big day for robberies, with so many Negro residents away from home, for the trip to Washington.
> But in the evening, the desk sergeant of the twenty-sixth precinct reported no robberies or other crime.

It has been our opinion that in the long run, the effects of the civil rights movement on the self-image and social behavior of the American Negro will be as important as the movement's direct effect on segregation patterns. Two of us have already written extensively about the student civil rights demonstrators themselves—their attitudes, behavior and motivations, and the psychological significance of antisegregation activities in their life histories to date. The present paper represents the initial phase of an inquiry into possible community-wide "side-effects" of the civil rights movement.

Data will be presented which, in a preliminary way, tend to document the existence of an association between well-organized direct action for civil rights and a substantial reduction in crimes of violence committed by Negroes. We shall discuss the findings, their limitations, and their implications and shall offer some thoughts about further research.

HISTORICAL NOTE

The historic Niagara Movement in 1905 was the foundation for a national organization whose declared purpose was to wage a war against racial injustice, The National Association for the Advancement of Colored People. Since its inception, the NAACP has sought the support of both Negroes and whites in an effort to mount an effective protest against lynching, unfair characterization of the Negro in the news and entertainment media, job and housing discrimination, and segregated public accommodations. Almost from the very beginning, the NAACP sought redress for racial injustice in the nation's courts. Citizen participation in NAACP efforts was invited largely in the area of fund-raising to support the enormous costs of litigation. There was very little the lower-class Negro citizen was asked to do, personally, to strike a blow for his rights.

During the World War I period, the National Urban League began its work of helping Negro immigrants from the rural South adjust to urban living. This organization typically worked on two levels. First, attempts were made to educate and train Negroes to live in an urban setting. Almost every segment of the Negro community was involved in teaching, learning, or fund-raising. Second, the Urban League undertook to negotiate with employers in an effort to open new opportunities for Negroes. Although the Urban League has been, in a sense, a "grass roots" organization it rarely has urged its constituency to mount a public protest against prevailing systems of injustice.

It has been said that the work of the NAACP and the Urban League has laid the economic, legal, and educational groundwork for the present civil rights movement. The 1954 Supreme Court decision and the successful adjustments to urban living made by many Negroes serve as testimony to the effectiveness of their efforts.

However, it is not the use of legal skill, negotiation, or education which is the focus of this paper. We are concerned here with the process of direct action which began on a large scale in the 1955 Montgomery, Alabama, bus boycott; found new expression in the student "sit-in" movement; was dramatized by the "Freedom Rides"; and continues to express itself in the street demonstrations and voter registration efforts of today. What is direct action? Whom does it involve? How does it differ from other civil rights activities?

In the context of the so-called Negro Revolt, direct action is a nonviolent confrontation between the prevailing power structure of the community and an emerging center of power which demands changes in the legal, social, political, and economic fabric of the community. The main thrust of direct action has been via nonviolent public demonstrations, civil disobedience, economic boycott, and various actions designed to test the legality of local laws and customs.

Direct action involves different segments of the Negro community, depending on the particular technique being used. Economic boycotts and voter registration campaigns often directly commit a majority of the Negro community to the effort. Sit-ins and street demonstrations traditionally involve college-age Negroes, but there is mounting evidence that a wider segment of the Negro population is becoming directly involved in these especially active forms of protest.

Those members of the Negro community not directly involved in direct action are often indirectly and vicariously involved nonetheless. The violent reactions of whites, that is often the price of direct action, strikes close to home. Friends and relatives are often directly involved. The "battle plans" are drawn up in the Negro areas and are often public knowledge there. Negroes are often questioned about the movement by their white employers. There is strong community pressure to actively join in the "fight for freedom."

Contrast, then, the community involvement characteristic of a direct action movement with that of a local community's involvement in a battery of NAACP lawyers fighting a legal battle in the Supreme Court in Washington. Clearly, the average man sees himself as more immediately involved in a direct action, where willingness to be counted is the major requirement for participation, than he is in a legal battle that requires long years of professional training for participation in the front line.

METHODOLOGY

For three cities (two in the Deep South and one in a border state) data were collected from various sources, including official crime reports, medical records, newspaper accounts, and individual interviews with residents. Originally, a systematic attempt had been made to obtain relevant and reliable crime records from sixteen cities, twelve of them Southern. This was largely unsuccessful because of a number of problems. For example, two cities with crucial roles in the history of the civil rights struggle had changed their crime reporting criteria and the organization of their reports from year to year within the period in which we were interested. In another city, a Negro colleague of professorial rank in a local college, was denied access to the police reports which he had seen on the shelves of the public library just the day before. A general problem in the crime statistics which we *were* able to obtain was the absence of racial breakdown in most of the data.

Two central crime information agencies were contacted for their help—The Uniform Crime Reporting Section of the Federal Bureau of Investigation and The Crime Information Center of the National Council on Crime and Delinquency. They were of limited assistance; and we have drawn some inferences from data from several cities; but we have found only one Southern city with the kind of published crime reports that would be maximally useful to us in this research, and that is "city Z." Using an alternate approach, we have obtained hospital emergency room statistics and other relevant data from a small town which we shall call "town X," and we have a fairly reliable picture of developments there. Finally, via interviews, we collected some important anecdotal material which describes direct interaction between delinquent gangs and a young civil rights leader in "city A."

In evaluating crime data our focus has been upon major crimes committed by Negroes, with special emphasis upon aggravated assaults. There are several reasons for this focus. Local police departments report major crimes to the FBI under the heading of "Part I Offenses." (Other offenses in this category aside from aggravated assault are homicide, manslaughter, rape, robbery, burglary, larceny, and auto theft. Minor offenses such as drunkenness or gambling are much less uniformly reported by police departments and are not considered accurate indices of local crime pictures.) Of major crimes against persons, aggravated assault is by far the most frequent, so that variations in the number of assaults from year to year (or month to month) are likely to be statistically more meaningful than would be variations in homicide or rape, for example. Furthermore, aggravated assaults frequently result in some kind of medical attention to the victims; so medical personnel in hospital emergency rooms may keep records that may usefully supplement what appears (or does not appear) in police reports. Finally, as the FBI *Manual on Uniform Crime Reporting (1964)*, states, assaults are a fairly sensitive "index of social disorder in a community."

Of course, one must always keep in mind that, except for homicide and armed robbery, *all* crime statistics are reflecting merely the top of an iceberg of unreported crime. Most criminal acts never come to the attention of the police.

There is another problem in doing a study of this kind. There is a paucity of written material about the chronological development of direct action for civil rights in various geographical areas. There is a great need, we feel, for someone to chronicle the contemporary history of these developments. For our part, we have relied upon the *New York Times Index* for cities Z and A, an unpublished document written by college students detailing developments in town X, and interview material for all three communities.

CITY Z

City Z is a large industrial and educational center located in the Deep South. The city has had a reputation for being "progressive," within the confines of segregation. Many of the city's Negro college students come from the North. The city has a well-established Negro middle class. Although the police force is interracial, the Negro officers customarily restrict their arrest power to Negro suspects.

The civil rights movement in city Z, according to local citizens, began in 1960 primarily as a student movement in response to the initial sit-ins in Greensboro, N.C. However, the white community's reaction to the students' increased pressure for equality soon welded the whole Negro community (and its established leaders) into a unified force in support of direct action.

Two economic boycotts of downtown stores with segregated facilities and employment practices were nearly one hundred percent effective in terms of participation. In the Christmas season of 1960 and again at Easter of 1961, reportedly no more than a handful of Negroes could be seen shopping downtown on any given day. In response to this boycott by the whole Negro community, as well as in response to numerous public demonstrations by students, the major downtown stores finally did upgrade employment opportunities for Negroes, and all their lunch counters were desegregated by the end of 1961. There was virtually no organized civil rights protest activity in 1962, in sharp contrast to the extremely active years of 1960 and 1961. (Late in 1963, public protests resumed, focusing upon segregated eating places.)

Crime statistics included in city Z's annual police reports reflect trends which suggest that civil rights activities may be related to a reduction of crime within the Negro community. The general police and crime activity over the four-year period 1959 through 1962 is reflected in Table 1.

TABLE 1

GENERAL POLICE AND CRIME ACTIVITY
1959–1962

Population	1959	1960*	1961*	1962
Population	487,000	Data missing	Data missing	504,000
Police-patrolmen	519	519	538	541
Total Part I Offenses (major crime)	16,809	17,290	19,414	20,431

* Years of sustained civil rights activity.

This indicates that city Z's slow increase in population was matched by a roughly proportional increase in patrolmen. Major crime has also increased in the city's general population.

Various direct action protests were common occurrences in city Z in 1960 and 1961; there were no such activities in 1959 and very few in 1962. Table 2 shows that in 1960 the number of Negro vs. Negro assaults coming to the attention of the police decreased thirty-one percent from the 1959 figure. During 1961, the Negro vs. Negro assaults remained at this low 1960 figure. However, in 1962—a year which saw civil rights activity in only one month—the annual rate for Negro vs. Negro assaults returned to the 1959 figure.

Aggravated assaults within the white community did *not* vary in the same manner as did the Negro vs. Negro assaults. On an annual basis, the figures for cross-race assaults are too small to be particularly noteworthy.

The known offense data concerning aggravated assault cases are reported not only annually but also on a month-by-month basis. Such figures would appear useful in making a closer inspection of the possible relationship between variations in civil rights activity and changes in Negro crime rates. These *monthly* data, however, are not broken down by race, as were the *annual* data reported in Table 2. Therefore, any inferences from these data of an association between civil rights activity and assaults by Negroes must be based on the knowledge that whites account for only a small proportion of the total reports of aggravated assault. For the period 1959–1962, only 16.5 percent of the reported and recorded assaults were attributed to whites; thus, in any given month, one might assume that Negroes account for about four out of five of the "known offenses" in the aggravated assault category.

TABLE 2

AGGRAVATED ASSAULTS (KNOWN OFFENSES, BY RACE)

	1959	*1960**	*1961**	*1962*
Negro attacks Negro	531	371	373	536
White attacks white	85	79	100	101
Negro attacks white	8	9	13	19
White attacks Negro	5	5	5	9

* Years of sustained civil rights activity.

It is of some interest to note, as in the top line of Table 3, monthly averages for assaults in city Z. In the period 1959 through 1962 there were sixteen months in which newsworthy civil rights protest activity occurred (fifteen months in 1960 and 1961, one month in 1962). The average number of assaults in these "civil rights months" was thirty-nine; the average number of assaults in "noncivil rights months" was fifty-two, one third higher than in the "civil rights months."

TABLE 3
AGGRAVATED ASSAULTS (KNOWN OFFENSES)

	1959	1960*	1961*	1962
Monthly average (all races)	52	38	41	59
Annual assaults by Negroes	539	380	386	575
Annual assaults by whites	90	84	105	110
Annual grand total	629	464	491	711

* Years of sustained civil rights activity.

Of all the forty-eight months from 1959 through 1961, only three had less than thirty reported assaults. These were the months of October, 1960 (27), November, 1960 (23), and January, 1961 (25). It turns out that this period (October, 1960–January, 1961) was an especially significant one in terms of the history of city Z's civil rights movement. We have already noted the successful boycott of downtown stores which occurred from about December 15, 1960, to January 15, 1961. But this was preceded by a peak of mass activity in October and November, 1960. Mass arrests of demonstrators and the confinement of the city's civil rights leaders both took place during these two months of unusually low rates of assault.

It is also interesting to note that, except for the period just mentioned it was largely in the warmer months of 1960 and 1961 that most of the civil rights activity took place. Crime, especially assault, is at its greatest during the warmer months. The months of May, June, and July in both 1960 and 1961 were all months of civil rights activity, whereas these same months in 1959 and 1962 were inactive, as far as direct action for civil rights is concerned. The average number of assaults in these civil rights months, compared with these noncivil rights months was forty-six vs. fifty-six.

Certain anecdotal material from interviews appears relevant to the process by which the direct action for civil rights might have affected a violence-prone segment of the Negro community in city Z.

In 1960 and 1961, a student civil rights leader decided to spend as much time as he could in poolrooms and bars talking with lower-class Negroes about "the issues" over which the civil rights groups were then doing battle with the "white power structure." Although his success in gaining really active recruits was limited, he discovered several surprising things. First of all, virtually everyone in the bars and poolrooms was well acquainted with all the details of the sit-ins and boycotts as they occurred. Secondly, the two issues of mistreatment by the police and segregated employment were very meaningful ones to these people, and they found common cause with the civil rights demonstrators over them. Thirdly, and most impressive, a sense of the hope and of the power of organized direct action began to creep into the lives of these ordinarily rather hopeless people. This is illustrated, somewhat humorously, in the following incident which the student observed from a distance. One afternoon during the boycott, a bartender became verbally abusive to a patron who was apparently speaking rather loudly. Some of the other patrons told the bartender, "Let him talk! Let him talk!" When the bartender persisted and became even more abusive, all the customers joined in telling him, "You better let him talk or we'll *all* leave." The bartender let him talk.

The student placed this incident in the perspective of a "definite change of attitude" in the lower-class people with whom he had chosen to acquaint himself. During this period of direct action civil rights activity, "a 'cat' would have something to live for—not just a five day week, then get it off his chest by getting drunk on Saturday night."

CITY A

Our second city, designated city A, is in the Deep South not far from city Z. It has a population of sixty thousand, virtually no Negro middle class, and a reputation for police brutality and unequal administration of justice. Details of the crime picture are not available from its Police Department. City A is brought up here only because the young leader of the civil rights movement there has been quite successful in converting members of delinquent juvenile gangs into nonviolent workers for civil rights. The leader was interviewed several times, and his reports were corroborated by others familiar with his work.

The leader's work with the gangs grew out of necessity, not design. Soon after he had begun organizing meetings and protest marches and had come into conflict with the police, he discovered that his group's activities were receiving unasked for "protection" of a violent sort. For example, young people from delinquent gangs would "protect" a civil rights meeting in a church by standing outside throwing bricks at white policemen. Soon the civil rights leader—a former seminary student—was able to persuade the delinquents that they were needed instead as guards *against* violence, assigning them the job of "policing the area to make sure no violence occurred and to make sure nobody was waiting outside who should be inside at the meeting."

Over the next two years, about two hundred members of four different gangs of out-of-school, out-of-work Negro teenagers received some training in nonviolent techniques and have become rather effective workers for voter registration, thus aiding the regular members of the local civil rights group, most of whom are in school or have jobs. Reportedly, delinquency among the gang members has diminished markedly, although sometimes the civil rights leader has had to personally "cool off" gang wars and personal rivalries to avert the bloodshed that used to be the order of the day.

TOWN X

Town X, which has a population of less than twenty thousand, is situated in a rural part of a border state. The Negro population is about one third of the total. The town is controlled by a small number of wealthy whites who are adamant segregationists.

At the time of the Civil War, at least half of the Negroes were enslaved, and town X was the major slave trading center for the area. Geographical factors have made the city isolated, and even today it lacks a train service. In the 1920s the city became a "Company town" in which almost the entire labor force, white and Negro, were employed by one firm. After the second World War, however, various factors caused the decline of the "Company," so that early in the 1950s its machinery finally ground to a reluctant halt.

This alteration in the economic status quo produced a meteoric rise in unemployment. A federal report in 1962 described the town as "economically distressed." Despite the founding of numerous small industries during the last ten years, the unemployment rate among Negroes is still between thirty percent and forty percent. The new factories, being obligated to the city council, apparently preferred white workers, and as more and more Negro job applications were ignored, the first stirrings of racial unrest were heard in the community. For the Negroes benevolent exploitation by a small group had been replaced by total inattention. The disintegration of the Company had removed the barriers of social structure which had, for years, kept the Negro community in a state of enforced "contentment." A Negro adult from town X summed it up recently: "At one time we coloreds here used to admire the whites and look up to them. But, then something happened—I don't know, everybody was out of work—and they didn't look so good any more."

Later in 1961, members of several interested organizations visited town X to investigate conditions there as they affected Negroes. Gradually, the local chapter of the NAACP (which had been virtually inactive for years and was composed mainly of middle-class Negroes) was superseded by the formation of a local committee for nonviolent direct action. Early in 1962 demonstrations took place which were met with resistance from the white community. Throughout the year outside help continued to arrive in the town, and further sit-ins and picketing took place. About ninety percent of those arrested for misdemeanors in 1962 civil rights activities were so-called Freedom Riders from outside town X. Because of some disagreements within the local movement, the winter of 1962–1963 was quiet and relatively uneventful.

The spring of 1963 heralded the arrival of Congress of Racial Equality (CORE) officials and members of student organizations. The local nonviolent action group was under new leadership, and demonstrations were in active progress by May. A mass arrest took place, which highlighted the movement in the national press. In June, the Negro community had an explosive reaction when two teenagers were sent to reform school for illegal demonstrating.

Prior to this incident, some local leaders had experienced difficulty in raising crowds to demonstrate; but now, they had to
beseech them to remain in their homes, lest violence should ensue
from inadequately planned demonstrations. An army of police
reinforcements occupied the town and the situation resembled one
of martial law for much of the summer. Gradually, the mutual fear
of violence eased, and negotiations were resumed. Demonstrations
were suspended in August and September while a temporary compromise was being worked out.

Perhaps the most important single fact about the movement in
town X is that it was conducted almost entirely by *lower-class*
Negroes. After the pattern of most revolutionary movements, a
few key leaders were middle class. But, in fact, most middle-class
Negroes remained aloof from the action, and by their passivity
incurred hostility and contempt as "Uncle Toms," with the result
that their property was sporadically damaged by angry youngsters
on the periphery of the movement.

Because of the longitudinal nature of the civil rights action
outlined above (five months of maximal organization in 1963,
some activity in 1962, none in 1961), town X was thought to be a
propitious place to investigate the incidence of crime among
Negroes in temporal relation to the movement. For the purpose of
the study it was decided to investigate the period of May through
September for the years 1961, 1962, and 1963. It is felt that this
period reflects the situation in terms of a progression from virtual
inactivity to explosive action. This progression seems to be reflected in data on major crime in the town. The police reports of
town X for the months of May through September show that the
number of Part I Offenses recorded during this five-month period
in 1963 was thirty-one, a very low figure. During this period in
previous years, records show forty-nine reported offenses in 1962
and seventy-three in 1961. By way of contrast, the number of
reported offenses in the four months *before* direct action began in
1963 and in the three months after it had subsided, showed
approximately the same crime rate as the previous two years (see
Table 4). Unfortunately, these figures do not include reports of
assaults, and there is no racial breakdown, although it is known

that Negroes *normally account for about fifty percent* of the arrests for "major crime" in town X.*

TABLE 4
TOWN X PART I OFFENSES
(Murder, Robbery, Burglary, Larceny)

	1961	1962	1963
May–September	73	49	31
January–April	38	49	35
October–September	21	31	30
Total (annual)	132	129	96
Total adult arrests by the police force—all offenses	(Data missing)	386	429

Because the relevant police records with racial breakdowns are unavailable, we thought of studying the Emergency Case records of the General Hospital in an effort to estimate the number of injuries resulting from assaults by Negroes during the time periods in question. Table 5 shows the incidences including those arising from racial rioting and police violence. The last line in Table 5 is corrected to exclude these cases, and represents the "routine" number of cases treated. Both tables exclude assaults perpetrated in the local labor camps, as it is felt that those were essentially nonconnected with the movement. We were told that the Negro migrant workers, who come to the area during the summer months to harvest the crops, would not associate themselves in any way with the movement, and, in fact, stayed away from the town

* An examination of Magistrate's Court's gross records of people arraigned on a variety of crimes indicates a similar trend. In the summer of 1962, 53 percent fewer *local Negroes* were arraigned on the various charges than were arraigned in the summer of 1961. The summer of 1963 saw a slight rise in the total, in that a reduction of only 25 percent below the 1961 figure was apparent. It is fair to assume, though, that the reason 1963 showed more cases than 1962 is that a substantial number of disorderly conduct and trespass arrests took place as part of 1963's civil rights effort by local Negroes. (The 1962 civil rights arrests, it will be recalled, were largely of people from out of town, though that year's efforts were obviously watched by the local populace with avid interest.)

because they were "scared." (Parenthetically, it *is* interesting to note that the incidence of assault among the migrant workers showed no appreciable change. Indeed a slight increase was apparent, whereas the "routine" cases from local Negroes diminished sharply.)

TABLE 5
TOWN X EMERGENCY ROOM CASES
ASSAULTS BY NEGROES

	May	June	July	Aug	Sept	Total
1961	1	7	7	2	4	21
1962	1	4	0	7	1	13
1963						
All cases	0	1	4	4	1	10
1963 "ordinary" cases	(0)	(0)	(0)	(4)	(1)	5

While it is felt that these figures do not represent the total number of assaults, they would seem to reflect a fairly constant proportion of the incidences and thus be suitable for our purposes. The one Negro physician in the community quite independently supported the accuracy of the trend shown in these hospital records in stating that "during the summer of 1963 I stitched only three or four cases, when in other years I would have seen a dozen in the same period of time."

Many local leaders were interviewed in conjunction with the study, and their anecdotal impressions are of some interest. For example, the Public Health Inspector, whose duty it is to control the spread of venereal disease, particularly among crime-prone lower-class Negroes well known to him, observed: "Many of the contacts I sought, who would normally have been in jail, were living at home or could be found with their friends."

One of the principal Negro leaders estimates that there was much less crime in general: "People became interested in the movement, and were reluctant to do anything to jeopardize its progress. Most of the 1962 arrests were Freedom Riders—not locals. By 1963 there was a unification of common interest, and people who before were indigent and depressed, suddenly found that they had something to live and fight for."

Another local movement leader had anticipated trouble from the "winos" (alcoholics) and for this reason she felt that they should not be included in the protest marches. However, she was surprised to find that with special attention from the sober and more responsible members, they behaved themselves admirably and turned out to be exemplary, if somewhat passive, demonstrators. A student leader attests to this and quotes the case of a young alcoholic who had a long history of arrests. "He apparently was accustomed to being in the County Jail, but while the movement was strong and active he never was in trouble, although he continued to drink." When the student returned to the town later in the year, months after all activity had ceased, he met the man leaving the jail; he had just been released and was heading for a bar.

Many factors may influence this apparent decrease in the incidence of crimes involving personal violence. Most of the local people quoted above mentioned that a temporary ban on retail sales of alcohol and the imposition of a curfew were important inhibitors. One reliable report, however, indicates that "bootlegged" alcohol was readily available for anyone who wanted it. Group identification and interest in the Cause, strengthened by the persuasion of the leaders, were the factors most commonly selected for mention. One leader said that during the marches "We found ourselves breaking ranks to intervene in sidewalk scuffles and family squabbles, so that there may well have been more than an indirect influence."

The civil rights struggle in town X was not totally devoid of incidental violence. A student civil rights worker, who spent the summer in town X, indicts a small splinter group for the violence which did occur in the early summer of 1963. "There was a great deal of interest during early July in the movement from this group—young, violent types. As soon as the police had a permanent hold, and the movement continued to threaten to demonstrate but never did, they provided the biggest lobby to continue demonstrations, even at gun and bayonet point, and constantly threatened to act on their own if the movement itself would not. They spoke to us often about this, because we (the college student staff) also wanted to resume demonstrations. They never carried out any of their major threats, although one assumes that they were the group responsible for the various crimes related to the movement from the Negro ward," such as throwing bricks at policemen and attacking the property of whites and so-called Uncle Toms.

Nevertheless, there are certain factors in town X that make it quite surprising that *more* violence did not occur. Among the lower-class Negroes of town X, there is a great contempt for the local police force. Arrests and jail sentences do not carry any social stigma; imprisonment is merely something unpleasant which must be endured. On one occasion during the summer, a group of jeering Negroes surrounded a white policeman who had drawn his gun, and dared him to shoot. The same attitude of sullen hostility was in evidence toward the dogs which were used occasionally by the police. (The dogs were returned to their kennels, we understand, when it became clear that they had failed to have the desired effect on the demonstrators.) In other words, town X could be considered a "tough" town with a "tough" population of unemployed Negroes, many of whom became actively involved in direct action programs for civil rights. The fact that crimes of violence apparently *decreased* during this tense summer would hardly have been a predictable phenomenon.

COMMENT

The material we have presented raises many questions, certainly raises more questions than it has answered. We hasten to state categorically that the findings are suggestive, by no means conclusive.

There seem to us to be four areas that warrant discussion and exploration:

1. To what extent are the data reliable?
2. Assuming the data *are* reliable and suggest a diminished incidence of crime committed by Negroes during periods of direct

action for civil rights, what are the possible explanations for this relationship?

3. What implications might all this have for an understanding of violence in populations of the poverty-stricken and socially disadvantaged?

4. What further research is indicated to shed light on the effect of organized social movements on the behavior of lower-class populations?

We have already remarked that probably the majority of criminal acts go unreported and that collection of crime data by police departments is often quite unreliable. One can never be sure what factors, including chance, may be operating to influence the crime reporting process. Even when one finds a police department (such as the one in city Z) that prides itself on its crime reporting, there is still much to be desired in the uniformity of crime reporting from city to city.

Nonetheless, even taking these limitations into account, it is interesting that the statistics we have collected show the definite trend that they do, and that supplementing the police statistics with hospital Emergency Room records (as we have done in town X) reveals the same trend. It is possible to argue that this apparent trend is based on a change in contact between the police and the Negro community. Perhaps the police were so busy with civil rights demonstrators that their contact with or recording of crimes of violence within the Negro community was altered; i.e., their attention and concentration of forces were elsewhere. Or, perhaps, during economic boycotts Negroes are more careful to shield crime from the eyes of the police and white authorities. If these be so, any drop in crime rate is more illusory than real.

While these are real possibilities, there is at least anecdotal evidence to the contrary. During periods of "racial tension" in the South, the police force generally pays particularly close attention to the Negro sections of town and keeps a close vigil for potential violence of all kinds. Furthermore, where we have been able to supplement police data with medical information, as in town X, the incidence of medically recorded injuries resulting from personal violence has shown a decrease during civil rights activity.

Obviously, it would further strengthen the case for our hypothesis if we could present parallel data from comparable communities which have had no direct action civil rights programs. Unfortunately, we have not yet been able to obtain appropriately comparative data.

Assuming for the time being, then, that the reduction in the incidence of crime was *real*, not merely apparent, how might this be explained?

Perhaps when there are important events upon which the attention of any community is focused there is distraction from the forms of behavior which might otherwise lead to crime. Is the reduction of crime in these instances an epiphenomenon of the focusing of group attention on unusual public events? (There are some reports, for example, that crime in Washington, D. C., was reduced somewhat during the period following President Kennedy's assassination. Would the same have been true of the 1962 Cuban Crisis or of a World Series?)

Or, perhaps the explanation lies in a deterrent effect of the increased number of policemen on patrol during periods of protest, or the potentiality of such an increase. In city Z, at least, this "deterrence" could not have been a large factor in the sustained diminution of assaults during 1960 and 1961. The major form of protest during that time was an economic boycott which did not involve the local police very extensively.

There is some sociological and psychological data that might suggest a basis for the possible existence of a causal relationship between organized direct action for civil rights and reduced crime among Negroes. A long-term effect of segregation upon lower-class Negroes has been a blocking off of their social and self-assertion—economically, socially, and psychologically (Kardiner and Ovesey, 1951; Fishman and Solomon 1963; and Solomon and Fishman 1964b). Open expression of their resentment against second class status has been blocked off in both South and North. We would agree with other authors that this damming-up of resentment is one reason for the high incidence of crime among lower-class Negroes (Kardiner and Ovesey, 1951; and Myrdal, 1944); this is further supported by the fact that the vast majority of violent acts by Negroes are directed toward other Negroes. To put it another way, one might say that for the lower-class Negro, avenues have been closed off by the social structure, so that violent crime against members of his own race is one of the channels of least resistance open to him for the expression of aggression. When he becomes aggressive *against segregation,* the Negro's sense of personal and group identity is altered; race pride partially replaces self-hatred, and aggression need not be directed so destructively at the self or the community. The concept of "prosocial acting out" has been set forth elsewhere (Fishman and Solomon 1963; and Solomon and Fishman, 1964a) to describe risky, aggressive, somewhat impulsive actions which the actor sees himself taking "for the good of society." These actions are thus distinguished from the diffuse lashing out against social institutions that characterizes "antisocial acting out"—although in some cases, the psychodynamic roots of the two types of behavior may be quite similar.

When large scale direct action civil rights activities are launched in a community, the leaders face a herculean task of community organization. The members of the community must be recruited, trained, and organized into a disciplined, nonviolent army. Networks of communication and transportation must be arranged, for large numbers of people must be united behind a single effort. It is the pooling of resources, the setting up and certifying of goals, priorities, and methods in a community effort to produce social change that draws neighbors together in an organization whose very existence would tend to discourage crime (particularly crimes of violence against each other). If the community organization process is successful, each man, through the combined strength of his and his neighbors' efforts, can have that seat at the "community bargaining table" that has traditionally been denied him. Each man learns that possibly his personal welfare and certainly the welfare of the movement requires unity in the Negro community. As a result of the need for unity, people begin to know their neighbors and their neighbors' problems. A spirit of common concern pervades the community and serves to discourage crimes of violence.

The data we have presented do not indicate any long-lasting effect of organized civil rights activity upon the crime pictures of city Z and town X—although seemingly permanent gains have been made with the juvenile gangs of city A. In looking at the crime data from city Z and town X, it is clear that after the major civil rights action had ceased, the number of reported crimes by Negroes returned fairly promptly to the frequency that was customary before the "movement" began. It is impressive, though, that a reduced crime rate for Negroes was sustained in city Z for two full years before going back up to former levels. Furthermore, when crime rates returned to frequencies comparable to earlier years, there was no "rebound phenomenon" of a net *increase* in violence which (had it occurred) might have been attributed to frustration of hopes which had been "stirred up" by the civil rights movement. Indeed, in city Z the 1962 frequency of assaults by Negroes is somewhat *below* what one would expect in view of the increase in population over 1959.

It is apparent from these data that direct or vicarious participation in the partial successes of civil rights direct action movements did not solve all the problems of violence-prone, socially disadvantaged Negroes. In recent months in town X, for example, the leaders of the civil rights movement have become less and less interested in equal access to public accommodations but increasingly adamant about obtaining federal relief of poverty and unemployment in the area. Whether civil rights leaders across the nation are feeling a continuing responsibility to plan for and press for improvements in the life conditions of the low-income Negro is a question that cannot be dealt with here, although there are several recent signs pointing in this direction.* This shift in emphasis by civil rights groups represents an increasingly sophisticated awareness of the multifaceted nature of the problems faced by Negroes, both North and South. In spite of successes in the

---

* For example, in November, 1963, the "militant" Student Nonviolent Coordinating Committee (SNCC) held its annual leadership conference on the theme of "Food and Jobs." The meeting was held in Washington and featured conference-workshops with federal officials on the subject of existing programs that could possibly be of aid to the rural Negro in the South.

South, however, the direct action civil rights groups have been largely unable to organize the socially disadvantaged Negroes of the North—perhaps because they have been perceived by the residents of Northern Negro slums as being mainly interested in public accommodations and voting rights. At this point in time, the deprived Northern Negro is cynical about the value of a public accommodations law or the right to vote. He lives in areas of the country where there are few statutory or semilegal sanctions to prevent him from eating at a lunch counter, going to a movie, or voting. Yet, he is still denied equal employment opportunities, good housing, and respect from police officers. The Northern slum Negro sees himself as still not being "free," and until effective methods are found to combat his problems, he will often choose between the unfortunate alternatives of either accepting his fate or lashing out with hate and violence. In our opinion it seems unlikely that the civil rights groups will be able to effectively organize the socially deprived Negro in the urban North; it may instead be the black "hate" groups that will be successful, unless substantial efforts are made to relieve the social and economic deprivation of the Northern Negro.

This brings us to our concluding remarks. We feel it should be emphasized that if our findings are verified, there is then a very strong argument that the kind of community organization and psychological mobilization inherent in the civil rights struggle may be of prime importance in the development and implementation of various crime prevention programs and "anti-poverty" programs. It would appear that such programs—which, after all, are often aimed at lower-class Negroes—could learn a great deal from the interactional and motivational processes involved in the direct action civil rights movement. Yet, surprisingly little research has been done or is being done on just *how* the movement functions and the process of its development. The study of process requires a multidimensional approach including both that of statistical reporting and anecdotal observations. This technique requires considerable further development. It is our hope that the need for such research will have been made more apparent by this presentation.

SUMMARY

Data are presented which suggest a substantial reduction in crimes of violence by Negroes in three cities during periods of organized protests and "direct action" for civil rights in those cities. The findings are based on official crime reports, medical records, newspaper accounts, and interviews with residents of the three communities (two cities in the Deep South and one in a border state).

It is hypothesized that Negroes release long dammed-up resentment of segregation by asserting themselves (directly or vicariously) in direct action for civil rights. Such emotional expression, when it occurs in a framework of community organization may reduce the need for aggressive outbursts of a violent sort, thus reducing the incidence of such crimes.

We note that further research into the functioning of the civil rights movement may produce fruitful implications for programs to prevent crime and battle poverty.

COMMENTARY on
THE LOCUS OF CONTROL AND
ACADEMIC PERFORMANCE AMONG RACIAL GROUPS

Some of the most exciting research in social psychology is being done on a variable known by the cumbersome label "internal versus external control of reinforcements" (or sometimes simply "locus of control"). By definition, the "internally controlled" person feels that he can largely control his life and that success in any endeavor depends on his own efforts. Further, he believes that political and social events are responsive to the influence of the average man. The "externally controlled" person, by contrast, feels at the mercy of chance or forces beyond his control and that his own effort is practically useless. Of course, in his view, the average person is powerless to influence social and political events. Considerable research indicates that locus of control correlates with other variables in a theoretically meaningful way and that its measurement is valid (Lefcourt 1966; Rotter 1966).

Blacks have been found, on the average, to be more externally oriented than whites (Coleman *13;* Lefcourt and Ladwig 1965; Thune 1967). These findings make sense. For insofar as discrimination exists, a black is judged by his race, not by his achievements. Thus effort fails to pay off. Insofar as discrimination exists, moreover, blacks have little political power. Consequently, decision-makers can, with impunity, pay little attention to their wishes and demands. Feelings of powerlessness and the irrelevance of effort, then, are a reflection of the social reality under which the black man has lived in American society. This interpretation is corroborated by data showing that blacks reared in a desegregated milieu tend to be more internally oriented than blacks reared under segregation (Coleman *13;* Bullough 1967).

The major importance of the locus of control variable is its power to illuminate the behavior of blacks. Internally oriented blacks, for example, are more likely than externally oriented blacks to participate in non-violent social action and in protest organizations devoted to the defense of blacks (Gore and Rotter 1963; Strickland 1965). Internally oriented blacks, moreover, are more willing to endure the frustrations necessary for finding housing in desegregated neighborhoods (Bullough 1967). In addition, there is evidence that, for blacks, external orientation discourages academic achievement (Gurin et al. *14;* Lao 1970). If you feel it's not going to get you anywhere, why study hard?

The relation between locus of control and academic achievement receives much attention in the excerpts of the Coleman Report reprinted here. A survey of more than six hundred thousand pupils throughout the United States, this investigation found that blacks lag behind whites in the acquisition of those intellectual "skills which are among the most important in our society for getting a good job, moving up to a better one, and for full participation in an increasingly technical world." In attempting to illuminate this finding, the authors examine ethnic differences with respect to attitudes and personality characteristics. Their most interesting datum is that black students feel less control over their environment (i.e., are more externally oriented) than white students. This finding is significant in view of the high correlation between sense of control and academic achievement. Thus if black children do poorly in school, it appears to be in part because they feel that their efforts are useless. To change this feeling and thereby improve the academic performance of blacks will require less discrimination and more equality of opportunity.

The Locus of Control and Academic Performance Among Racial Groups

JAMES S. COLEMAN, ERNEST Q. CAMPBELL,
CAROL J. HOBSON, JAMES McPARTLAND,
ALEXANDER M. MOOD, FREDERIC D. WEINFELD,
and ROBERT L. YORK*

All of the findings reported here are based on responses to questionnaires filled out by public school teachers, principals, district school superintendents, and pupils. The data were gathered in September and October of 1965 from 4,000 public schools. All teachers, principals, and district superintendents in these schools participated, as did all pupils in the third, sixth, ninth, and twelfth grades. First grade pupils in half the schools participated.† More than 645,000 pupils in all were involved in the survey. About thirty percent of the schools selected for the survey did not participate; an analysis of the nonparticipating schools indicated that their inclusion would not have significantly altered the results of the survey.

ACHIEVEMENT IN THE PUBLIC SCHOOLS

The schools bear many responsibilities. Among the most important is the teaching of certain intellectual skills such as reading, writing, calculating, and problem solving. One way of

*Excerpted from *Equality of Educational Opportunity* by permission of James S. Coleman. Published by the U. S. Government Printing Office, Washington, D. C., 1966.

† The analysis of attitudes, which is the focus of the selection reprinted here, however, is limited to pupils in the sixth, ninth, and twelfth grades.—Ed.

assessing the educational opportunity offered by the schools is to measure how well they perform this task. Standard achievement tests are available to measure these skills, and several such tests were administered in this survey to pupils at grades one, three, six, nine, and twelve.

These tests do not measure intelligence, nor attitudes, nor qualities of character. Furthermore, they are not, nor are they intended to be, "culture free." Quite the reverse: they are culture bound. What they measure are the skills which are among the most important in our society for getting a good job and moving up to a better one, and for full participation in an increasingly technical world. Consequently, a pupil's test results at the end of public school provide a good measure of the range of opportunities open to him as he finishes school—a wide range of choice of jobs or colleges if these skills are very high; a very narrow range that includes only the most menial jobs if these skills are very low.

Table 1 gives an overall illustration of the test results for the various groups by tabulating nationwide median scores (the score which divides the group in half) for first-grade and twelfth-grade pupils on the tests used in those grades. For example, half of the white twelfth-grade pupils had scores above fifty-two on the nonverbal test and half had scores below fifty-two. (Scores on each test at each grade level were standardized so that the average over the national sample equaled fifty and the standard deviation equaled ten. This means that for all pupils in the Nation, about sixteen percent would score below forty and about sixteen percent above sixty.)

With some exceptions—notably Oriental Americans—the average minority pupil scores distinctly lower on these tests at every level than the average white pupil. The minority pupils' scores are as much as one standard deviation below the majority pupils' scores in the first grade. At the twelfth grade, results of tests in the same verbal and nonverbal skills show that, in every case, the minority scores are farther below the majority than are the first-graders. For some groups, the relative decline is negligible; for others, it is large.

Furthermore, a constant difference in standard deviations over the various grades represents an increasing difference in grade level gap. For example, Negroes in the metropolitan Northeast are about 1.1 standard deviations below whites in the same region at grades six, nine, and twelve. But at grade six this represents 1.6 years behind; at grade nine, 2.4 years; and at grade twelve, 3.3 years. Thus, by this measure, the deficiency in achievement is progressively greater for the minority pupils at progressively higher grade levels.

TABLE 1

NATIONWIDE MEDIAN TEST SCORES
FOR 1ST- AND 12TH-GRADE PUPILS, FALL 1965

| | | | *Racial or ethnic group* | | | |
Test	*Puerto Ricans*	*Indian Americans*	*Mexican Americans*	*Oriental Americans*	*Negro*	*Majority*
1st grade:						
Nonverbal	45.8	53.0	50.1	56.6	43.4	54.1
Verbal	44.9	47.8	46.5	51.6	45.4	53.2
12th grade:						
Nonverbal	43.3	47.1	45.0	51.6	40.9	52.0
Verbal	43.1	43.7	43.8	49.6	40.9	52.1
Reading	42.6	44.3	44.2	48.8	42.2	51.9
Mathematics	43.7	45.9	45.5	51.3	41.8	51.8
General information	41.7	44.7	43.3	49.0	40.6	52.2
Average of the 5 tests	43.1	45.1	44.4	50.1	41.1	52.0

For most minority groups, then, and most particularly the Negro, schools provide little opportunity for them to overcome this initial deficiency; in fact they fall farther behind the white majority in the development of several skills which are critical to making a living and participating fully in modern society. Whatever may be the combination of nonschool factors—poverty, community attitudes, low educational level of parents—which put minority children at a disadvantage in verbal and nonverbal skills when they enter the first grade, the fact is the schools have not overcome it.

Some points should be borne in mind in reading the table. First, the differences shown should not obscure the fact that some minority children perform better than many white children. A difference of one standard deviation in median scores means that about eighty-five percent of the children in the lower group are below the median of the majority students—but fifty percent of the white children are themselves below that median as well.

A second point of qualification concerns regional differences. By grade twelve, both white and Negro students in the South score below their counterparts—white and Negro—in the North. In addition, Southern Negroes score farther below Southern whites than Northern Negroes score below Northern whites. The consequences of this pattern can be illustrated by the fact that the twelfth-grade Negro in the nonmetropolitan South is 0.8 standard deviation below—or, in terms of years, 1.9 years behind—the Negro in the metropolitan Northeast, though at grade one there is no such regional difference.

Finally, the test scores at grade twelve obviously do not take account of those pupils who have left school before reaching the senior year. In the metropolitan North and West, twenty percent of the Negroes of ages sixteen and seventeen are not enrolled in school—a higher dropout percentage than in either the metropolitan or nonmetropolitan South. If it is the case that some or many of the Northern dropouts performed poorly when they were in school, the Negro achievement in the North may be artificially elevated because some of those who achieved more poorly have left school.

ASPIRATIONS AND MOTIVATION

The orientations of the children themselves are important indicators of both school and family environments. For these orientations—how they feel about themselves, their motivations in school, their aspirations toward further education and toward desirable occupations—are partly a result of the home and partly a result of the school. They play a special role, for they are in part an outcome of education, and in part a factor which propels the child toward further education and achievement. Consequently, they will be examined later in this section in both these capacities: as a factor affected by the school, and as a factor that itself affects school achievement. For quite clearly, if a school does not motivate its students toward learning, it can hardly expect achievement from them. At this point, we shall merely give an overview of the orientations and motivations shown by students in these different racial and ethnic groups and for Negroes and whites, in the different regions.

When asked the question, "If something happened and you had to stop school now, how would you feel," nearly half the twelfth grade students responded that they "would do almost anything to stay in school." All groups were similar in this. Negroes and whites were slightly higher than the others, and only Puerto Rican children indicated in any number (15.9 percent) that they would like to quit school. There is little regional variation, except that for both Negroes and whites, both in and outside metropolitan areas, the reported motivation to stay in school is slightly higher in the South and Southwest than in the North and West.

When asked about whether they wanted to be good students, a higher proportion of Negroes than any other group—over half—reported that they wanted to be one of the best in the class. In every region, a considerably higher proportion of Negroes than of whites gave this response. And again, as in the preceding question, both Negroes and whites more often showed this high level of motivation in the South and Southwest—fifteen to twenty percent more among the Negroes, and ten to fifteen percent more among the whites. Puerto Ricans again were unique in the proportion who responded that they were satisfied just to get by.

Negroes report also more studying outside school than any group except the Oriental Americans. Here again, they—though not the whites—report more studying in the South and Southwest than in any other region.

Negroes report a sharply lower frequency of staying away from school because they "didn't want to come" than do whites, in every region of the country, matched only by the Oriental Americans. The regional differences show a similar pattern to the previous questions, with slightly less voluntary absenteeism in the South and Southwest for both Negroes and whites. Also, for both Negroes and whites, students from the nonmetropolitan areas report slightly less such absenteeism than do those in the metropolitan areas.

Consistent with the general pattern of Negro-white differences in the preceding questions, slightly fewer Negroes than whites report having read no books during the past summer.

Turning to college plans and aspirations, the pattern is slightly different. A smaller proportion of Negroes than of whites report wanting to go no further than high school, in each region, though a slightly smaller proportion report wanting to finish college or go beyond. More Negroes report wanting to go to technical, nursing, or business school after college. Among the other groups, the Oriental Americans show by far the highest aspirations toward college of any group in the entire sample, sixty-four percent reporting wanting to finish college or go beyond.

The concrete plans for college next year expressed by these students show two tendencies in comparing Negroes with whites: fewer Negroes have definite plans for college, but fewer have definite plans not to attend. This indicates the lesser concreteness in Negroes' aspirations, the greater hopes, but lesser plans.

The greater uncertainty in Negro students' plans about college than those of whites is shown also in the lower proportion who have seen a college catalog or written to a college.

The very high educational aspirations of all groups is shown by the equally high occupational aspirations. For every group, by far the largest category of occupation indicated as the one they "think they will have" is professional. Overall, thirty-five percent of the twelfth-grade students report planning to have a professional occupation—though only the whites (in seven regions) and the Oriental Americans are above this overall average.

For each group, the proportion with this aspiration is unrealistically high, since professionals constitute only thirteen percent of the total labor force in this country. But again the question shows the high educational and occupational aspirations that students in all these groups have.

Altogether, the responses that these children gave to questions about their present motivation in school and their future plans show some rather unexpected differences between groups. Apart from the generally high levels for all groups, the most striking differences are the especially high level of motivation, interest, and aspirations reported by Negro students. These data are difficult to reconcile with the facts of Negroes' lower rates of completion of school, and lower college-going rate. They appear to show at least one thing: Negroes are especially strongly oriented toward the school as a path for mobility. This finding is consistent with other research that has shown greater aspirations for college among Negroes than among whites of comparable economic levels. But the results suggest as well a considerable lack of realism in aspirations, especially among Negroes whose responses deviate most from actual rates of college-going and completion of high school.

There is another set of orientations of these children that may be important both as a factor affecting their school achievement and as a consequence of school for achievement in later life. These are general attitudes toward themselves and their environment. In this survey, two such attitudes have been studied. The first is the child's sense of his own ability, his "self-concept." If a child's self-concept is low, if he feels he cannot succeed, then this will affect the effort he puts into the task and thus, his chance of success. It is true, of course, that his self-concept is affected by his success in school and it is thus hard to discover the effect of self-concept upon achievement. But as a factor in its own right, it is an important outcome of education.

Three questions were used at the twelfth- and ninth-grade levels to obtain an indication of the child's self-concept. These are:

(1) How bright do you think you are in comparison with the other students in your grade.

(2) Agree or disagree: I sometimes feel that I just can't learn.

(3) Agree or disagree: I would do better in schoolwork if teachers didn't go so fast.

In general, the responses to these questions do not indicate differences between Negroes and whites, but do indicate differences between them and the other minority groups. Negroes and whites show similar levels of response to these items, though there are variations among regions. Each of the other groups shows lower self-concept on each of these questions than does either the Negro sample or the white sample.

It is puzzling to some analysts that the Negro children report levels of self-esteem as high as white when there is so much in their social environment to reduce the self-esteem of a Negro, and those analysts conjecture that these responses may not mean what their face value suggests. In any case it will be valuable to examine how school factors affect such self-esteem, because many of these children do report low levels of self-esteem, and it is clear that experiences in school may have an effect upon this.

The second attitudinal factor that is included in this examination is the child's sense of control of his environment. If a child feels that his environment is capricious, or random, or beyond his ability to alter, then he may conclude that attempts to affect it are not worthwhile, and stop trying. Such a response to one's environment may be quite unconscious, but merely a general attitude that has developed through long experience. The particular relevance of this factor for groups that have been the subject of discrimination is that they have objectively had much less control of their environment than have members of the majority groups. This has been particularly true for Negroes.

Three items from the questionnaire are used to measure the child's sense of control of his environment—

(1) Agree or disagree: Good luck is more important than hard work for success (Table 2).

(2) Agree or disagree: Every time I try to get ahead, something or somebody stops me.

(3) People like me don't have much of a chance to be successful in life.

On all these items, Negroes and other minority children show much lower sense of control of their environment than do whites. In metropolitan areas, about twice the proportion of Negroes as of whites give a low-control response to the "good luck" question. Outside metropolitan areas, the proportion is about three times as great. For the other minority groups, the low-control response is similarly high, being highest among the Puerto Ricans, and lowest among the Oriental Americans.

Similar differences are found between whites and the minority groups for the other two questions, though the differences are not quite as great. It is clear that the average child from each of these minority groups feels a considerably lower sense of control of his environment than does the average white child. It appears that the sense of control is lowest among Puerto Ricans, and among Negroes lowest for those outside metropolitan areas, and that except for the whites it is highest for the Oriental Americans.

As indicated earlier, there is an objective basis for this difference in feelings of control, since these minority children have

TABLE 2

Percent of 12th-grade pupils who reported that they feel that good luck is more important for success than is hard work, for white and Negro pupils in metropolitan and nonmetropolitan areas by region, and for selected minority groups for the United States, fall 1965.

Race and area	Agree	Not sure	Dis-agree	Nonre-sponse
White, nonmetropolitan:				
South	4	6	89	2
Southwest	4	4	89	3
North and West	4	6	89	2
White, metropolitan:				
Northeast	4	7	88	2
Midwest	4	6	89	2
South	4	5	89	2
Southwest	4	5	87	4
West	4	7	84	5
Negro, nonmetropolitan:				
South	15	15	57	12
Southwest	14	15	59	12
North and West	14	17	64	5
Negro, metropolitan:				
Northeast	9	9	70	11
Midwest	9	11	73	7
South	10	11	60	20
Southwest	11	10	66	13
West	10	12	58	20
Mexican Americans, total	11	12	68	9
Puerto Ricans, total	19	15	53	14
Indian Americans, total	11	15	68	6
Oriental Americans, total	8	10	78	3
Other, total	14	16	62	9
TOTAL, all races	6	7	82	5

Source: U–102.

less chance to control their environment than do the majority whites. What is not clear, however, is how much of this can be accounted for by school factors, how much by family difference, and how much by their general position in society. It also remains to be examined just how much effect this attitudinal factor has upon the child's achievement in school. Both of these questions will be examined in study of the effects of school.

ATTITUDES OF STUDENTS

Three expressions of student attitude and motivation were examined in relation to achievement. One was the student's interest in school and his reported pursuit of reading outside school; another was his self-concept, specifically with regard to learning, and success in school; and a third was what we have called his sense of control of the environment. The criterion of achievement was the student's score on the verbal ability test, a vocabulary test measuring verbal skills.

As indicated in an earlier section, both Negro and white children expressed a high self-concept, as well as high interest in school and learning, compared to the other groups. Negroes, however, were like the other minority groups in expressing a much lower sense of control of the environment than whites.

Of all the variables measured in the survey, including all measures of family background and all school variables, these attitudes showed the strongest relation to achievement, at all three grade levels. The zero-order correlations of these attitudes with achievement were higher than those of any other variables, in some cases as high as the correlation of some test scores with others (between .4 and .5). Taken alone, these attitudinal variables account for more of the variation in achievement than any other set of variables (all family background variables together, or all school variables together). When added to any other set of variables, they increase the accounted-for variation more than does any other set of variables.

Whatever measure is chosen, the attitudinal variables have the strongest relation to achievement. It is, of course, reasonable that self-concept should be so closely related to achievement, since it represents the individual's own estimate of his ability. The relation of self-concept to achievement is, from one perspective, merely the accuracy of his estimate of his scholastic skills, and is probably more a consequence than a cause of scholastic achievement. His interest in learning, it can be assumed, partly derives from family background, and partly from his success in school. Of the three attitudinal variables, however, it is the weakest, especially among minority groups, where it shows inconsistent relations to achievement at grades nine and twelve. The absence of a consistent relation for Negroes, along with the data which showed Negroes even more interested in learning than whites, gives a picture of students who report high interest in academic achievement, but whose reported interest is not translated through effective action into achievement. Thus the causal sequence which is usually assumed to occur, in which interest leads to effort and thereby to achievement, appears not to occur in this way for Negroes and other minority groups.

Clues to the causal sequence that may occur are provided by the relation of the two other attitudes to achievement. One of these clues lies in the second important result of this section: At grade twelve, for whites and Oriental Americans, self-concept is more highly related to verbal skills before or after background is controlled than is control of environment; for all the other minority groups, the relative importance is reversed: the child's sense of control of environment is most strongly related to achievement.

This result is particularly impressive because this attitude has no direct logical relation to achievement in school or to ability. The three questions on which it is based are a statement that "good luck is more important than hard work for success," a statement that "every time I try to get ahead, something or someone stops me," and a statement that "people like me don't have much of a chance to be successful in life." Yet for minority groups which achieve least well, responses to these statements (individually or together) are more strongly related than any other variable to achievement. It was evident earlier . . . that children from these groups are much more likely to respond to these statements in terms showing a sense of lack of control of the environment. Now the present data show that children in these minority groups who do exhibit a sense of control of the environment have considerably higher achievement than those who do not. The causal sequence in this relation is not implied by the relationship itself. It may very well be two-directional, with both the attitude and the achievement affecting each other. Yet in the absence of specific evidence about causal direction, it is useful to examine one direction at length—the possible effect of such an attitude, that is, feeling a high or low sense of control of the environment, on achievement.*

Table 3 shows, for each minority group, and separately for Negroes and whites in the North and South, the average verbal achievement scores for boys and girls who answer "good luck" and those who answered "hard work" on one of these questions. Those minority group students who give "hard work" or "control" responses score higher on the tests than do whites who give "no control" responses.

The special importance of a sense of control of environment for achievement of minority-group children and perhaps for disadvantaged whites as well suggests a different set of predispositional factors operating to create low or high achievement for children from disadvantaged groups than for children from advantaged groups. For children from advantaged groups, achievement or lack of it appears closely related to their self-concept: what they believe about themselves. For children from disadvantaged groups, achievement or lack of achievement appears closely related to what they believe about their environment: whether they believe the environment will respond to reasonable efforts, or whether they believe it is instead merely random or immovable. In different words, it appears that children

---

* In this regard, a recent social-psychological experiment is relevant. Negro and white adults were offered an alternative between a risky situation in which the outcome depended on chance, and one in which the outcome, though no more favorable altogether, was contingent on their own response. Negro adults less often chose the alternative contingent on their own behavior, more often chose the chance alternative, as compared to whites (Lefcourt 1965).

from advantaged groups assume that the environment will respond if they are able enough to affect it; children from disadvantaged groups do not make this assumption, but in many cases assume that nothing they will do can affect the environment—it will give benefits or withhold them but not as a consequence of their own action.

TABLE 3

Verbal achievement scores of grade-9 pupils who have differing responses to the question: "Agree or disagree: Good luck is more important than hard work for success."

Group and region	Agree (good luck)	Disagree (hard work)
Mexican American	38.6	46.8
Puerto Rican	38.5	45.5
Indian American	39.9	47.3
Oriental	44.0	52.5
Negro, South	36.6	43.3
Negro, North	40.0	47.1
White, South	42.9	52.5
White, North	45.4	54.8

One may speculate that these conceptions reasonably derive from the different experiences that these children have had. A child from an advantaged family most often has had all his needs satisfied, has lived in a responsive environment, and hence can assume that the environment will continue to be responsive if only he acts appropriately. A child from a disadvantaged family has had few of his needs satisfied, has lived in an unresponsive environment, both within the family (where other demands pressed upon his mother) and outside the family, in an outside and often unfriendly world.* Thus he cannot assume that the environment will respond to his actions. Such a state of affairs could be expected to lead to passivity, with a general belief in

* Recent research on Negro mothers and their four-year-old children has shown that those mothers with a sense of futility relative to the environment have children with lower scores on Stanford-Binet IQ tests, after other aspects of the mother's behavior, including her own IQ score, are statistically controlled (Bear, Hess and Shipman 1966).

luck, a belief that the world is hostile, and also a belief that nothing he could ever do would change things. He has not yet come to see that he can affect his environment, for it has never been so in his previous experience.

Thus, for many disadvantaged children, a major obstacle to achievement may arise from the very way they confront the environment. Having experienced an unresponsive environment, the virtues of hard work, of diligent and extended effort toward achievement appear to such a child unlikely to be rewarding. As a consequence, he is likely to merely "adjust" to his environment, finding satisfaction in passive pursuits.

It may well be, then, that one of the keys toward success for minorities which have experienced disadvantage and a particularly unresponsive environment—either in the home or the larger society—is a change in this conception.

There is a further result in these data which could provide some clues about the differential dynamics of these attitudes among children from disadvantaged and advantaged groups, or from different kinds of families. When all three attitudes are examined together as predictors of verbal achievement, then the following shifts from grade six to nine and twelve occur: (*a*) At grade six, professed interest in school is related to achievement for all groups; but this relation vanishes at grades nine and twelve except for Oriental Americans and whites; (*b*) control of environment is strongly related to achievement for all groups at grade six; but this relation declines for Oriental Americans and whites in grades nine and twelve, while it increases for the other minority groups.

These data indicating changes in the relationships must be viewed with caution, since some differences existed between grade six and grades nine and twelve in the measures themselves. However, the data suggest that the child's sense of control of his environment (which is lower at grade six, and increases with age) is important in the early achievement of children from all groups, but that it is the children from disadvantaged groups whose sense of control of environment continues to be associated with an important difference in later achievement. These results of course are only suggestive, and indicate the need for further investigations of the dynamics of attitudes and achievement among disadvantaged groups in society. Because of the likely mutual dependence of these attitudes and achievement, such investigations will require special care in determining the extent to which each influences the other.

It is useful to inquire about the factors in the school and the home which affect children's self-concept and sense of control of the environment. First, this study provides little evidence concerning the effect of school factors on these attitudes. If family background characteristics are controlled, almost none of the remaining variance in self-concept and control of environment is accounted for by the school factors measured in this survey. One variable, however, is consistently related to control of environment and self-concept. For each group, as the proportion white in the school increases, the child's sense of control of environment increases, and his self-concept decreases. This suggests the possibility that school integration has conflicting effects on attitudes of minority group children: it increases their sense of control of the environment or their sense of opportunity, but decreases their self-concept. This relationship may well be an artifact, since the achievement level of the student body increases with percent white, and may be the proximate cause of these opposite relationships. If so, these effects are merely effects of achievements and motivations of fellow students, rather than direct effects of integration. Whatever the time structure of causation, the relations, though consistent, are in all cases small.

It appears reasonable that these attitudes depend more on the home than the school. Reference was made earlier to a study which suggests that a mother's sense of control of the environment affects her young child's cognitive skills. It appears likely that her child's sense of control of environment depends similarly on her own. Such inquiry into the source of these attitudes can best be carried out by such intensive studies on a smaller scale than the present survey. However, some results from the present survey may be stated as clues to the sources of these attitudes.

At grades six, nine, and twelve, the simultaneous relation of eight family background factors to the two attitudes was studied.

These background factors are:

Structural integrity of the home (father's presence, primarily).
Number of brothers and sisters.
Length of residence in an urban area.
Parents' education.
Economic level of home environment.
Reading material in home.
Parents' interest in child's schooling.
Parents' desires for child's further education.

The pattern of relationships between these factors and the two attitudes is similar for all groups in the survey with minor exceptions noted below. First, only a small fraction of the variance in these attitudes, averaging less than ten percent, is accounted for by all these background factors, combined. For minority groups other than Negroes, control of environment is better accounted for by these background factors than is self-concept. For Negroes, both are about the same; and for whites self-concept is better accounted for than control of environment.

For both attitudes and for all groups, the parents' desires for the child's further education have the largest unique contribution to positive self-concept and a sense of control of environment. For self-concept, the only other variables which show a consistent relation (positive) are parents' education and the amount of reading material in the home. For the child's sense of control of the environment, there is in addition a consistent relation to the economic level of the home and the structural integrity of the home. That is, children from homes with a higher economic level, and children from homes where the father is present, show a higher sense of control of the environment than do children from homes with lower economic level or children from homes where the father is absent.

These results can be seen only as minor indications of the source of these attitudes in children's backgrounds. The major result of this section, which appears of considerable importance and warrants further investigation, is the different role these two attitudes appear to play for children from advantaged and disadvantaged backgrounds.

COMMENTARY on
INTERNAL-EXTERNAL CONTROL
IN THE MOTIVATIONAL DYNAMICS OF NEGRO YOUTH

As scientists, social researchers are continually reevaluating "accepted truths." In few other places can a better illustration of this be found than in the work on locus of control. As fruitful as the use of this variable has been in studies such as the Coleman Report (*13*), Patricia Gurin and her associates argue in the following selection that locus of control, as formulated by Rotter (1966), is too global a variable to fit black Americans. It is useful, they claim, to make certain distinctions.

Accordingly, these investigators differentiate three separate dimensions:

1. Control ideology refers to a person's beliefs about the determinants of success in the *society at large*. Does he feel that people are able to shape their own lives? Or does he feel that success is determined by external forces, forces beyond the control of most individuals?

2. Personal control refers to the degree to which a respondent believes that he controls *his own life* and that his effort and ability will bring him rewards.

3. Individual-system blame has to do with how a person accounts for the disabilities suffered by blacks in American society. Does he view these disabilities as the fault of the black individual himself—the result of his lack of knowledge, skill, or initiative? Or does he place the blame on the system—on discrimination and the absence of equal opportunity?

These dimensions differ in their relations to other variables. Gurin and her associates, for example, find that the races have similar responses to items gauging control ideology: blacks are just as likely as whites to believe that the society at large operates according to the traditional virtues of the Protestant Ethic. On the personal control dimension, however, blacks tend to be more external than whites. It is in their own lives, in other words, that blacks doubt that effort and ability pay off.

To illuminate a person's level of aspiration and to predict his performance at school and on the job, we should, the following study suggests, gauge the degree to which he believes he has power over his own life. If, on the other hand, our interest is in a black's inclination to join social action organizations and to participate in protest activity, we should find out where he puts the blame for the disabilities of black Americans.*

According to other data (Forward and Williams 1970), attitudes toward violence are related to both personal control and individual-system blame. But the correlations are in opposite directions. That is, a black's approval of violence goes with an internal orientation on personal control (i.e., a strong feeling of personal control) but with an external orientation on individual-system blame (i.e., a belief that the system is to blame). These data support the view that black rioters have high aspirations and great confidence in their ability to fulfil these aspirations, combined with the feeling that it is discrimination, not their own inadequacies, that frustrates their ambitions.

The separate dimensions of locus of control, then, enhance our understanding of the behavior of black Americans in a way that a single, global measure never could. Thus the distinctions made by Gurin and her colleagues have proven fruitful.

* For findings that parallel those of Gurin and her colleagues here, see Lao (1970).

Internal-External Control in the Motivational Dynamics of Negro Youth

PATRICIA GURIN, GERALD GURIN,
ROSINA C. LAO, and MURIEL BEATTIE *

The concept of internal-external control has now gained prominence in many diverse areas of research. As defined by Rotter, internal control represents a person's belief that rewards follow from, or are contingent upon, his own behavior (Rotter 1966). Conversely, external control represents the belief that rewards are controlled by forces outside himself and thus may occur independently of his own actions.

A number of studies of motivation and performance of Negro student populations suggest that Negro students, in comparison with whites, are less likely to hold strong beliefs in internal control; that social class and race probably interact so that lower-status Negroes particularly stand out as externally-oriented; that internal control is a critical determinant of academic performance. A well-known example of the relevance of this concept appears in the Coleman report on *Equality of Educational Opportunity* (Coleman, *et al 13*). In the Coleman study, internal control proved in two ways to be unusually important for Negro students. It explained more of the variance in achievement for Negro than for white students; furthermore it explained more variance for Negro students than any other measure included in that massive survey of academic behavior.

*Excerpted from the *Journal of Social Issues,* vol. 25, number 3 (Summer 1969), pp. 29-53 by permission from the publisher, The Society for the Psychological Study of Social Issues, and Patricia Gurin.

In addition to these direct uses of the concept of internal-external control, a number of closely related concepts have also become prominent in studies of low-income and minority groups. For example, a major focus in the current poverty literature is on the concept of powerlessness. Seeman (1959) defines powerlessness as the expectancy or probability held by the individual that his own behavior cannot determine the occurrence of the outcomes, or reinforcements, he seeks. This definition is very similar to Rotter's construct of internal-external control; indeed, the Internal-External Control scale is frequently used to measure this sense of powerlessness.

DISTINCTIONS WITHIN THE CONCEPT OF INTERNAL-EXTERNAL CONTROL

One of the complexities in the concept [of internal-external control] springs from the fact that the writings in this area have not distinguished between the belief that internal or external control operates *generally* in society and the application of this to one's own personal situation. It has been implicitly assumed in the literature that a belief in internal control represents a person's evaluation of his own life experience, that he can influence the outcomes of situations through his own actions. Yet, questions in the Rotter Internal-External Control scale include two types of items that have not been distinguished—those which do refer explicitly to the respondent's own life situation and those which seem to tap beliefs about what causes success or failure for people generally. In our research we have been interested in whether this *self-other distinction* is meaningful to respondents and whether these two types of questions predict different behaviors.

We question still another implicit assumption in the way internal control has been interpreted, particularly with respect to poverty and minority groups. It has usually been assumed that internal beliefs represent a positive affirmation. What has been neglected in the literature is the fact that an internal orientation may also have negative implications. When associated with success, an internal orientation can lead to feelings of competence and efficacy. When associated with failure, however, it can lead to self-derogation and self-blame.

This distinction between *responsibility for success* and *responsibility for failure* should assume heightened significance whenever we are trying to understand the motivation and behavior of people who have a history of much failure and whose failures are tied to real external obstacles they have faced. We would expect it to be particularly helpful in studying the subgroup of Negro youth who have encountered social constraints associated not only with race but also with low income and lower-class status. For such young people, an internal orientation based on responsibility for their failures may be more reflective of intrapunitiveness [i.e., self-derogation and self-blame] than of efficacy [i.e., a feeling of mastery over the self and the environment]. An internal response reflecting acceptance of blame for one's failures, which might be considered "normal" in the typical middle-class experience, may be extreme and intrapunitive for a Negro youngster growing up in poverty in the ghetto.

EXTERNAL CONTROL—BLAMING CHANCE OR A FAULTY SYSTEM?

The implication that the meaning of internal control is complicated by the reality obstacles the individual has faced points to a distinction that has not been made on the external end of the continuum. Almost all of the research on internal and external bases of control has examined just two bases—skill versus chance. The experimental studies have varied characteristics of the situation to produce perceptions that success and failure are the result of either skill or chance; the personality measure of internal-external control developed by Rotter and his associates requires the individual to choose between two explanations for success and failure—an internal explanation asserting that what happens in life is the result of skill, ability, or effort, and an external explanation asserting that success and failure are determined by fate or chance. These may be the most pertinent bases for people whose advantaged position in the social structure limits the operation of other external determinants of success and failure.

But low income groups experience many external obstacles that have nothing to do with chance—the operation of the labor market which can lead to layoffs over which individuals have no control, poor transportation facilities which reduce their possibilities in the job hunt, the tendency of employers to hire within the social network of those already on the payroll, etc. In addition, there are class-tied obstacles to many kinds of opportunities and to resources which open up other opportunities, which may be perceived correctly by low-income persons as external but not a matter of randomness or luck. For Negroes there is also the external factor of racial discrimination which operates over and beyond the class constraints they may or may not experience. Discrimination may be perceived as operating quite the opposite of chance—systematically, predictably, and reliably.

We suspect that this distinction is a crucial one, that it matters motivationally for groups disadvantaged by social conditions whether the external orientation refers to chance or to these more systematic, constraining forces. Although the literature to date indicates that people who believe in external control are less effectively motivated and perform less well in achievement situations, these same effects may not follow for low-income persons, particularly Negroes, who believe that economic or discriminatory factors are more important than individual skill and personal qualities in explaining why they succeed or fail. Instead of depressing motivation, focusing on external forces may be motivationally healthy if it results from assessing one's chances for success against systematic and real external obstacles rather than the exigencies of an overwhelming, unpredictable fate. Therefore, we have placed considerable emphasis in our work with Negro students on their causal explanations for the status of Negroes in American society. Do they follow an internal explanation by blaming the social position of Negroes on their own inadequacies, or are they more externally oriented by stressing the importance of racial or social discrimination?

This distinction between *individual and system blame* has often been drawn in psychological and sociological analyses of minority groups. The literature generally supports the view proposed in this paper that an internal orientation, when it involves excessive self-blame or blame of one's group, can be damaging to minority group members. Psychologists and psychoanalysts, such as Kardiner and Ovesey (1951) and Fanon (1967), have emphasized the psychic damage that results when this self-blaming orientation turns into hatred of the group and the self. Sociologists, following Merton's (1957) classic statement of the issue, have pointed out the social dysfunctionality of such beliefs for the minority group members. Merton notes that when people subordinated in a social system react with invidious self-deprecation rather than against the system, they accept a rationale for the existing system that serves to perpetuate their subordinate position. This distinction also has obvious relevance to the current scene with its increasing emphasis on black nationalism and black pride, since rejection of the more conventional "individual inadequacy" explanation is primary in the rhetoric of black militants.

Still, even though this distinction has been discussed in the literature on minority groups, it has not been related to the literature on internal-external control. In this paper we are interested in making this connection. In a later section we will present some correlates of individual-system blame and the implications of these results for the more usual interpretations of internal-external control.

MEANINGFULNESS AND SIGNIFICANCE OF DISTINGUISHING SELF FROM OTHER AND INDIVIDUAL FROM SYSTEM BLAME

Several studies, conducted recently at the Survey Research Center, have explored how meaningful the self-other and individual-system blame distinctions are to Negroes as they think about issues of control and whether these distinctions make a difference in explaining their goals, motivation, or performance. One is a study of students attending ten predominantly Negro colleges in the Deep South; another is a study of Negro high school dropouts attending a job training program in a large northern city; a third is a national study of both white and Negro adults taking part in retraining programs all over the country. The results show that these different groups of Negroes respond to questions about internal control in ways which support the meaningfulness and significance of these distinctions.

THE SELF-OTHER DISTINCTION

Evidence for the meaningfulness of the self-other distinction comes, first of all, from a factor analysis of a pool of items bearing on internal control which were administered in the study of college students. Included in the factor analysis were the twenty-three items from the Rotter Internal-External Control scale,* the three items from the Personal Efficacy scale,† and a set of questions, phrased in the same forced-choice format, which were written specifically for this study to tap students' beliefs about the operation of personal and external forces in the race situation in the United States. The factor analysis of these items resulted in four factors with approximately the same structure for both male and females.

The items loading on Factors I and II (Control Ideology and Personal Control) are distinguishable in terms of *whose* success or failure is referred to in the question. The five items with the highest loadings on Factor II are all phrased in the *first person.* The student who consistently chooses the internal alternative on these five items believes that he can control what happens in his *own* life. He has a strong conviction in his own competence or what we have called a sense of *personal control.* In contrast, only one of the items loading on Factor I explicitly uses the first person. Referring instead to people generally, these items seem to measure the respondent's ideology or general beliefs about the role of internal and external forces in determining success and failure in the culture at large. Endorsing the internal alternative on these items means rejecting the notion that success follows from luck, the right breaks or knowing the right people, and accepting a traditional Protestant Ethic explanation. Such a person believes that hard work, effort, skill, and ability are the important determinants of success in life. We have called this factor a measure of the respondent's *control ideology.*

---

* Some of these items were slightly rephrased in ways we felt would be more meaningful to the study population.

† The Personal Efficacy scale items were adapted from a scale that has been used in many studies at the Survey Research Center over the past ten years. The questions are phrased in the same forced-choice format as the Rotter items. They focus on the respondent's feelings of control over his own life, not his general beliefs about what makes for control in life.

The difference between these two factors can be seen in the contrast of the highest loading items on each factor. Defining the sense of personal control is the assertion that "when I make plans, I am almost certain that I can make them work," rather than "it is not always wise to plan too far ahead because many things turn out to be a matter of good or bad fortune anyhow." Defining the general ideology measure, on the internal control end of the dimension, is the assertion that "people will get ahead in life if they have the goods and do a good job; knowing the right people has nothing to do with it"; on the external end of the dimension is the assertion that "knowing the right people is important in deciding whether a person will get ahead."

SEPARATION OF PERSONAL AND IDEOLOGICAL LEVELS

This separation of self from other, or the personal and the ideological levels, is not typical of factor analytic results from studies of white populations. Rotter and others report finding one general factor which includes both types of questions (Rotter 1966). The addition of items from the Personal Efficacy scale to our pool of items may have encouraged the emergence of this separation since it provides a few more items which are cast clearly in personal terms. We believe, however, that the separation of personal and ideological levels is likely to be a valid rather than an artifactual difference between Negro and white populations.

Why would we expect Negroes, but not whites, to distinguish self from other in the way they think about internal control? Our rationale is that Negroes may very well adopt the general cultural beliefs about internal control but find that these beliefs cannot always be applied in their own life situations. Without the same experiences of discrimination and racial prejudice, whites are less likely to perceive an inconsistency between cultural beliefs and what works for them. Therefore, Negro students may endorse general cultural beliefs in the Protestant Ethic just as strongly as would their white peers; at the same time, they may express much less certainty that they can control the outcomes of their own lives. Evidence that this seems to be the case is found in several studies. For example, in the Coleman study of educational opportunity, Negro students in college are *equally, if not more, internal* than white students in responding to statements which sound very much like our measure of control ideology; e.g., "If people are not successful, it is their own fault." In contrast, race differences do appear in questions which use a personal referent. Negro students are *less internal* than their white peers in answering questions about their own life experiences, for instance, in responding to the statement "every time I try to get ahead, something or somebody stops me."

This same pattern of race results also characterizes the adults in our own study of job retraining programs. There were no differences between Negro and white trainees in response to questions tapping general Protestant Ethic ideological beliefs, including some items adapted from the Rotter scale. However, there were clear race differences in responses to questions on the sense of efficacy and control over one's own life, with white trainees indicating a greater sense of this personal control.

THE SEPARATION OF LEVELS. . . PARTICULARLY CHARACTERISTIC OF NEGROES?

In addition to this pattern (the great convergence of Negroes and whites in endorsing general cultural beliefs and yet considerable divergence in their feelings of control over their own lives), still other data support the possibility that this separation of levels is particularly characteristic of Negroes. Results from our own studies indicate much greater unanimity in the general ideologies held by Negro youth than in their assessments of their competence to control their own lives. When questions were phrased at a very general level, asking what generally makes for success in life, the great majority (approximately seventy-five to eighty percent) of the students in our study of Negro colleges agreed with a Protestant Ethic ideology. In contrast, when the questions were phrased in terms of what control they themselves had over their lives, many more (approximately fifty percent) answered in ways indicating some questioning of this sense of control. This difference in endorsement rates for ideological and personal questions also holds for the high school dropouts we studied in a job training program. Despite rather frequent feelings of lack of control in their own personal lives, most of these trainees, like the college students, endorsed the cultural beliefs that hard work rather than luck makes for success in life.

THE "PERSONAL LEVEL" MOTIVATES

More important than this difference in the proportion of Negroes who endorse the ideological and personal questions on internal-external control are the further results that these two types of questions are differentially related to a number of motivational and performance indicators. It is the personal, rather than the ideological, measure that operates significantly in motivation and performance. We have seen this in our studies of Negro college students as well as our study of young dropouts in the retraining program.

In the college study we examined relationships between three control scores—the sense of personal control, control ideology, and the total Rotter Internal-External Control scale—and a variety of motivational and performance measures. Only rarely do the measures of personal control and control ideology operate the same way. Usually it is the sense of personal control, but not control ideology, that differentiates motivation and performance. Students who have a high sense of personal control over their own lives also express heightened expectancies of success and self-confidence about their abilities for academic and job performance; they also aspire to jobs that are more *prestigeful, demanding,* and *realistic* in terms of their own abilities and interests, three characteristics of job aspirations that have been related to high achievement motivation in many studies in the achievement literature. In contrast, the students' beliefs about what generally determines success and failure have nothing to do with their self-confidence, personal expectancies, or aspirations. It is not surprising, therefore, that the total Internal-External Control scale, which includes items at both the personal and the ideological levels, predicts to these aspects of motivation either very weakly or not at all.

In the performance area we find that the two control measures, the personal and the ideological, work in opposite ways. Students who are strongly internal in the personal sense have higher achievement test scores, achieve higher grades in college, and perform better on an anagrams task which was included in the instruments administered in the study. In contrast, students who are strongly internal in the sense of believing that internal forces are the major determinants of success in the culture at large [ideological] perform *less* well than the more externally-oriented students. Given that these opposing results from the two types of control measures cancel each other, the total Rotter score understandably bears no relationship to these performance indicators.

The motivational significance of the personal rather than the more ideological measure is also clear in our research on the high school dropouts. In that study, responses to questions at the general ideological level bore no relationship to the trainee's job success in the period following his training. Questions tapping the trainee's sense of personal control or powerlessness were very clearly related to job success.

These results would suggest that if the concept of internal control is to capture the personal level intended in Rotter's definition, then questions asked of Negroes probably need to be cast in personal instead of general cultural terms. At least this self-other, or personal-ideological, distinction seems to be meaningful in the Negro populations we have studied.

INDIVIDUAL-SYSTEM BLAME

Several questions were written specifically for the study of college students to measure beliefs about the role of external and personal forces in the race situation. A second factor analysis was done on just the fourteen race-related questions. This subanalysis also resulted in four factors which have much the same structure for male and female students.

Our primary interest in this paper is with Factor III from this analysis. This factor seems to be a direct measure of the concept of concern in this paper, the student's explanation for social or economic failure among Negroes. We have called it a measure of *individual-system blame.* Consistently choosing the internal alternative on these four items means resting the burden for failure on Negroes themselves, specifically on their lack of skill, ability, training, effort, or proper behavior. In contrast, choosing the external alternative means attributing the responsibility for failure to the social system because of lack of opportunities and racial discrimination.

What are the implications of this blame-attribution variable for predicting the types of aspirations and performance criteria that have been traditional in the studies of achievement and internal-external control? Our main data bearing on this question come from the study of Negro college students where we related our measure of *individual-system blame* to the same set of motivational and performance indicators that were discussed in the preceding section.

An interesting difference appears when we compare the relationships obtained with the blame-attribution measure and those obtained with the measure of personal control. It will be recalled that personal control was related positively to a number of performance and aspiration measures that have often been associated with high achievement motivation—for instance, higher performance on tests of academic competence, greater expectations among entering freshmen that they would complete their college careers, stronger aspirations for occupations that are high in their prestige and ability demands. On the other hand, none of these performance and aspiration criteria were in any way related—either positively or negatively—to our measure of individual-system blame.

However, these performance and aspiration criteria commonly used in achievement studies represent a limited point of view about achievement. For one, they are *traditional* criteria, oriented toward achievement according to the most obvious societal standards—doing well in school, getting a prestigeful job. They do not represent the less traditional achievements which may be more innovative in nature. Secondly, they are *individual* criteria. Thus, these criteria point to individual mobility rather than to group-identified collective actions as the solution to the problems of poverty and minority populations.

TWO OTHER SETS OF CRITERIA

We felt that a broader conception of achievement and effectiveness-relevant behavior was needed in a study of Negroes at this stage of history. Therefore, we added two other sets of criteria to our analyses of internal-external control in the study of Negro college students. First, in the area of occupational aspiration, we included a concept of *nontraditionality of job aspirations,** as well as the usual concepts of prestige and ability demands. At a time of expanding job opportunities for Negro college students, when occupational arenas traditionally closed to Negroes (such as engineering and business) have begun to open up, the readiness of a Negro student to be an occupational pioneer becomes a critical achievement indicator. As a second nontraditional "innovative" criterion, the study also included a number of questions on students' attitudes toward and participation in *collective action* in the civil rights area. Given the magnitude of the problems facing Negroes and the increasing recognition—in the civil rights movement, in the emphasis on black pride, black power, and decentralized control of social institutions—that these problems demand collective attempts to change aspects of the social system as well as individual attempts to rise within it, we felt that involvement in these collective coping behaviors might be viewed as an important effectiveness criterion.

When we related personal control and individual-system blame to these nontraditional occupational aspirations and involvement in collective action, we found a very different pattern of results from those obtained with the traditional individual performance and aspiration criteria. The sense of personal control, which was associated with aspiring for jobs of high prestige and ability demands, was *not* associated with aspiring for jobs that are less traditional for Negroes. Conversely, individual-system blame, which was not related to prestige and ability demands, was clearly related to nontraditionality of aspiration. The students who were more sensitive to discrimination, who tended to blame the social system rather than individual qualities of Negroes for the problems that Negroes face, more often aspired for jobs that are less traditional for Negroes. In this instance, as we had pre-

---

* Each student's occupational choice was given a nontraditionality score by using the 1960 census breakdown of the percent Negro in that occupation. The occupations with the smallest proportion of Negroes in 1960 are the most nontraditional choices.

dicted, the external rather than internal orientation was associated with greater aspirations.

THE READINESS TO ENGAGE IN COLLECTIVE ACTION

A similar pattern of results was obtained when we related the personal control and individual-system blame measures to students' readiness to engage in collective action. Attitudes in this area were measured by a scale . . . [dealing with] the extent to which students felt that *individual effort and mobility* or *group action* represented the best way to overcome discrimination. This was clearly related to the blame attribution measure. Students on the external end of the continuum—i.e., those who tended to blame the system—were much more in favor of group rather than individual action to deal with discrimination. In contrast, the personal control measure showed no relationship to this individual-collective orientation.

Similar results appeared when the behavioral implications of these individual-collective attitudes were related to the individual-system blame and personal control measures. Individual-system blame was related to civil rights activity; students who blamed the system had engaged in many more civil rights activities such as demonstrations, picketing, and boycotting than had those who tended to see Negroes themselves as responsible for their subordinate position. Again, the personal control measure showed no relationship with civil rights activity.

To summarize, our results indicate that when internal-external control refers to Negroes' conceptions of the causes of their condition as Negroes, and these conceptions are related to more innovative, coping criteria, it is the external rather than the internal orientation that is associated with the more effective behaviors. When an internal orientation implies self-blame as a Negro, it also seems to involve a readiness to accept traditional restraints on Negroes' behavior. It might be noted, in this connection, that at the time of the study in 1964, the majority of the Negro college students fell on the "internal" end of the individual-system blame continuum; i.e., they tended to see the cause of Negroes' problems in personal inadequacies of Negroes rather than in the social system. Since self-blame for Negroes' problems was the majority point of view among these students, it is not surprising that students holding this view also supported the conventional and traditional view that individual self-betterment is the best approach to dealing with the problems.

These results on the correlates of individual-system blame are particularly consistent with sociological analyses that have highlighted the dysfunctionality for minority group members of self-blame beliefs which rationalize their subordinate position and inhibit behavior which might challenge the system determinants of their condition. We have already noted Merton's germinal statement of this point of view. A recent statement of this position appears in Paige's (1968) study of ghetto rioters. Paige demonstrates that rioting is clearly associated with rejecting a set of beliefs he refers to as the "culture of subordination," with self-blame rather than system-blame being a central aspect of these beliefs.

In this section we have presented the different attitudinal and behavioral implications that follow from our two concepts of internal-external control: personal control and individual-system blame. One further question remains. What is the relationship of these two concepts to each other? We will explore this question and some of the issues it raises in the concluding section of this paper.

RELATIONSHIP BETWEEN PERSONAL CONTROL AND INDIVIDUAL–SYSTEM BLAME

Individual mobility and collective action are often viewed, particularly in the sociological literature on subordinate groups, as alternative, and to some extent mutually exclusive, approaches that individuals in minority groups can take to cope with their problem of subordination. Therefore, one might expect that high personal control, which was associated with traditional individual mobility aspiration, would be negatively related to system-blame, which was associated with collective modes of dealing with discrimination. Yet, data from the college study indicate that personal control and individual-system blame are not related, either positively or negatively, to each other (Tau = +.04). This is not surprising considering the nature of the civil rights movement, particularly at the time the college study was done. To a large extent the collective assaults on the system represented in this movement have reflected an attempt to remove the barriers to Negro mobility within the system, rather than a desire to overthrow or opt out of it. Therefore, individual mobility and collective action orientations would not necessarily be polarized, even among the activist students.

Rather than predicting a simple relationship between personal control and individual-system blame, it might be more fruitful to expect the relationship to vary under different conditions, particularly those which affect individual payoffs produced by collective efforts. That we did not find a polarization of individual and collective orientations among Negro college students in 1964 is understandable. It was the peak of the success and optimism of the civil rights movement. The collective efforts of Negroes had not only overcome legal and social barriers but had job recruiters flocking to the Negro campuses. At that time, we might have found more polarization in noncollege Negro groups whose lack of skills did not permit them to maximize the possibilities afforded by expanding opportunities for Negroes. Today we might find more polarization even among college groups. Although the payoffs for individual Negro college students may still be expanding, the heightened concern on Negro campuses with black identity has probably promoted closer identification with the frustrations of the bulk of the Negro population for whom system rewards are not changing appreciably.

RACIAL MILITANTS—LOW PERSONAL CONTROL,
HIGH SYSTEM BLAME

There is some evidence from our college study that this greater polarization may come with increasing disenchantment and militancy. . . . *Racial militancy* measures the extent to which students reject methods of accommodation and consensus as ways of dealing with racial discrimination in favor of strategies of protest, confrontation, and conflict. This militancy was related to individual-system blame in a way that parallels the results on individual-collective orientations and civil rights activities. In addition to being more collectively oriented in their attitudes and engaging in more civil rights activity, the students who blamed the system were also more militant in supporting the necessity for confrontation tactics. What is interesting is that personal control, which was not related to individual-collective orientations or to involvement in civil rights activities, was actually *negatively* related to racial militancy. Of all the measures discussed in this paper, racial militancy was the only one that suggests a polarization between personal control and individual-system blame by showing a negative relationship with the former and a positive relationship with the latter.

If the tide of events should increasingly force motivationally effective Negroes to feel they have to choose between individual and collective expressions of their effectiveness, the social implications are obviously of paramount concern. Such a polarization would also sharpen some of the questions we have raised about the usual assumption in the internal-external control literature that effective motivation almost always flows from internal orientations.

Selected Bibliography

The first heading includes the general surveys of the modal personality characteristics of blacks. Each of the remaining headings refers to a personality variable (or set of related variables) discussed in the reader. Almost all the items in this bibliography appear in the alphabetically arranged list of sources that are cited in this book. That list immediately follows this bibliography.

GENERAL

Baughman, E. Earl. 1971. *Black Americans: A Psychological Analysis.* New York: Academic Press.

Dreger, Ralph Mason and Kent S. Miller. 1968. Comparative psychological studies of Negroes and whites in the United States 1959–65. *Psychological Bulletin* (Monograph Supplement) vol. 7, pp. 1–58.

———. 1960. Comparative psychological studies of Negroes and Whites in the United States. *Psychological Bulletin* vol. 57, pp. 361–402.

Goldschmid, Marcel L., ed. 1970. *Black Americans and White Racism: Theory and Research.* New York: Holt, Rinehart and Winston.

Pettigrew, Thomas F. 1964. *A Profile of the Negro American.* Princeton: Van Nostrand.

RACIAL PREFERENCE

Asher, Steven R. and Vernon L. Allen. 1969. Racial preference and social comparison processes. *Journal of Social Issues* vol. 25 (January), pp. 157–66.

Bayton, J. A., L. J. Austin and K. R. Burke. 1965. Negro perception of Negro and white personality traits. *Journal of Personality and Social Psychology,* vol. 1, pp. 250–53.

Butts, Hugh F. 1963. Skin color perception and self-esteem. *Journal of Negro Education*, vol. 32, pp. 122–28.

Clark, Kenneth B. and Mamie P. Clark. 1947. Racial identification and preference in Negro Children. In *Readings in Social Psychology*, T. M. Newcombe and E. L. Hartley, eds. New York: Holt, Rinehart and Winston.

Derbyshire, Robert L. and Eugene B. Brody. 1964. Identity and Ethnocentrism in American Negro college students. *Mental Hygiene*, vol. 48, pp. 202–08.

Gregor, A. James and D. A. McPherson. 1966a. Racial attitudes among white and Negro children in a deep-South standard metropolitan area. *Journal of Social Psychology*, vol. 68, pp. 95–106.

——. 1966b. Racial preference and ego-identity among white and Bantu children in the Republic of South Africa. *Genetic Psychology Monographs*, vol. 73, pp. 217–53.

Grossack, Martin M. 1956. Group belongingness among Negroes. *Journal of Social Psychology*, vol. 43, pp. 167–80.

——. 1957b. Group belongingness and authoritarianism in southern Negroes— a research note. *Phylon*, vol. 18, pp. 261–66.

Hoetker, James and Gary Siegel. 1970. Three studies of the preferences of students of different races for actors in interracial theatre productions. *Journal of Social Issues*, vol. 26 (Autumn), pp. 87–103.

Johnson, David W. 1966. Racial attitudes of Negro freedom school participants and Negro and white civil rights participants. *Social Forces*, vol. 45, pp. 266–72.

Johnson, Robert B. 1957. Negro reactions to minority group status. In *American Minorities*. Milton L. Barron, ed. New York: Knopf.

Kirkhart, Robert O. 1963. Minority group identification and group leadership. *Journal of Social Psychology*, vol. 59, pp. 111–17.

Maliver, Bruce L. 1965. Anti-Negro bias among Negro college students. *Journal of Personality and Social Psychology*, vol. 2, pp. 770–75.

Martin, James G. 1964. Racial ethnocentrism and judgment of beauty. *Journal of Social Psychology*, vol. 63, pp. 59–63.

Middleton, Russell and John Moland. 1959. Humor in Negro and white subcultures: a study of jokes among university students. *American Sociological Review*, vol. 24, pp. 61–69.

Morland, J. Kenneth. 1966. A comparison of race awareness in northern and southern children. *American Journal of Orthopsychiatry*, vol. 36, pp. 22–31.

——. 1963b. Racial self-identification: a study of nursery school children. *American Catholic Sociological Review*, vol. 24, pp. 231–42.

——. 1962. Racial acceptance and preference of nursery school children in a southern city. *Merrill-Palmer Quarterly*, vol. 8, pp. 271–80.

Noel, Donald L. 1964. Group identification among Negroes: an empirical analysis. *Journal of Social Issues,* vol. 20 (April), pp. 71–84.

Proshansky, Harold and Peggy Newton. 1968. The nature and meaning of Negro self-identity. In *Social Class, Race, and Psychological Development.* Martin Deutsch and others, eds. New York: Holt, Rinehart & Winston.

Rosenberg, Morris and Roberta G. Simmons. 1971. Black and white self-esteem: the urban school child. Unpublished manuscript.

Stevenson, H. W. and E. C. Stewart. 1958. A developmental study of racial awareness in young children. *Child Development,* vol. 29, pp. 399–409.

Trent, Richard D. 1957. The relation between expressed self-acceptance and expressed attitudes toward Negroes and whites among Negro children. *Journal of Genetic Psychology,* vol. 91, pp. 25–31.

SELF-ESTEEM

Baughman, E. Earl and W. Grant Dahlstrom. 1968. *Negro and White Children: A Psychological Study in the Rural South.* New York: Academic Press.

Butts, Hugh F. 1963. Skin color perception and self-esteem. *Journal of Negro Education,* vol. 32, pp. 122–28.

Carpenter, Thomas R. and Thomas V. Busse. 1969. Development of self concept in Negro and white welfare children. *Child Development,* vol. 40, pp. 935–39.

Clark, Kenneth B. 1965. *Dark Ghetto: Dilemmas of Social Power.* New York: Harper & Row.

Deutsch, Martin. 1960. Minority group and class status as related to social and personality factors in scholastic achievement. *Society of Applied Anthropology,* Monograph No. 2.

Gibby, Robert G. and Robert Gabler. 1967. The self-concept of Negro and white children. *Journal of Clinical Psychology,* vol. 23, pp. 144–48.

Grossack, Martin M. 1957a. Some personality characteristics of southern Negro students. *Journal of Social Psychology,* vol. 46, pp. 125–31.

Kardiner, Abram Lionel Ovesey. 1951. *The Mark of Oppression: Explorations in the Personality of the American Negro.* New York: Norton.

Keller, Suzanne. 1963. The social world of the urban slum child. *American Journal of Orthopsychiatry,* vol. 33, pp. 823–31.

Lang, Barbara H. and Edmund H. Henderson. 1968. Self-social concepts of disadvantaged school beginners. *Journal of Genetic Psychology,* vol. 113, pp. 41–51.

Liebow, Elliot. 1967. *Tally's Corner: A Study of Negro Streetcorner Men.* Boston: Little, Brown.

McCarthy, John D. and William L. Yancey. 1971. Uncle Tom and Mr. Charlie: metaphysical pathos in the study of racism and personal disorganization. *American Journal of Sociology*, vol. 76, pp. 648–72.

Rosenberg, Morris and Roberta G. Simmons. 1971. Black and white self-esteem: the urban school child. Unpublished manuscript.

Trent, Richard D. 1957. The relation between expressed self-acceptance and expressed attitudes toward Negroes and whites among Negro children. *Journal of Genetic Psychology*, vol. 91, pp. 25–31.

Williams, Robert L. and Harry Byars. 1968. Negro self-esteem in a transitional society. *Personnel and Guidance Journal*, vol. 47, pp. 120–25.

ACHIEVEMENT MOTIVATION

Atkinson, John W. and Norman T. Feather, eds. 1966. *A Theory of Achievement Motivation*. New York: Wiley.

Baughman, E. Earl and W. Grant Dahlstrom. 1968. *Negro and White Children: A Psychological Study in the Rural South.* New York: Academic Press.

Birney, Robert C. 1968. Research on the achievement motive. In *Handbook of Personality Theory and Research*. Edgar F. Borgatta and William W. Lambert, eds. Chicago: Rand McNally.

Katz, Irwin. 1967. Some motivational determinants of racial differences in intellectual achievement. *International Journal of Psychology*, vol. 2, pp. 1–12.

Mingione, Ann D. 1968. Need for achievement in Negro, white, and Puerto Rican children. *Journal of Consulting and Clinical Psychology*, vol. 32, pp. 94–95.

——. 1965. Need for achievement in Negro and white children. *Journal of Consulting Psychology*, vol. 29, pp. 108–11.

Mussen, Paul H. 1953. Differences between TAT responses of Negro and white boys. *Journal of Consulting Psychology*, vol. 17, pp. 373–76.

Veroff, J., J. W. Atkinson, S. C. Feld and G. Gurin. 1960. The use of thematic apperception to assess motivation in a nationwide interview study. *Psychological Monographs*, vol. 74, No. 449.

ALIENATION AND ANOMIE

Angell, Robert. 1962. Preference for moral norms in three problem areas. *American Journal of Sociology*, vol. 67, pp. 650–72.

Baughman, E. Earl and W. Grant Dahlstrom. 1968. *Negro and White Children: A Psychological Study in the Rural South.* New York: Academic Press.

Harrison, Robert H. and Edward H. Kass. 1967. Differences between Negro and white pregnant women on the MMPI. *Journal of Consulting Psychology*, vol. 31, pp. 454–63.

Lefton, Mark. 1968. Race, expectations, and anomie. *Social Forces*, vol. 46, pp. 347–52.

McCarthy, John D. and William L. Yancey. 1971. Uncle Tom and Mr. Charlie: Metaphysical pathos in the study of racism and personal disorganization. *American Journal of Sociology*, vol. 76, pp. 648–72.

Orbell, John M. 1967. Protest participation among southern Negro college students. *American Political Science Review*, vol. 61, pp. 446–56.

Robinson, John P. and Phillip R. Shaver. 1969. *Measures of Social Psychological Attitudes.* Ann Arbor: Institute for Social Research, University of Michigan.

SEX-ROLE ORIENTATION

Baughman, E. Earl and W. Grant Dahlstrom. 1968. *Negro and White Children: A Psychological Study in the Rural South.* New York: Academic Press.

Biller, Henry B. 1968. A note on father absence and masculine development in lower-class Negro and white boys. *Child Development*, vol. 39, pp. 1003–06.

Dager, Edward Z. 1964. Socialization and personality development in the child. In *Handbook of Marriage and the Family.* Harold T. Christensen, ed. Chicago: Rand McNally.

Hetherington, E. Mavis. 1966. Effects of paternal absence on sex-typed behaviors in Negro and white preadolescent males. *Journal of Personality and Social Psychology*, vol. 4, pp. 87–91.

Hokanson, J.E. and G. Calden. 1960. Negro-white differences on the MMPI. *Journal of Clinical Psychology*, vol. 16, pp. 32–33.

Keil, Charles. 1966. *Urban Blues.* Chicago: University of Chicago Press.

Lott, Albert J. and Bernice E. Lott. 1963. *Negro and White Youth: A Psychological Study in a Border State Community.* New York: Holt, Rinehart & Winston.

Mussen, Paul H. 1969. Early sex-role development. In *Handbook of Socialization Theory and Research.* David A. Goslin, ed. Chicago: Rand McNally.

INTERNAL-EXTERNAL CONTROL OF REINFORCEMENTS

Bullough, Bonnie. 1967. Alienation in the ghetto. *American Journal of Sociology*, vol. 72, pp. 469–78.

Forward, John R. and Jay R. Williams. 1970. Internal-external control and black militancy. *Journal of Social Issues*, vol. 26 (Winter), pp. 75–92.

Gore, Pearl M. and Julian B. Rotter. 1963. A personality correlate of social action. *Journal of Personality*, vol. 31, pp. 58–64.

Lao, Rosina C. 1970. Internal-external control and competent and innovative behavior among Negro college students. *Journal of Personality and Social Psychology*, vol. 14, pp. 263–70.

Lefcourt, Herbert M. 1966. Internal versus external control of reinforcements: a review. *Psychological Bulletin*, vol. 65, pp. 206–20.

Lefcourt, Herbert M. and Gordon W. Ladwig. 1965. The American Negro: a problem in expectancies. *Journal of Personality and Social Psychology*, vol. 1, pp. 377–80.

Ransford, H. Edward. 1968. Isolation, powerlessness, and violence. *American Journal of Sociology*, vol. 73, pp. 581–91.

Rotter, Julian B. 1966. Generalized expectancies for internal versus external control of reinforcement. *Psychological Monographs*, vol. 80, pp. 1–28, No. 609.

Strickland, Bonnie Ruth. 1965. The prediction of social action from a dimension of internal-external control. *Journal of Social Psychology*, vol. 66, pp. 353–58.

Thune, Jeanne M. 1967. Racial attitudes of older adults. *Gerontologist*, vol. 7, pp. 179–82.

MINNESOTA MULTIPHASIC PERSONALITY INVENTORY (MMPI)

Carson, Robert C. 1969. Interpretative manual to the MMPI. In *MMPI: Research Developments and Clinical Applications.* James Neal Butcher, ed. New York: McGraw Hill.

Harrison, Robert H. and Edward H. Kass. 1967. Differences between Negro and white pregnant women on the MMPI. *Journal of Consulting Psychology*, vol. 31, pp. 454–63.

Miller, C., S.C. Knapp and C.W. Daniels. 1968. MMPI study of Negro mental hygiene clinic patients. *Journal of Abnormal Psychology*, vol. 73, pp. 168–73.

FRUSTRATION, ANGER, AND AGGRESSION

Baughman, E. Earl and W. Grant Dahlstrom. 1968. *Negro and White Children: A Psychological Study in the Rural South.* New York: Academic Press.

Brazziel, William F. 1964. Correlates of southern Negro personality. *Journal of Social Issues*, vol. 20 (April), pp. 46–53.

Breen, Michael. 1968. Culture and schizophrenia: a study of Negro and Jewish schizophrenics. *International Journal of Social Psychiatry*, vol. 14, pp. 282–89.

Dollard, John. 1957. *Caste and Class in a Southern Town.* New York: Doubleday Anchor, 3rd edition.

Federal Bureau of Investigation. 1970. *Uniform Crime Reports for the United States, 1969.* Washington, D.C.: U.S. Government Printing Office.

Figelman, Matthew. 1968. A comparison of affective and paranoid disorders in Negroes and Jews. *International Journal of Social Psychiatry*, vol. 14, pp. 277–81.

Gibbs, Jack P. 1966. Suicide. In *Contemporary Social Problems.* Robert K. Merton and Robert A. Nisbet, eds. New York: Harcourt, Brace and World. 2nd. edition.

Gold, Martin. 1958. Suicide, homicide, and the socialization of aggression. *American Journal of Sociology,* Vol. 63, pp. 651–61.

Grindstaff, Carl F. 1968. The Negro, urbanization, and relative deprivation in the deep south. *Social Problems,* Vol. 15, pp. 342–52.

Grossack, Martin M. 1957a. Some personality characteristics of southern Negro students. *Journal of Social Psychology*, vol. 46, pp. 125–31.

Hammer, E.F. 1953. Frustration-aggression hypothesis extended to socioracial areas: comparison of Negro and white children's H-T-P's. *Psychiatric Quarterly*, vol. 27, pp. 597–607.

Kardiner, Abram and Lionel Ovesey. 1951. *The Mark of Oppression: Explorations in the Personality of the American Negro.* New York: Norton.

Karon, Bertram P. 1958. *The Negro Personality: A Rigorous Investigation of the Effects of Culture.* New York: Springer.

Katz, Irwin, et al. 1964. The influence of race of the experimenter and instructions upon the expression of hostility by Negro boys. *Journal of Social Issues*, vol. 20 (April), pp. 54–60.

Lalli, Michael and Stanley H. Turner. 1968. Suicide and homicide; a comparative analysis by race and occupational levels. *Journal of Criminal Law, Criminology, and Police Science*, vol. 59, pp. 191–200.

Lane, Ellen A. 1968. The influence of sex and race on process-reactive ratings of schizophrenics. *Journal of Psychology*, vol. 68, pp. 15–20.

McCary, James L. 1956. Picture frustration study normative data for some cultural and racial groups. *Journal of Clinical Psychology*, vol. 12, pp. 194–95.

——. 1950. Ethnic and cultural reactions to frustration. *Journal of Personality,* vol. 18, pp. 321–26.

Mussen, Paul H. 1953. Differences between TAT responses of Negro and white boys. *Journal of Consulting Psychology*, vol. 17, pp. 373–76.

National Advisory Commission on Civil Disorders. *1968 Report*. Washington, D.C.: U.S. Government Printing Office.

Pettigrew, Thomas F. 1971. *Racially Separate or Together?* New York: McGraw-Hill.

Portnoy, Bernard and Chalmers L. Stacey. 1954. A comparative study of Negro and white subnormals on the children's form of the Rosenzweig P-F Test. *American Journal of Mental Deficiency*, vol. 59, pp. 272–78.

Prange, Arthur J. and M. M. Vitals. 1962. Cultural aspects of the relatively low incidence of depression in southern Negroes. *International Journal of Social Psychiatry*, vol. 8, pp. 104–12.

Ransford, H. Edward. 1968. Isolation, powerlessness, and violence. *American Journal of Sociology*, vol. 73, pp. 581–91.

Sears, David O. and John B. McConahay. 1970. Racial socialization, comparison levels, and the Watts riot. *Journal of Social Issues*, vol. 26 (Winter), pp. 121–40.

Touchstone, F. V. 1957. A comparative study of Negro and white college students' aggressiveness by means of sentence completion. *Dissertation Abstracts*, vol. 17, pp. 1588–89

Winslow, Charles N. and James E. Brainerd. 1950. A comparison of the reactions of whites and Negroes to frustration as measured by the Rosenzweig Picture-Frustration Test. *American Psychologist*, vol. 5, p. 297 (Abstract).

Wolfgang, Marvin E. 1968. Crime: homicide. *International Encyclopedia of the Social Sciences*, vol. 3, pp. 490–95.

References

A selection of these sources is arranged by topic in the preceding Selected Bibliography.

Abrahams, Roger D. 1962. Playing the dozens. *Journal of American Folklore* vol. 75, pp. 209–20.

———. 1964. *Deep Down in the Jungle . . . Negro Narrative Folklore from the Streets of Philadelphia.* Hatboro: Folklore Associates.

Adorno, T. E., et al 1950. *The Authoritarian Personality.* New York: Harper & Row.

Angell, Robert. 1962. Preference for moral norms in three problem areas. *American Journal of Sociology,* vol. 67, pp. 650–72.

Asher, Steven R. and Vernon L. Allen. 1969. Racial preference and social comparison processes. *Journal of Social Issues,* vol. 25, pp. 157-66.

Atkinson, John W. and Norman T. Feather, eds. 1966. *A Theory of Achievement Motivation.* New York: Wiley.

Ausubel, D. P. and P. Ausubel. 1963. Ego development among segregated Negro children. In *Education in Depressed Areas,* A. H. Passow, ed. New York: Columbia University Press.

Azrin, N. H., R. R. Hutchinson and D. F. Hake. 1966. Extinction-induced aggression. *Journal of the Experimental Analysis of Behavior,* vol. 9, pp. 191–204.

Bakke, E. Wright. 1940. *Citizens Without Work.* New Haven: Shoestring Press.

Baldwin, James. 1963. *The Fire Next Time.* New York: Dial Press.

Barnes, J. A. 1954. Class and committees in a Norwegian island parish. *Human Relations,* vol. 7, pp. 39–58.

Baughman, E. Earl. 1971. *Black Americans: A Psychological Analysis.* New York: Academic Press.

Baughman, E. Earl and W. Grant Dahlstrom. 1968. *Negro and White Children: A Psychological Study in the Rural South.* New York: Academic Press.

Bayton, J. A., L. J. Austin and K. R. Burke. 1965. Negro perception of Negro and white personality traits. *Journal of Personality and Social Psychology,* vol. 1, pp. 250–53.

Bear, Roberta M., Robert D. Hess and Virginia C. Shipman. 1966. Social class difference in maternal attitudes toward school and the consequences for cognitive development in the young child. Mimeographed. Urban Child Center: University of Chicago.

Berdie, Ralph F. 1947. Playing the dozens. *Journal of Abnormal and Social Psychology,* vol. 42, pp. 120–21.

Berger, Bennett M. 1967. Soul searching. Review of Urban Blues (Keil 1966). Trans*action,* vol. 4, June, pp. 54–57.

Berger, Peter L., and Thomas Luckmann. 1966. *The Social Construction of Reality.* Garden City: Doubleday.

Berkowitz, L. 1965. The concept of aggressive drive. In *Advances in Experimental Social Psychology,* L. Berkowitz, ed. New York: Academic Press.

———. 1968. *Roots of Aggression: A Re-examination of the Frustration-Aggression Hypothesis.* New York: Atherton Press.

Berkowitz, L. and A. Le Page. 1967. Weapons as aggressive-eliciting stimuli. *Journal of Personality and Social Psychology,* vol. 7. pp. 202–07.

Bernard, Jessie. 1966. *Marriage and Family among Negroes.* Englewood Cliffs: Prentice-Hall.

Biller, Henry B. 1968. A note on father absence and masculine development in lower-class Negro and white boys. *Child Development,* vol. 39, p. 1003.

Birdwhistell, Ray. 1966. The American family: some perspectives. *Psychiatry,* vol. 29, pp. 203–12.

Birney, Robert C. 1968. Research on the achievement motive. In *Handbook of Personality Theory and Research.* Edgar F. Borgatta and William W. Lambert, eds. Chicago: Rand McNally.

Blauner, Robert. 1970. Black culture: myth or reality? In *Old Memories, New Moods.* Peter I. Rose, ed. New York: Atherton.

Bogardus, Emory S. 1959. Race reactions by sexes. *Sociology and Social Research,* vol. 48, p. 441.

Bott, Elizabeth. 1957. *Family and Social Networks.* London: Tavistock.

Brazziel, William F. 1964. Correlates of southern Negro personality. *Journal of Social Issues,* vol. 20, April, pp. 46–53.

Breen, Michael. 1968. Culture and schizophrenia: a study of Negro and Jewish schizophrenics. *International Journal of Social Psychiatry* vol. 14, pp. 282–89.

Brown, Roger. 1965. *Social Psychology.* New York: Free Press.

Bullough, Bonnie. 1967. Alienation in the ghetto. *American Journal of Sociology,* vol. 72, pp. 469–78.

Burgess, T. 1913. *Greeks in America.* Boston: Sherman, French.

Burton, Roger V., and John W. M. Whiting. 1961. The absent father and cross-sex identity. *Merrill-Palmer Quarterly,* vol. 7, pp. 85–95.

Butcher, J. N. and W. G. Dahlstrom. 1965. Equivalence of the booklet and taped forms of the MMPI for use with college normals. Unpublished materials.

Butts, Hugh F. 1963. Skin color perception and self-esteem. *Journal of Negro Education,* vol. 32, pp. 122–28.

Byrne, Donn. 1966. *Introduction to Personality: A Research Approach.* Englewood Cliffs: Prentice-Hall.

Carpenter, Thomas R. and Thomas V. Busse. 1969. Development of self concept in Negro and white welfare children. *Child Development* vol. 40, pp. 935–39.

Carson, Robert C. 1969. Interpretative manual to the MMPI. In *MMPI: Research Developments and Clinical Applications.* James Neal Butcher, ed. New York: McGraw-Hill.

Cartwright, Dorwin. 1950. Emotional dimensions of group life. In *Feelings and Emotions.* New York: McGraw-Hill.

Child, Irwin L. 1968. Personality in culture. In *Handbook of Personality Theory and Research.* Edgar F. Borgatta and William W. Lambert, eds. Chicago: Rand McNally.

Christie, Richard and Marie Jahoda, eds. 1954. *Studies in the Scope and Method of the Authoritarian Personality.* New York: Free Press.

Clark, Kenneth B. 1965. *Dark Ghetto: Dilemmas of Social Power.* New York: Harper & Row.

Clark, Kenneth B. and Mamie P. Clark. 1947. Racial identification and preference in Negro children. In *Readings in Social Psychology.* T. M. Newcombe and E. L. Hartley, eds. New York: Holt, Rinehart & Winston.

Cohen, Albert K., and Harold M. Hodges. 1963. Characteristics of the lower-blue-collar-class. *Social Problems,* vol. 10, no. 4, pp. 303–34.

Coleman, J. S., et al. 1966. *Equality of Educational Opportunity.* U. S. Department of Health, Education and Welfare. Washington: U.S. Government Printing Office, 1966.

Dager, Edward Z. 1964. Socialization and personality development in the child. In *Handbook of Marriage and the Family.* Harold T. Christensen, ed. Chicago: Rand McNally.

Dahlstrom, W. G. and G. S. Welsh. 1960. *An MMPI Handbook: A Guide to Use in Clinical Practice and Research.* Minneapolis: University of Minnesota Press.

Danzig, D. 1964. The meaning of the Negro strategy. *Commentary,* February, pp. 41–46.

Davie, M. 1936. *World Migration.* New York: Macmillan.

Davies, J. C. 1962. Toward a theory of revolution. *American Sociological Review,* vol. 17, pp. 5–19.

Davis, Allison, Burleigh B. Gardner and Mary Gardner. 1944. *Deep South: A Social Anthropological Study of Caste and Class.* Chicago: University of Chicago Press.

Dean, Dwight G. 1961. Alienation: its meaning and measurement. *American Sociological Review*, vol. 26, pp. 753–58.

Derbyshire, Robert L., Eugene B. Brody and Carl Schleifer. 1963. Family structure of young adult Negro male patients: preliminary observations from urban Baltimore. *Journal of Nervous and Mental Disease*, vol. 136, pp. 245–51.

Derbyshire, Robert L. and Eugene B. Brody. 1964. Identity and ethnocentrism in American Negro college students. *Mental Hygiene*, vol. 48, pp. 202–08.

Deutsch, Martin. 1960. Minority group and class status as related to social and personality factors in scholastic achievement. *Society of Applied Anthropology*, Monograph No. 2.

Dollard, John. 1939. The dozens: dialect of insult. *American Imago*, vol. 1, pp. 3–25.

——. 1957. *Caste and Class in a Southern Town.* New York: Doubleday Anchor, 3rd edition.

Dollard, John, et al. 1939. *Frustration and Aggression.* New Haven: Yale University Press, p. 3.

Drake, St. Clair. 1965. *The Social and Economic Status of the Negro in the United States.* Daedalus, Fall, p. 772.

Drake, St. Clair and Horace R. Cayton. 1962. *Black Metropolis: A Study of Negro Life in a Northern City*, 2 vols. New York: Harper & Row.

Dreger, Ralph Mason and Kent S. Miller. 1960. Comparative psychological studies of Negroes and whites in the United States. *Psychological Bulletin*, vol. 57, pp. 361–402.

——. 1968. Comparative psychological studies of Negroes and whites in the United States: 1959–65. *Psychological Bulletin* (Monograph Supplement), vol 70, pp. 361–58.

Dunbar, Leslie W. 1964. The changing mind of the South: the exposed nerve. In *The American South in the 1960s.* New York: Praeger.

Ellison, Ralph. 1964. *Shadow and Act.* New York: Random.

Epstein, A. L. 1961. The network and urban social organization. *Human Problems in British Central Africa*, vol. 29, pp. 29–62.

Erickson, Erik H. 1959. Identity and the life cycle. *Psychological Issues, I.*

Fanon, F. 1967. *Black Skin, White Masks.* New York: Grove Press.

Featherman, David L. 1971. The socioeconomic achievement of white religio-ethnic subgroups: social and psychological explanations. *American Sociological Review*, vol. 36, pp, 207–22.

Federal Bureau of Investigation. 1964. *Manual for Uniform Crime Reporting.* Department of Justice.

———. 1970. *Uniform Crime Reports for the United States, 1969.* Washington, D. C.: U. S. Government Printing Office.

Feierabend, I. K., and R. L. Feierabend. 1966. Aggressive behaviors within politics, 1948–1962: a cross-national study. *Journal of Conflict Resolution,* vol. 10, pp. 249–71.

Figelman, Matthew. 1968. A comparison of affective and paranoid disorders in Negroes and Jews. *International Journal of Social Psychiatry,* vol. 14, pp. 277–81.

Fishman, J. R., and F. Solomon. 1963. Youth and social action: I. Perspectives on student sit-in movement. *American Journal of Orthopsychiatrics,* vol. 33, pp. 872–82.

Floyd, James A., Jr. 1969. Self-concept development in black children. Senior thesis, Princeton University.

Forward, John R. and Jay R. Williams. 1970. Internal-external control and black militancy. *Journal of Social Issues,* vol. 26 (Winter), pp. 75–92.

Franklin, John Hope. 1956. *From Slavery to Freedom.* New York: Knopf.

Frazier, E. Franklin. 1932. *The Negro Family in Chicago.* Chicago: University of Chicago Press.

———. 1934. Traditions and patterns in Negro family life in the United States. In *Race and Culture Contacts.* E. B. Reuter, ed. New York: McGraw-Hill.

———. 1939. *The Negro Family in the United States.* Chicago: University of Chicago Press. Revised and abridged edition 1948. New York: Dryden. Paperback edition of 1948 edition 1966, Chicago: University of Chicago Press.

———. 1949. *The Negro in the United States.* New York: Macmillan. 2nd edition, 1957.

Galbraith, J. K. 1958. *The Affluent Society.* Boston: Houghton Mifflin.

Gans, Herbert J. 1962. *The Urban Villagers.* New York: Free Press.

———. 1967. The Negro family: reflections on the Moynihan report. In *The Moynihan Report and the Politics of Controversy.* Lee Rainwater and William L. Yancey, eds. Cambridge: M.I.T. Press.

Gibbs, Jack P. 1966. Suicide. In *Contemporary Social Problems.* Robert K. Merton and Robert A. Nisbet, eds. New York: Harcourt, Brace and World. 2nd edition.

Gibby, Robert G. and Robert Gabler. 1967. The self-concept of Negro and white children. *Journal of Clinical Psychology,* vol. 23, pp. 144–48.

Gilberstadt, H. and Jan Duker. 1965. *A Handbook for Clinical and Actuarial MMPI Interpretation.* Philadelphia: Saunders.

Glazer, N. 1958. The American Jew and the attainment of middle-class rank: some trends and explanations. In M. Sklare, ed. *The Jews: Social Patterns of an American Group.* Glencoe: Free Press.

Glock, Charles Y. 1964. Images of man and public opinion. *Public Opinion Quarterly,* Winter.

Goffman, Irving. 1961. *Asylums.* Garden City, N.Y.: Doubleday.

Gold, Martin. 1958. Suicide, homicide, and the socialization of aggression. *American Journal of Sociology,* vol. 63, pp. 651–61.

Goldschmidt, Marcel L., ed. 1970. *Black Americans and White Racism: Theory and Research.* New York: Holt, Rinehart and Winston.

Goodenough, Ward. 1963. *Cooperation and Change.* New York: Russell Sage.

Goodman, M. E. 1946. Evidence concerning the genesis of interracial attitudes. *American Anthropologist,* vol. 48, pp. 624–30.

———. 1964. *Race Awareness in Young Children.* Rev. ed. New York: Collier Books.

Gore, Pearl M. and Julian B. Rotter. 1963. A personality correlate of social action. *Journal of Personality,* vol. 31, pp. 58–64.

Gouldner, Alvin W. 1958. Reciprocity and autonomy in functional theory. In *Symposium on Sociological Theory.* Llewellyn Gross, ed. Evanston: Harper & Row.

Green, Arnold W. 1941. The Cult of Personality and Sexual Relations. *Psychiatry,* vol. 4, pp. 343–48.

Greenwald, H. J., and D. B. Oppenheim. 1968. Reported magnitude of self-misidentification among Negro children—artifact? *Journal of Personality and Social Psychology,* vol. 8, pp. 49–52.

Gregor, A. James and D. A. McPherson. 1966a. Racial attitudes among white and Negro children in a deep-south standard metropolitan area. *Journal of Social Psychology,* vol. 68, pp. 95–106.

———. 1966b. Racial preference and ego-identity among white and Bantu children in the Republic of South Africa. *Genetic Psychology Monographs,* vol. 73, pp. 217–53.

Grindstaff, Carl F. 1968. The Negro, urbanization, and relative deprivation in the deep south. *Social Problems,* vol. 15, pp. 342-52.

Grossack, Martin M. 1956. Group belongingness among Negroes. *Journal of Social Psychology,* vol. 43, pp. 167–80.

———. 1957a. Some personality characteristics of southern Negro students. *Journal of Social Psychology,* vol. 46, pp. 125–31.

———. 1957b. Group belongingness and authoritarianism in southern Negroes—a research note. *Phylon,* vol. 18, pp. 261–66.

Hammer, E. F. 1953. Frustration-aggression hypothesis extended to socio-racial areas: comparison of Negro and white children's H-T-P's. *Psychiatric Quarterly,* vol. 27, pp. 597–607.

Hammond, Boone. 1965. The contest system: a survival technique. Masters Honors paper, Washington University.

Harrison, Robert H. and Edward H. Kass. 1967. Differences between Negro and white pregnant women on the MMPI. *Journal of Consulting Psychology,* vol. 31, pp. 454–63.

Herskovits, Melville J. 1941. *The Myth of the Negro Past.* New York: Harper. Paperback edition 1958. Boston: Beacon Press.

Herzog, Elizabeth. 1967. Is there a "breakdown" of the Negro family? In *The Moynihan Report and the Politics of Controversy.* Lee Rainwater and William L. Yancey, eds. Cambridge: M.I.T. Press.

Hess, Robert D. and Gerald Handel. 1959. *Family Worlds.* Chicago: University of Chicago Press.

Hetherington, E. Mavis. 1966. Effects of paternal absence on sex-typed behaviors in Negro and white preadolescent males. *Journal of Personality and Social Psychology,* vol. 4, pp. 87–91.

Hoetker, James and Gary Siegel. 1970. Three studies of the preferences of students of different races for actors in interracial theatre productions. *Journal of Social Issues,* vol. 26 (Autumn), pp. 87–103.

Hokanson, J. E. and G. Calden. 1960. Negro-white differences on the MMPI. *Journal of Clinical Psychology,* vol. 16, pp. 32–33.

Hollinshead, A. B., and F. C. Redlich. 1953. Social stratification and psychiatric disorders. *American Sociological Review,* vol. 18, pp. 163–69.

Inkeles, Alex and Daniel J. Levinson. 1969. National character: the study of modal personality and sociocultural systems. In *The Handbook of Social Psychology.* Gardner Lindzey and Elliot Aronson, eds. 2nd edition, Reading: Addison-Wesley.

Jahoda, Gustav, T. Venessa and I. Pushkin. 1966. Awareness of ethnic differences in young children: proposals for a British study. *Race,* vol. 8, p. 63.

James, William. 1950. *The Principles of Psychology.* Dover Publications (originally published in 1890).

Johnson, David W. 1966. Racial attitudes of Negro freedom school participants and Negro and white civil rights participants. *Social Forces,* vol. 45, pp. 266–72.

Johnson, Robert B. 1957. Negro reactions to minority group status. In *American Minorities.* Milton L. Barron, ed. New York: Knopf.

Jones, Le Roi. 1963. *Blues People.* New York: William Morrow & Co.

Josephson, Eric and Mary Josephson, eds. 1962. *Man Alone: Alienation in Modern Society.* New York: Dell.

Kalijarvi, T. 1942. French-Canadians in the United States. *Annals, American Academy of Political and Social Science,* September.

Kardiner, Abram and Lionel Ovesey. 1951. *The Mark of Oppression: Explorations in the Personality of the American Negro.* New York: Norton.

Karon, Bertram P. 1958. *The Negro Personality: A Rigorous Investigation of the Effects of Culture.* New York: Springer.

Katz, Irwin. 1967. Some motivational determinants of racial differences in intellectual achievement. *International Journal of Psychology,* vol. 2, p. 1.

Katz, Irwin, et al. 1964. The influence of race of the experimenter and instructions upon the expression of hostility by Negro boys. *Journal of Social Issues,* vol. 20 (April), pp. 54–60.

Keil, Charles. 1966. *Urban Blues.* Chicago: University of Chicago Press.

Keller, Suzanne. 1963. The social world of the urban slum child. *American Journal of Orthopsychiatry,* vol. 33, pp. 823–31.

Kelman, H. and J. Barclay. 1963. The F Scale as a measure of breadth of perspective. *Journal of Abnormal and Social Psychology.*

Killian, Lewis M. and Charles M. Grigg. *1962. Urbanism, Race, and Anomie. American Journal of Sociology,* vol. 67.

King, Martin Luther. 1958. *Stride Toward Freedom.* New York: Ballantine Books.

——. 1964. A challenge to the churches and synagogues. In *Challenge to Religion.* M. Ahmann, ed. Chicago: Henry Regnery Company.

Kirkhart, Robert O. 1963. Minority group identification and group leadership. *Journal of Social Psychology,* vol. 59, pp. 111–17.

Kleinmuntz, Benjamin. 1967. *Personality Measurement: An Introduction.* Homewood (Ill.): Dorsey Press.

Kluckhohn, F. 1950. Dominant and substitute profiles of cultural orientations. *Social Forces,* vol. 28, pp. 376–93.

Kluckhohn, Clyde and Henry A. Murray. 1956. Personality formation: the determinants. In *Personality in Nature, Society, and Culture.* Clyde Kluckhohn, ed. 2nd edition. New York: Knopf.

Komarovsky, Mirra. 1960. *The Unemployed Man and His Family.* New York: Octagon.

——. 1964. *Blue Collar Marriage.* New York: Random.

Koss, Earl L. 1946. *Families in Trouble.* New York:

Lalli, Michael and Stanley H. Turner. 1968. Suicide and homicide: a comparative analysis by race and occupational levels. *Journal of Criminal Law, Criminology, and Police Science,* vol. 59, pp. 191–200.

Lane, Ellen A. 1968. The influence of sex and race on process-reflective ratings of schiziphrenics. *Journal of Psychology,* vol. 68, pp. 15–20.

Lang, Barbara H. and Edmund H. Henderson. 1968. Self-social concepts of disadvantaged school beginners. *Journal of Genetic Psychology,* vol. 113, pp. 41–51.

Lao, Rosina C. 1970. Internal-external control and competent and innovative behavior among Negro college students. *Journal of Personality and Social Psychology*, vol. 14, 263–70.

Lefcourt, Herbert M. 1965. Risk-taking in Negro and white adults. *Journal of Personality and Social Psychology*, vol. 2, pp. 765–70.

———. 1966. Internal versus external control of reinforcements: a review. *Psychological Bulletin*, vol. 65, pp. 206–20.

Lefcourt, Herbert M. and Gordon W. Ladwig. 1965. The American Negro: a problem in expectancies. *Journal of Personality and Social Psychology*, vol. 1, pp. 377–80.

Lefton, Mark. 1968. Race, expectations, and anomie. *Social Forces*, vol. 46, pp. 347–52.

Levison, P. K. and J. P. Flynn. 1965. The objects attacked by cats during stimulation of the hypothalamus. *Animal Behavior*, vol. 13, pp. 217–20.

Lewis, Hylan. 1955. *Blackways of Kent*. Chapel Hill: University of North Carolina Press.

———. 1967. The family—resources for change. In *The Moynihan Report and the Politics of Controversy*. Lee Rainwater and William L. Yancey, eds. Cambridge: M.I.T. Press.

Liebow, Elliot. 1967. *Tally's Corner: A Study of Negro Streetcorner Men*. Boston: Little, Brown.

Lorenz, Konrad. 1966. *On Aggression*. New York: Harcourt Brace & World.

Lott, Albert J. and Bernice E. Lott. 1963. *Negro and White Youth: A Psychological Study in a Border State Community*. New York: Holt, Rinehart & Winston.

McCarthy, John D. and William L. Yancey. 1971. Uncle Tom and Mr. Charlie: metaphysical pathos in the study of racism and personal disorganization. *American Journal of Sociology*, vol. 76, pp. 648–72.

McCary, James L. 1950. Ethnic and cultural reactions to frustration. *Journal of Personality*, vol. 18, pp. 321–26.

———. 1956. Picture frustration study normative data for some cultural and racial groups. *Journal of Clinical Psychology*, vol. 12, pp. 194–95.

McClelland, D. C. 1955. Some social consequences of achievement motivation. In *Nebraska Symposium on Motivation*. M. R. Jones, ed. Lincoln: University of Nebraska Press.

McClelland, D. C., A. Rindlisbacher, and R. C. deCharms. 1955. Religious and other sources of parental attitudes towards independence training. In *Studies in Motivation*. D. C. McClelland, ed. New York: Appleton-Century-Crofts.

McClelland, D. C., J. Atkinson, R. Clark and E. Lowell. 1953. *The Achievement Motive.* New York: Appleton-Century-Crofts.

Mailer, Norman. n. d. *The White Negro.* San Francisco: City Lights Books.

Maliver, Bruce L. 1965. Anti-Negro bias among Negro college students. *Journal of Personality and Social Psychology,* vol. 2, pp. 770–75.

Mallick, S. K. and B. R. McCandless. 1966. A study of catharsis of aggression. *Journal of Personality and Social Psychology,* vol. 4, pp. 591–96.

Marks, P. A. and W. Seeman. 1963. *Actuarial Description of Abnormal Personality.* Baltimore: Williams & Wilkins.

Martin, James G. 1964. Racial ethnocentrism and judgment of beauty. *Journal of Social Psychology,* vol. 63, pp. 59–63.

Mayer, Adrian C. 1966. The significance of quasi-groups in the study of complex societies. In *The Social Anthropology of Complex Societies.* Michael Banton, ed. New York: Praeger.

Meeks, D. E. 1967. The white ego ideal: implications for the bi-racial treatment relationship. *Smith College Studies in Social Work,* vol. 37, pp. 93–105.

Merton, Robert K. 1957. *Social Theory and Social Structure.* Glencoe: Free Press. Revised edition, 1964.

Middleton, Russell and John Moland. 1959. Humor in Negro and white subcultures: a study of jokes among university students. *American Sociological Review,* vol. 24, pp. 61–69.

Mignione, Ann D. 1965. Need for achievement in Negro and white children. *Journal of Consulting Psychology,* vol. 29, pp. 108–11.

———. 1968. Need for achievement in Negro, white, and Puerto Rican children. *Journal of Consulting and Clinical Psychology,* vol. 32, pp. 94–95.

Miller, C., S. C. Knapp and C. W. Daniels. 1968. MMPI study of Negro mental hygiene clinic patients. *Journal of Abnormal Psychology,* vol. 73, 168–73.

Miller, S. M. 1964. The American lower classes: a typological approach. In *Blue Collar World.* Arthur B. Shostak and William Gomberg, eds. Englewood Cliffs: Random.

Miller, Walter B. 1958. Lower class structure as a generating milieu of gang delinquency. *Journal of Social Issues,* vol. 14, p. 3.

Miner, H. 1939. *St. Dennis: a French-Canadian Parish.* Chicago: University of Chicago Press.

Mitchell, J. Clyde. 1966. Theoretical orientations in African urban studies. In *The Social Anthropology of Complex Societies.* Michael Banton, ed. New York: Praeger.

Mizruchi, Ephraim. 1954. *Success and Opportunity: A Study of Anomie.* New York: Free Press.

Morland, J. Kenneth. 1958. Racial recognition by nursery school children in Lynchburg, Virginia. *Social Forces*, vol. 37, pp. 132–37.

———. 1962. Racial acceptance and preference of nursery school children in a southern city. *Merrill-Palmer Quarterly*, vol. 8, pp. 271–80.

———. 1963a. The development of racial bias in young children. *Theory into Practice*, vol. 2, pp. 120–27.

———. 1963b. Racial self-identification: a study of nursery school children. *American Catholic Sociological Review*, vol. 24, pp. 231–42.

———. 1966. A comparison of race awareness in northern and southern children. *American Journal of Orthopsychiatry*, vol. 36, pp. 22–31.

Moynihan, Daniel Patrick. 1965. *The Negro Family: The Case for National Action*. Washington, D. C.: Government Printing Office. Prepared for the Office of Policy Planning and Research of the Department of Labor.

———. 1970. *Memorandum for the President*. Reprinted in the *New York Times*, 1 March.

Mussen, Paul H. 1953. Differences between TAT responses of Negro and white boys. *Journal of Consulting Psychology*, vol. 17, pp. 373–76.

———. 1969. Early sex-role development. In *Handbook of Socialization Theory and Research*. David A. Goslin, ed. Chicago: Rand McNally.

Myrdal, G. 1944. *American Dilemma*. New York: Harper & Brothers.

National Advisory Commission on Civil Disorders. 1968. *Report*. Washington, D. C.: U. S. Government Printing Office.

National Opinion Research Center. 1947. Jobs and occupations: a popular evaluation. *Opinion News*, no. 9.

Nettler, Gwynn. 1957. A measure of alienation. *American Sociological Review*, vol. 22, pp. 670–77.

Noel, Donald L. 1964. Group identification among Negroes: an empirical analysis. *Journal of Social Issues*, vol. 20, April, pp. 71–84.

Orbell, John M. 1967. Protest participation among southern Negro college students. *American Political Science Review*, vol. 61, pp. 446–56.

Paige, J. 1968. Collective violence and the culture of subordination. Unpublished doctoral dissertation, University of Michigan.

Parsons, Talcott and Robert F. Bales. 1955. *Family, Socialization and Interaction Process*. Glencoe: Free Press.

Pettigrew, Thomas F. 1964. *A Profile of the Negro American*. Princeton: Van Nostrand.

———. 1971. *Racially Separate or Together?* New York: McGraw-Hill.

Portnoy, Bernard and Chalmers L. Stacey. 1954. A comparative study of Negro and white subnormals on the children's form of the Rosenzweig P-F Test. *American Journal of Mental Deficiency*, vol. 59, pp. 272–78.

Powdermaker, Hortense. 1939. *After Freedom*. New York: Viking.

Prange, Arthur J. and M. M. Vitals. 1962. Cultural aspects of the relatively low incidence of depression in southern Negroes. *International Journal of Social Psychiatry* 8:104–12.

Proshansky, Harold and Peggy Newton. 1968. The nature and meaning of Negro self-identity. In *Social Class, Race, and Psychological Development*. Martin Deutsch, et al, eds. New York: Holt, Rinehart & Winston.

Prothro, James W. and Charles U. Smith. 1957. Ethnic differences in authoritarian personality. *Social Forces*, vol. 35, pp. 334–38.

Rainwater, Lee. 1964a. *Family Design*. Chicago: University of Chicago Press.

———. 1964b. Marital sexuality in four cultures of poverty. *Journal of Marriage and the Family*, vol. 26, p. 4.

———. 1966a. Work and identity in the lower class. In *Planning for a Nation of Cities*. Sam Bass Warner Jr., ed. Cambridge: M.I.T. Press.

———. 1966b. Crucible of identity: the Negro lower-class family. *Daedalus*, Winter. Abridgement in this publication.

Rainwater, Lee, Richard P. Coleman and Gerald Handel. 1959. *Workingman's Wife*. New York: Oceana.

Rainwater, Lee and William L. Yancey. 1967. *The Moynihan Report and the Politics of Controversy*. Cambridge: M.I.T. Press.

Randall, J. H. 1926. *The Making of the Modern Mind*. Boston: Houghton Mifflin.

Ransford, H. Edward. 1968. Isolation, powerlessness, and violence. *American Journal of Sociology*, vol. 73, pp. 581–91.

Reiss, Ira L. 1964. Premarital sexual permissiveness among Negroes and whites. *American Sociological Review*, vol. 29, p. 5.

Roach, Jack L. and Orville R. Gursslin. 1967. An evaluation of the concept "culture of poverty." *Social Forces*, vol. 45, pp. 383–92.

Roberts, John. 1964. The self-management of cultures. In *Explorations in Cultural Anthropology*. Ward H. Goodenough, ed. New York: McGraw-Hill.

Robinson, John P. and Phillip R. Shaver. 1969. *Measures of Social Psychological Attitudes*. Ann Arbor: Institute for Social Research, University of Michigan.

Rodman, Hyman. 1963. The lower-class value stretch. *Social Forces*, vol. 42, pp. 405–15.

Rohrer, John H. and Munro S. Edmonson. 1960. *The Eighth Generation Grow Up*. New York: Harper & Row.

Rose, Arnold. 1948. *The Negro's Morale: Group Identification and Protest*. Minneapolis: University of Minnesota Press.

Rosen, Bernard C. 1952. Cultural factors in achievement. Mimeographed.

———. 1956. The achievement syndrome: a psychocultural dimension of social stratification. *The American Sociological Review,* vol. 21, pp. 203–11.

———. 1957. The psychosocial origins of achievement motivation. Mimeographed progress report to the National Institute of Mental Health.

Rosenberg, Morris and Roberta G. Simmons. 1971. Black and white self-esteem: the urban school child. Unpublished manuscript.

Rosenthal, Jack. 1971a. Census finds rise in Negro families headed by women. *New York Times,* 26 February.

———. 1971b. Census data shows blacks still poor. *New York Times,* 12 February.

Rotter, Julian B. 1966. Generalized expectancies for internal versus external control of reinforcement. *Psychological Monographs,* No. 609, vol. 80, pp. 1–28.

Saloutos, T. 1945. The Greeks in the U. S. *The South Atlantic Quarterly,* vol. 4.

Schwartz, Michael and George Henderson. 1964. The culture of unemployment: some note on Negro children. In *Blue Collar World.* Arthur B. Shostak and William Gomberg, eds. Englewood Cliffs: Random.

Sears, David O. and John B. McConahay. 1970. Racial socialization, comparison levels, and the Watts riot. *Journal of Social Issues,* vol. 26, Winter, pp. 121–40.

Seeman, Melvin. 1959. On the meaning of alienation. *American Sociological Review,* vol. 24, pp. 783–91.

Sheatsley, P. 1966. White attitudes toward the Negro. *Daedalus,* Winter, pp. 217–38.

Short, James F., and Fred L. Strodtbeck. 1965. *Group Process and Gang Delinquency.* Chicago: University of Chicago Press.

Silverberg, William V. 1953. *Childhood Experience and Personal Destiny.* New York: Springer Publications.

Simpson, George E. and J. Milton Yinger. 1965. *Racial and Cultural Minorities.* 3rd edition. New York: Harper & Row.

Solomon, F. and J. R. Fishman. 1964a. Youth and social action: II, action and identity formation in first student sit-in demonstration, *Journal of Social Issues,* vol. 20, pp. 36–45.

———. 1964b. Psychosocial meaning of nonviolence in student civil rights activities. *Psychiatry,* vol. 27, pp. 91–99.

Spiegel, John P. 1960. The resolution of role conflict with the family. In *A Modern Introduction to the Family.* Norman W. Bell and Ezra F. Vogel, eds. Glencoe: Free Press.

Srole, Leo. 1956. Social integration and certain corollaries: an exploratory study. *American Sociological Review,* vol. 21, pp. 709–16.

Stampp, Kenneth. 1956. *The Peculiar Institution*. New York: Random.

Stevenson, H. W. and E. C. Stewart. 1958. A developmental study of racial awareness in young children. *Child Development*, vol. 29, pp. 399–409.

Stone, Gregory. 1962. Appearance and the self. In *Human Behavior in Social Process*. Arnold Rose, ed. Boston: Houghton Mifflin.

Strickland, Bonnie Ruth. 1965. The prediction of social action from a dimension of internal-external control. *Journal of Social Psychology*, vol. 66, pp. 353–58.

Strodtbeck, F. L. 1958a. Jewish and Italian immigration and subsequent status mobility. In *Talent and Society*. D. McClelland, A. Baldwin, U. Bronfenbrenner and F. Strodtbeck, eds. Princeton: Van Nostrand.

———. 1958b. Family interactions, values and achievement. In *Talent and Society*, D. McClelland, A. Baldwin, U. Bronfenbrenner and F. Strodtbeck, eds. Princeton: Van Nostrand.

Strodtbeck, F. L., M. McDonald, and B. C. Rosen. 1957. Evaluation of occupations: a reflection of Jewish and Italian mobility differences. *American Sociological Review*, vol. 22, pp. 546–53.

Talese, G. 1963. A happy day in Harlem. *New York Times*, 29 August.

Tannenbaum, Frank. 1946. *Slave and Citizen: the Negro in the Americas*. New York: Random.

Thune, Jeanne M. 1967. Racial attitudes of older adults. *Gerontologist*, vol. 7, pp. 179–82.

Touchstone, F. V. 1957. A comparative study of Negro and white college students' aggressiveness by means of sentence completion. *Dissertation Abstracts*, vol. 17, pp. 1588–89.

Townsend, Peter. 1957. *The Family Life of Old People*. London: Routledge and Kegan Paul.

Trager, H. G., and M. Yarrow. 1952. *They Learn What They Live*. New York: Harper.

Trent, Richard D. 1957. The relation between expressed self-acceptance and expressed attitudes toward Negroes and whites among Negro children. *Journal of Genetic Psychology*, vol. 91, pp. 25–31.

Ulrich, R. E. and N. H. Azrin. 1962. Reflexive fighting in response to aversive stimulation. *Journal of the Experimental Analysis of Behavior*, vol. 5, pp. 511–20.

United States Bureau of Labor Statistics and United States Census Bureau. 1968. *Recent Trends in the Social and Economic Conditions of Negroes in the United States*. BLS Report No. 347. Washington, D. C.: U. S. Government Printing Office.

———. 1971. *The Social and Economic Status of Negroes in the United States, 1970*. BLS Report No. 394. Washington, D. C.: U. S. Government Printing Office.

United States Department of Labor. 1965. *The Negro Family: The Case for National Action.* Washington, D. C.: U. S. Government Printing Office.

Valentine, Charles A. 1968. *Culture and Poverty.* Chicago: University of Chicago Press.

Van Den Berghe, Pierre L. 1967. *Race and Racism: A Comparative Perspective.* New York: Wiley.

Vaughan, G. M. 1963a. Concept formation and the development of ethnic awareness. *Journal of Genetic Psychology,* vol. 103, pp. 93–103.

———. 1963b. The effect of the ethnic grouping of the experimenter upon children's responses to tests of an ethnic nature. *British Journal of Social and Clinical Psychology,* vol. 2, pp. 66–70.

———. 1964a. The development of ethnic attitudes in New Zealand school children. *Genetic Psychology Monographs,* No. 70, pp. 135–75.

———. 1964b. Ethnic awareness in relation to minority group membership. *Journal of Genetic Psychology,* vol. 105, pp. 119–30.

Veroff, J., J. W. Atkinson, S. C. Feld and G. Gurin. 1960. The use of thematic apperception to assess motivation in a nationwide interview study. *Psychological Monographs,* 74, number 499.

Warner, W. L. and L. Srole. 1945. *The Social Systems of American Ethnic Groups.* New Haven: Yale University Press.

Watson, Jeanne. 1958. A formal analysis of sociable interaction. *Sociometry,* vol. 21, pp. 269–81.

Weinstein, Eugene A., and Paul Deutschberger. 1963. Some dimensions of altercasting. *Sociometry,* vol. 26, pp. 454–66.

Welsh, G. S. and W. G. Dahlstrom, eds. 1956. *Basic Readings on the MMPI in Psychology and Medicine.* Minneapolis: University of Minnesota Press.

Westie, F. R. 1964. Race and ethnic relations. In *Handbook of Modern Sociology,* R. E. L. Faris, ed. Chicago: Rand McNally.

Whyte, W. H. 1957. *The Organization Man.* New York: Simon and Schuster.

Whyte, William F. 1943a. *Street Corner Society.* Chicago: University of Chicago Press.

———. 1943b. A slum sex code. *American Journal of Sociology,* vol. 49, p. 1.

Williams, J. E. 1964. Connotations of color names among Negroes and Caucasians. *Perceptual and Motor Skills,* vol. 18, 721–31.

———. 1966. Connotations of racial concepts and color names. *Journal of Personality and Social Psychology,* vol. 3, pp. 531–40.

Williams, J. E. and D. J. Carter. 1967. Connotations of racial concepts and color names in Germany. *Journal of Social Psychology,* vol. 72, pp. 19–26.

Williams, J. E., J. K. Morland, and W. L. Underwood. n. d. Connotations of color names in the United States, Europe, and Asia. *Journal of Social Psychology.*

Williams, J. E. and J. K. Roberson. 1967. A method for assessing racial attitudes in preschool children. *Educational and Psychological Measurement*, vol. 27, pp. 671–89.

Williams, P. H. 1938. *South Italian Folkways in Europe and America*. New Haven: Yale University Press.

Williams, R. M., Jr. 1951. *American Society*. New York: Knopf.

Williams, Robert L. and Harry Byars. 1968. Negro self-esteem in a transitional society. *Personnel and Guidance Journal*, vol. 47, pp. 120–25.

Wiltse, Kermit T. 1963. Orthopsychiatric programs for socially deprived groups. *American Journal of Orthopsychiatry*, vol. 33, no. 5.

Winslow, Charles N. and James E. Brainerd. 1950. A comparison of the reactions of whites and Negroes to frustration as measured by the Rosenzweig Picture-Frustration test. *American Psychologist*, vol. 5, p. 297.

Winterbottom, M. 1958. The relation of need for achievement to learning experiences in independence and mastery. In *Motives in Fantasy, Action and Society*. J. Atkinson, ed. Princeton: Van Nostrand.

Wolfgang, Marvin E. 1968. Crime: homicide. *International Encyclopedia of the Social Sciences*, vol. 3, pp. 490–95.

Woods, F. J. 1956. *Cultural Values of American Ethnic Groups*. New York: Harper.

Yancey, William L. n. d. The culture of poverty: not so much parsimony. Social Science Institute: Washington University. Unpublished.

Zybrowski, M. and E. Herzog. 1952. *Life Is With People*. New York: International University Press.